The Clothing of Clio

A study of the representation of history in
nineteenth-century Britain and France

STEPHEN BANN

Reader in Modern Cultural Studies
University of Kent

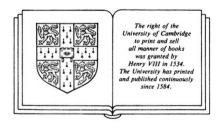

- use of rhetoric as formalizing
  structure to analysis
- change in form of rhetoric → change
  in underlying epistomology → change
  in era/discourse.
- but does not really discuss why
  or the effect on 19th c - why does irony
  arise.
- also does not discuss changes in
  the type of history asserted → values
  in rep. that relate to contemp. society

The right of the
University of Cambridge
to print and sell
all manner of books
was granted by
Henry VIII in 1534.
The University has printed
and published continuously
since 1584.

CAMBRIDGE UNIVERSITY PR

Cambridge
London   New York   New Rochelle
Melbourne   Sydney

CAMBRIDGE UNIVERSITY PRESS
Cambridge, New York, Melbourne, Madrid, Cape Town, Singapore,
São Paulo, Delhi, Dubai, Tokyo, Mexico City

Cambridge University Press
The Edinburgh Building, Cambridge CB2 8RU, UK

Published in the United States of America by Cambridge University Press, New York

www.cambridge.org
Information on this title: www.cambridge.org/9780521180887

First published 1984
First paperback edition 2010

A catalogue record for this publication is available from the British Library

Library of Congress Catalogue Card Number: 83–20909

ISBN 978-0-521-25616-2 Hardback
ISBN 978-0-521-18088-7 Paperback

The Clothing of Clio

A study of the representation of history in
nineteenth-century Britain and France

To my parents
who introduced me to history and poetry

History, not wanted yet,
Lean'd on her elbow, watching Time, whose course
Eventful, should supply her with a theme . . .

William Cowper, 'Yardley Oak' (1791)

History is the Muse of our time; we are, I think, the first who have
understood the past . . .

Albertine de Broglie, letter to Prosper de Barante (1825)

Contents

Illustrations

viii

FIGURES

Preface and acknowledgements

The academic paternity of an interdisciplinary study like this one is bound to be rather diverse. I owe a debt of gratitude first of all to the late Sir Herbert Butterfield, for agreeing to supervise the doctoral thesis on Prosper de Barante which was the origin of my interest in the different forms of historical representation; and also to the late Leland Lyons, who as founding Professor of History at the University of Kent took care that history of historiography should be taught there. Successive generations of students on the course which he set up have persuaded me that such an interest need not be entirely peripheral.

Colleagues and friends have helped me to see how the elusive concepts of historical representation might be investigated and understood. In particular, I should mention Hayden White, Lionel Gossman and Frank Kermode. To set oneself in such company may appear hazardous. But while I would not wish to associate them with the limitations of my approach, I can certainly say that I have been stimulated by the originality, acuity and elegance of their works. I am also especially grateful to Francis Haskell for reading through a preliminary draft of Chapter 2, and to Natalie Zemon Davis for commenting on my first stab at a conclusion. Elinor Shaffer deserves thanks for piloting my first chapter on its initial voyage through the Cambridge University Press.

The Rockefeller Foundation generously appointed me a Scholar in Residence at the Villa Serbelloni in the late Spring of 1982, thus enabling me to spend part of my study leave from the University of Kent in intelligent company and delightful surroundings. Though regrettably brief, this period provided me with the essential stimulus to complete this book.

Prior versions of three chapters have been published before: Chapter 1 in *Comparative Criticism Yearbook*, 3 (1981); Chapter 2 in *20th Century Studies*, 3 (1970); Chapter 4 in *History and Theory*, 17, 3 (1978). I am grateful for permission to reprint the substance (though not usually the letter) of these earlier studies.

Mrs Maxwell-Scott, of Abbotsford, kindly gave me permission to include a photograph of the house, as it appears in the official guide-book; Miss Pamela Wood, Keeper responsible for Newstead Abbey, allowed me a similar facility. Provenance of the other plates is given in the preceding list except where they have been prepared from my own materials with the expert aid of Jim Styles and John West.

For the final re-typing of the manuscript, I had the patient co-operation of Susan Davies and Mary Thomas. I am pleased to acknowledge, finally, the helpful comments of Terence Moore, of the Cambridge University Press, who was trusting enough to encourage this project at a stage when it was still very far from completion.

Quotations from foreign languages have been translated, except where the precise form of the original is judged to be important. In such cases, both the original language and the translation are included. Except where stated otherwise, the translations are my own.

S. B.

Canterbury, March 1983

1. *Maternal sustenance and grave example:* bas-relief of History by Clodion, from the *Palais de la Légion d'honneur*

Introduction

Clio, the Muse of History, invites a varied iconography. In Agostino di Duccio's fifteenth-century bas-relief at the Tempio Malatestiano, Rimini, she balances precariously on the Earth's surface. Her long hair ripples in the wind. Her left hand balances the long trumpet of Fame, while her right hand clasps the book of epic deeds to her breast. In the bas-relief which Clodion sculpted for Napoleon's Palais de la Légion d'Honneur, she adopts a position of watchful repose. Stern and unwavering, she gazes towards the tablet on which an attendant cherub is tracing out her message. With her right hand, she steadies the sharp stylus on her knee, while with her left she draws her loose gown away from her breast. What does she mean to convey to the young Napoleon whose meditative bust lies to the far side of the composition? Perhaps that History offers maternal sustenance, as well as stern example. Her annals may be graven in stone, but her generous gesture belies the original impression of severity.

This study is a response to the generosity of the nineteenth-century Clio. It takes as its subject the wide variety of representational forms which were utilised throughout this period to express a new vision of the past. That there was such a forcing period for 'historical-mindedness' in Britain, France and the remainder of the western world is an acknowledged fact which is close to a commonplace. Albertine de Broglie was not untypical of her age when, in 1825, she confided to the historian Prosper de Barante that 'we are . . . the first who have understood the past'.[1] Yet the traditional way of accounting for the appeal of the 'new' history has been to point to the emergence, in the early nineteenth century, of a new, professional historiography, bringing with it unprecedented standards of critical accuracy.

This approach was strongly endorsed at the end of the century by Lord Acton, in his famous inaugural lecture at Cambridge which accredited Leopold von Ranke as 'the representative of the age which instituted the modern study of History'.[2] Yet even Acton was obliged to note the relationship of the new professionalised historiography to a much broader context of cultural change. The revitalised history emerged, as he explained, 'from the Romantic School'. It was itself in a sense a by-product, rather than the effective cause, of this unprecedented preoccupation with the past.

Acting as the Devil's advocate, we could in fact put forward a position almost antithetical to that of Acton. The distinguishing mark of the period between 1750 and 1850 – in England at any rate – would be not the new professional practice of history but the increasingly expert production of pseudo-historical forgeries. There is Macpherson's Ossian, and Chatterton's medieval poetry. Perhaps most telling of all, there is Charles Bertram's forged Chronicle of Richard of Cirencester. Published in 1757 under the auspices of the antiquarian Stukeley, this document retained its currency in English historical circles for over a century, and was even republished as authentic as late as 1878, more than a decade after the Librarian of Windsor Castle had exposed Bertram's handwriting as being a mixture of incompatible styles! By this stage, the effect of the successful hoax had thoroughly permeated the historical study of Roman Britain, with effects that were to take many decades to eradicate.

Of course, it may be argued that the significant point about the previous example is not the temporary success of the hoax, but the fact that newly developed skills in orthography finally enabled the Librarian to pin it down. This period was certainly one in which long-established but unfounded myths about the past were finally exposed – as when James Raine investigated the shrine of St Cuthbert in Durham Cathedral in 1827, and concluded that the supposed body of the saint was in fact a piously reconstituted fraud.[3] But it is as difficult to attribute the motive for such an investigation to pure and disinterested science, as it is to put the forgeries down to a mere desire for monetary gain. The critical preoccupation with authenticity, and the transgressive wish to simulate authenticity, are, in a certain sense, two sides of the same coin.

We can put the issue in a different way by posing a series of questions. Why did a man like Charles Bertram choose to invent a record of the past? Why was Stukeley so ready and willing to accept his forgery as veracious? What fine sense of discrimination did the Librarian have to employ to identify the forgery beyond doubt? And how had this been developed? Of course, European history offers many prior examples of forgery – such as the notorious 'Donation of Constantine' – and many exposers of forgery – Peter Abelard and Lorenzo Valla among them. But such earlier forgeries had indeed been carried out, for the most part, with a specific political or financial end in view. By the middle of the eighteenth century, the concern with historical recreation is gradually beginning to overhaul the motive of deception. To put the issue graphically, we can choose to see Bertram as an anti-Ranke, in which case the final exposure of the false Chronicle is a triumph of historical method over perverse antiquarianism. Or we can see him as a proto-Scott, in which case the antiquarian's fascination with the detail of authenticity becomes a foreshadowing of the immense imaginative achievement of the Waverley Novels. And who can doubt that the Waverley Novels, though in the strictest sense a deception, gave their readers a new capacity for fine discrimination between what was authentic and what was false in a historically concrete milieu?

This mention of Scott leads me to note that he is one of the pioneers in the rediscovery of the past who pervades this study. But the fact that he is only in the forefront of the stage in one chapter is an indication of the approach which has been chosen. Rather than concentrate attention on the individual figures and their achievements, I have focused upon characteristic types of historical discourse and representation, juxtaposing particular examples in order to bring out common structural features and significant sequences. In a general sense, this is an exercise in 'arthrology' – the term coined by Michel Foucault for a science of the 'joints' between forms of discourse within an overall epistemological configuration. Accepting the likelihood that these 'joints' lie a little way below the surface, I have tried to locate them through the comparison of materials which may sometimes appear to have been brought together hastily or at random. To cover, in any inclusive sense, the emergence and development of historical-mindedness in the nineteenth century (even in Britain and France, which form the main focus of this study) would require a truly encyclopedic amalgamation of sources. Although I do not claim to have done this, I hope to offer some guidelines for the study of historical representation in this period, and indeed at the present day. It is remarkable how little effort has been directed, up to now, to the task of seeing the field as a whole. And it is clear that various individual aspects, which have for different reasons received attention, have had their significance obscured or distorted in consequence.

My concern is therefore with historical representation in the broadest sense of the term. I try to analyse the fictional element in such representation, and to identify common devices and strategies which might in aggregate add up to a 'historical poetics'. But what are the concepts, heuristic or otherwise, which could possibly claim to make sense of this vast and sprawling domain, which extends from historiography proper, through historical novels to visual art, spectacle and the historical museum? In his pioneering study, *Metahistory – The Historical Imagination in Nineteenth Century Europe,* Hayden White argued in 1974 that the historiography and the philosophies of history current in the nineteenth century shared the same rhetorical structures, and were 'emplotted' according to the same archetypal models of development as Northrop Frye had discerned in the western literary tradition. White's work is undoubtedly the most substantial recent contribution to the problem which I have outlined. It greatly aided the germination of my own work in this area, which had begun in 1970 with the study of 'A cycle in historical discourse', included here in a revised version. Yet, precisely because of the originality and impact of *Metahistory,* and because of the subsequent debate on the pertinence of rhetorical analysis to this area, I must make clear from the outset what claims are being put forward here.

A great deal turns upon the status of the linguistic and rhetorical terms which (as the reader will quickly notice) are used to penetrate the outer layer of discourse: recurrent figures or devices like metonymy, metaphor, synecdoche, chiasmus, catachresis and so on. Now, up to a point, the use of these terms can be defended on purely exegetic grounds. They belong to the traditional apparatus of literary criticism, even though that apparatus may have only quite recently been rescued from neglect. They identify, in a single economical word, recurrent patterns like 'the part substituting for the whole' (metonymy) which it would otherwise be cumbersome to indicate. An entrenched popular usage like 'the crown', as a way of referring to the monarchy, is sufficient proof that such figures are neither esoteric in their currency, nor confined strictly to the domain of literature. But to concede this point is to admit no specific claims about the cognitive status of these figures.

Here I would put forward a dual justification, both strictly heuristic and linked to a more speculative type of argument. Jonathan Culler defines the first approach when he describes the figures of rhetoric as 'the names of possible interpretive moves one can make when confronted with a textual problem'.[4] As he implies, we can try to make sense of a text, or any other significant pattern, through applying to it a limited number of formal schemata, and seeing if any of them will 'fit'. Yet this formulation brings with it a fundamental problem. What is the cognitive basis for this 'fit' between textual practice and the schemata which we project upon the text? The anthropologist Dan Sperber makes a valuable suggestion in his aptly named article on 'cognitive rhetoric':

The figure is not in the text, and it is not a function of the text alone. It is in the conceptual representation of the text; it is a function both of the text and of the shared knowledge. Rhetoricians argue about the issue whether there are figures of thought, as well as figures of phonology, syntax and semantics. I want to suggest that there are nothing but figures of thought, in relation to which phonological, syntactic or semantic properties could play the role of supplementary focalisers, without ever being either necessary or sufficient, to engage the mechanism of figural interpretation.[5]

Sperber's hypothesis is particularly appropriate for the diverse materials of this study. He is arguing against the traditional view of the rhetorical figure as a 'departure' from the ideal of a plain, unadorned, non-figurative language. As he rightly points out, this is a mythic notion – the neutral 'zero degree' from which the figure 'departs' simply does not exist. Instead we are to think of the figure as a 'function both of the text and of the shared knowledge' of those who interpret it. The process of interpretation is a dialectical one, in which 'figures of thought' are used to detect and explore those self-same figures, as they have been 'focalised' in the material of the text.

What are the special implications of this view for the study of historical representation? Clearly historiography in the strict sense of the term presents distinctive claims to 'scientific' truth. To this extent, it resists analysis in terms of 'style' or figure. Borrowing the phrase which Jacques Derrida has used in his 'deconstruction' of philosophical language, we might say that historiography has its own 'White Mythology'. Transparency to the 'facts' is the historian's code of literary practice, even though he is using figures of speech and narrative structures like any other literary craftsman. Peter Gay has commented usefully on this institutionalised 'double-think' in his study of *Style in History*, where he points out that the very Ranke praised for his 'colourless, critical' writing by Lord Acton in fact abounds in vivid rhetorical figures.[6] It is true that Ranke's contemporary, the French historian Prosper de Barante, took a more unequivocal path, striving to achieve as far as possible complete neutrality of style. But the very fact that Barante has to go to so much trouble to contrive a 'zero degree' of narration, and the dubious character of his achievement, both go to show *a contrario* the stylistic loading of the historical text.

Barante's contribution to historiography will be clearly outlined in the first chapters of this study, and his telling contrast with Ranke will be one of the keys used to unlock the 'historical-mindedness' of the age. But Sperber's hypothesis is useful not only in its implications for historiography proper – it also enables us to justify extending the investigation through historical fiction and historical painting to other forms of organised discourse which can be regarded as 'texts'. By emphasising the primacy of 'figures of thought' which are focalised in language, Sperber also opens up the possibility that such figures could be focalised in other material conditions. This is the guiding assumption of my chapter on the formation of two nineteenth-century historical museums, Lenoir's Musée des Petits-Augustins and Du Sommerard's Musée de Cluny. The conditions of assembling and exhibiting material objects are admittedly not as specific as those of literary composition. Yet I hope to demonstrate through comparison of the two museums that particular mechanisms are at work, and that these determine both the characteristic configurations of objects displayed there, and the overall notion of history experienced by the nineteenth-century visitor. A strictly parallel study is the following chapter on 'The Historical Composition of Place', which compares the personal and poetic investments of Scott and Byron in the architectural environments of Abbotsford and Newstead Abbey.

The central sections of this study therefore advance a claim for the existence of a 'historical poetics', which is distinctive to the early nineteenth century. In the eighteenth century, it would have been a commonplace to assert that the writing of history involved rhetorical procedures. In the early nineteenth century, emphasis on the compositional basis of historiography is gradually replaced by a stringent concern for cognitive values, which is marked in particular by Ranke's sharp distinction between primary and secondary sources. But at the same time, historians, painters, poets, novelists, collectors (and their public) are experiencing the elation of a new and concrete vision of the past, which is linked with but not (as it were) uniquely guaranteed by the new cognitive standards. *Why* this should have been so is a difficult issue in intellectual history, which will receive some attention at the beginning and at the end of this study. *How* it came to be so is the main concern of the central sections of the book, which trace the crucial shift from a reductive rhetorical strategy to an integrative poetics underpinning the new notion of history.

Yet this imaginative achievement of what Hayden White has called the 'Golden Age' of historiography was itself open to radical challenge by the middle of the century. Where Chapters 2, 3, 4 and 5 retrace the formation of a historical poetics, the remaining two chapters show how it was exposed to the onslaught of irony: precisely because the compelling rhetoric of the earlier period had worn thin, and historical science continued to assert more and more rigid standards of authenticity, the successors of Scott were forced to undertake new, and ever more extreme, stylistic subterfuges. Here the divergence of my approach from other existing studies of history in the nineteenth century will be plain enough. J. W. Burrow begins his account of 'Victcrian historians and the English past', entitled *A Liberal Descent*, with the statement that: 'The thirty years between 1848 and 1878 saw a remarkable flowering of English narrative history and a new intensity and elaboration in the interpretation of what arguably had been the three great crises in the history of the English as a nation.'[7] Measured against the substantial achievements of major English historians like Macaulay, Froude and Freeman, the texts with which I am concerned at this stage may appear to be peripheral and slight. Yet writers like Barham, Thackeray and Reade are the other side of the coin to the magisterial historians of the mid-century. Together with an aesthetic critic like Ruskin and an inventor like Fox Talbot, they can reveal the ingenious ways in which the test of historical authenticity survived the ironic stage, and yet at the same time engendered attitudes and outlooks which still persist in the historical culture of the modern world.

It would, however, be artificial to imply that the historical physiognomy of the nineteenth century was a crude succession of stages – a period of creative optimism followed by a period of artful doubt. Flaubert confessed in a famous letter of 1859, which referred to his own elaborate historical forgery, the historical novel *Salammbô*: 'Few people will guess how sad one had to be, in order to undertake to resuscitate Carthage.'[8] This world-weary tone may seem appropriate to its author and its period. But over a century before, when introducing his forged Chronicle of Richard of Cirencester, the elusive Charles Bertram had adduced the deficiency of the present age as a reason for his own publication: 'It contains many fragments of a better time, which would now in vain be sought for elsewhere.'[9] Even Albertine de Broglie, writing at the height of the Romantic period and placing herself among 'the first who have understood the past', adds the sobering observation: 'and that is largely the result of the fact that our own impressions are not strong enough'.[10] The magnitude of the achievement of the 'historical poetics' of the early nineteenth century must be measured, no doubt, against the increasing sense of world-weariness which it sought to combat, as well as by its own constructive procedures.

For Mme de Broglie, then, Clio is the Muse of the times. But she is not, like Agostino's Muse, an emblem of the vivid existential experience of the historical process. As conveyed in Clodion's relief, she reclines comfortably, with the elaborate folds of her clothing draped around her. The bust of the young Napoleon inclines towards the stone tablet on which the epic deeds of modern history are to be recorded. But we should not ignore the fact that Clio offers a more immediate, maternal sustenance; this primary relationship is also, no doubt, part of what Henry James called 'The Sense of the Past'.

1 The historian as taxidermist: Ranke, Barante, Waterton

What would be 'the most famous statement in all historiography'?[1] For Leonard Krieger, a recent commentator on the work of Leopold von Ranke, the answer lies unequivocally to the credit of his subject: 'History has had assigned to it the task of judging the past, of instructing the present for the benefit of ages to come. The present study does not assume such a high office; it wants to show only what actually happened (*wie es eigentlich gewesen*).'

Renke

Supplied with its appropriate glosses, and supplemented by other quotations, the 'statement' reads off the page unexceptionally enough, in spite of its celebrity. Yet we may find ourselves pausing momentarily at the point where the commentator brackets and italicises the four-word phrase from the original German. Is this phrase included merely to recall us to the fact that the original language was indeed German? Does it hint maybe at a need for precision that is not entirely fulfilled by the English translation? Given that the latter is the case, why has this particular part of the 'statement' been singled out for special attention? Is it because it is even more 'famous' than the remainder and therefore deserves such special recognition?

These questions are not, I would submit, entirely frivolous. There are at present two accessible English versions of the full Preface from which this statement is taken. The first makes exactly the same parenthetic nod towards the original: 'It wants only to show what actually happened (*wie es eigentlich gewesen*).'[2] The second, however, diverges sharply from this practice, and leads us to conclude that the underlined 'dictum' has been singled out for special attention at the price of dismissing the real problem of interpretation which it poses. 'Indeed Ranke's oft quoted dictum, "*wie es eigentlich gewesen*", has generally been misunderstood in this country as asking the historian to be satisfied with a purely factual recreation of the past.'[3] Evidently, in the view of this authority, it is a matter of mere mistranslation. The 'dictum' is reabsorbed into the 'statement' once again. But the word *eigentlich* has been retranslated, and the prominence of this new reading is emphasised by flanking commas: 'To history has been given the function of judging the past, of instructing men for the profit of future years. The present attempt does not aspire to such a lofty undertaking. It merely wants to show how, essentially, things happened.'[4]

Let us make one tentative comment at this point. If the 'statement' or the 'dictum' within the statement is indeed so 'famous' (to take two further

8

qualifications, 'classic',[5] and, *mea culpa*, 'time-honoured'[6]), then this is not necessarily because of what Ranke meant. It may be more accurately a question of what Ranke has been taken to mean. Our second translator stakes his case on the claim that the 'dictum', at least, has been widely misinterpreted 'in this country' – presumably America. Less circumspect opinion might go so far as to say that the misunderstanding has gone further afield. A recent attack on the premisses of traditional British historiography has used the 'dictum' to epitomise the positivism of late-nineteenth-century British historians: 'The task of the historian in Ranke's much quoted dictum, was "simply to show how it really was" – in other words to ascertain the facts.'[7] But if Gareth Stedman Jones is wrong in his translation and in his interpretation, and Messrs Iggers and von Moltke right, then what conclusions must we draw? That Ranke's 'dictum' genuinely did become the slogan of positivist historiography, but that he himself intended something quite different? There would then be a neat distinction between the original intention and the falsifying myth, between Ranke the straw positivist 'satisfied with a purely factual recreation of the past' and the genuine Ranke who held that it is 'the emphasis on the essential that makes an account historical'.[8]

Any growing impatience of the reader at this stage may well be given expression through Herbert Butterfield's sage judgement on the matter. Without deeming it necessary to give additional currency to the 'statement' or the 'dictum', he rightly discerns that Ranke has served as a mythic repository for the attitudes of the 'new' historiography of the nineteenth century, and that his originality has in all probability been exaggerated for that reason:

The world in general, when it discusses the basic ideas which are here in question, seems to find it useful to examine them as they are embodied in the work and views of Ranke; and possibly it is true that Ranke had the principal share in the development of the nineteenth-century tradition. There would be grounds for saying, however, that some of the main ideas and decisions go back beyond Ranke: and this may be true to even a greater degree than is suggested below.[9]

The reminder is salutary, and impels us to define the scope of this investigation more precisely. At least since the publication of Meinecke's *Die Entstehung des Historismus* in 1959, it has been customary to view Ranke's work as the culmination of a mighty tradition of historical thinking, which arose within the specific intellectual and cultural circumstances of eighteenth-century Germany. Significantly enough, Meinecke leads us up to Ranke, through Möser, Herder and Goethe, but he does not actually discuss Ranke except as a 'supplement' to the main body of the text.[10] The inference to be drawn is clear enough. Meinecke's concern is with historical thinking, and with the nature of history itself. Ranke is the bridge through which 'Historism' passes from its period of incubation in eighteenth-century philosophy to its maturity in the historiography of the nineteenth century. Yet, for all the importance that it accords to Ranke, this valuation tells us little about the character of Ranke's contribution to historiography. Meinecke himself admits, in the preliminary remarks which introduce his great work: 'I do not deal with the history of historical writing... but only with the history of the standards of value and formative principles in general lying at the back of all historical thought.'[11] Such a distinction is perfectly fair. But it leaves more than a mere 'supplement' for further consideration.

We thus have, on the one hand, Meinecke's Ranke, whose 'historical thought' is the culmination of an eighteenth-century German tradition. But we also have, as Butterfield implies, another very different image to contend with: that of the Ranke incorporated by Lord Acton into the British historical tradition, who has come to seem – if not to the 'world in general', at least to the historical profession – the exemplary progenitor of a 'new', professional historiography. Ranke's meta-historical pronouncements, such as they are, have had to bear the weight of this mythic load. And if we wish to understand their relevance, both to the placing of Ranke within the intellectual context of his times and to the singular tenacity of the Rankean myth, we cannot accept the alibi of Meinecke's 'Historism'. Meinecke's method, expressed in suitably Alpine imagery, was 'to undertake a kind of mountain journey along the ridges, attempting to get across from one high peak to the next, in the course of which it [would] also be possible to get glimpses of mountains and valleys that [could not] actually be visited'.[12] The present chapter presumes less ideal weather conditions. It aspires simply to clear away the mist from one part of the mountain.

That there is mist around can easily be demonstrated. Let us go back to one of Ranke's most immediate and distinguished precursors, Wilhelm von Humboldt. When Humboldt lectured on 'The Historian's Task' in 1821 (three years, that is, before the publication of Ranke's Preface), he began with the following, strangely familiar statement: 'The historian's task is to present what actually happened.'[13] Our immediate reaction is to proclaim a direct source for Ranke's dictum. So – it was not even original! Yet recourse to the German text of Humboldt's lecture reveals this opening sentence: 'Die Aufgabe des Geschichtschreibers ist die Darstellung des Geschehenen.'[14] In other words, through the misleading approximations of the English translation, Ranke has succeeded in casting his shadow backwards, against time. 'What actually happened' – *wie es eigentlich gewesen*: even if we retranslate, or qualify it as mythic, we are not going to get rid of it so easily.

The interests of precision seem to dictate, at this stage, that there should be a full quotation from Ranke's original German, not merely of the 'dictum' but of the full 'statement' within which it occurs. The statement comes (as if that information were necessary) from the Preface to Ranke's first substantial historical work: *Geschichten der romanischen und germanischen Völker von 1494 bis 1514*. The Preface bears the date 'October 1824'.

Man hat der Historie das Amt, die Vergangenheit zu richten, die Mittwelt zum Nutzen zukünftiger Jahre zu belehren, beigemessen: so hoher Aemter unterwindet sich gegenwärtiger Versuch nicht: er will bloss zeigen, wie es eigentlich gewesen.[15]

Certain obvious points arise from the detailed comparison between the original and the translation initially quoted. The 'statement' is indeed a coherent whole, not only because it is in effect a single sentence, divided by colons, but also because of the anaphora involved (and abandoned in the English) when the word *Amt* is picked up for a second time made prominent by subject/object inversion. But the statement is also, beyond doubt, an ironical one. That is to say, the renunciation of 'so high an office' cannot fail to appear disingenuous when set in the context of Ranke's claims for the new methodology. The second part of the statement is moreover constructed as an oxymoron: *merely* to show what *essentially* happened. Is there not a piquant contrast here? And, finally, the concluding phrase can hardly be regarded other than as a conspicuous litotes. After rejecting the 'high office', Ranke proposes that he will show us 'merely' what 'essentially' happened. Is this in any way, or could it possibly be conceived as, a simple task?

That Ranke is a highly accomplished rhetorician is by no means a new case to be sustained. Indeed, attention has been specifically drawn to his use of the gap between 'books' of a work to obtain a specific rhetorical effect.[16] In an analogous, though more modest way, the closure of the paragraph with 'wie es eigentlich gewesen' here accentuates the daring of the (understated) claim. We catch in our breath, as it were, before picking up the thread of the argument: 'But whence the sources for such a new investigation?' And in that momentary interruption and resumption of discourse, we have been shifted from one realm of assertion to another. In the first paragraph, Ranke was claiming to 'show' (*zeigen*), in the second he talks about 'investigating' (*erforscht*). If Ranke has indeed taken note of the substance of Humboldt's lecture, then he has carefully ignored the fact that Humboldt is specifically making a point about representation:

The historian's task is to present what actually happened. The more purely and completely he achieves this, the more perfectly has he solved his problem. A simple presentation [*Die einfache Darstellung*] is at the same time the primary, indispensable condition of his work and the highest achievement he will be able to attain. Regarded in this way, he seems to be merely receptive and reproductive, not himself active and creative. [*Von dieser Seite betrachtet, scheint er nur auffassend und wiedergebend, nicht selbstthätig und schöpferisch.*][17]

For Humboldt, therefore, the apparent paradox of the historian's self-efface-ment is resolved by the acknowledgement that it is a stylistic effect. The historian must *seem* to be 'merely receptive and reproductive'. His vocation is to aspire only to the modest fulfilment of a 'simple presentation'. We may glimpse Ranke's originality, by comparison, in the very movement from *darstellen* to *zeigen*, and in the effective elision of the question of representation which is involved.

Ranke's statement has thus become 'famous', we may be sure, not because of its explicit and understandable content, but because it represents in itself a form of evasion. It presents, with exemplary concision, the Utopia of historical discourse in the nineteenth century, which is to lie entirely outside the province of 'poetry' and of style – even in so far as style is envisaged in the self-immolating guise of Humboldt's programme. Naturally, as the century progressed, Ranke's commentators and translators were obliged to admit that the exemplary historian had, in effect, a style. But the very ways in which they make the concession indicate the paradoxical force of Ranke's formulation. Antoine Guilland, whose French *parti pris* helped him to dismiss the image of Ranke's political innocence, also took care to assert the disingenuousness of the famous statement: '"Je veux raconter simplement les choses, comme elles ont été réellement" ... Il ne suffit pas, en effet, de le vouloir pour y arriver, il faut encore une grâce particulière qui n'est accordée qu'à bien peu.'[18] ('"I wish simply to recount things as they have really been" ... It is not enough, in fact, to want this in order to achieve it, it is still necessary to have a particular kind of grace which is only granted to very few.') Innocently or not, however, Guilland has re-positioned and remade his target before shooting. Ranke does not use the personalised formula of *Je veux raconter*; he chooses the impersonal *er will bloss zeigen*. To narrate, to tell a story, this is an activity which fits well within the traditional terms of representation. But what, we may ask again, is the force of *showing*? To answer this question, we must in the first place divest ourselves of the elaborate apparatus which the later nineteenth century employed to inspect the problem of truth. If Truth is, as Nietzsche liked to imagine, a woman, then style is the sharp instrument which pierces the veils that conceal her.[19] Or, as Kipling put it in his clever short story 'A Matter of Fact', the only resource of the writer in possession of the remarkable story is to 'tell it as a lie': 'for Truth is a naked lady, and if by accident she is drawn up from the bottom of the sea, it behoves a gentleman either to give her a print petticoat or to turn his face to the wall and vow that he did not see'.[20] Against the orthodoxy of this position, Ranke raises up, in the days of his chivalrous youth, a redoubtable standard. For Truth, that abstract and over-extended lady, is substituted the homelier figure of Clio. And Clio, or History personified, will be revealed in untrammelled nakedness: is not the primary sense of *bloss* (*er will bloss zeigen*) precisely that of nakedness? *Eigentlich*, whether we translate it 'actually' or 'essentially', becomes no more than a means of assuring us that all the veils are off: there is not even a print petticoat for the sake of her modesty, and *a fortiori*, no need of the probing style (*stylus*) to make intrusive jabs into her secret places.

Let us, however, return to the formulation of our own problem, which is, or has been up to this point, the progressive unveiling of an elusive Ranke – the Ranke of the 'statement' and the 'dictum'. There are at least two layers to be removed, it would appear, in the process of our attempt to attain that area of primary meaning. On the one hand, and clearly in view, is the Ranke of our contemporary manuals of historiography. Despite his benefit from the more exact interpretations and translations of the present period, he remains, in the last resort, problematic. After all, does it really advance us very far to replace the translation of 'actually' with 'essentially', to proffer the by no means self-explanatory statement that Ranke's concern is 'not factuality but the emphasis on the essential'?[21] Equally, we may ask if it is anything more than an outer layer of Ranke that is identified when a modern exploder of 'Historians' Fallacies' insists that the historian's business is 'not to tell what actually *was*, but what actually *happened*'.[22] Again there is the shift from 'show' to 'tell', and the consequent elision of the problem of representation, which appears crucial – by its very absence – in the celebrated statement.

A considerable further step is taken if we attempt to reconstruct a nineteenth-century viewpoint, in which it is precisely the obfuscation of this problem and the unvarnished nakedness of his Clio, that secures Ranke's standing. Tzvetan Todorov has written about the genre of the fantastic, that it is 'nothing more than the uneasy conscience of the positivist nineteenth century. But nowadays we can no longer believe in an external immutable reality, nor in a literature which would merely be the transcription of this reality. Words have gained an autonomy which things have lost.'[23] If the fantastic was the uneasy conscience of positivism, then clearly Ranke's historiography was its good conscience, held within exactly the same economy of fact and fiction but fulfilling an opposite role. This economic requirement is doubtless responsible for the fact that Ranke's highly rhetorical and indeed dramatic style, which cannot fail to strike us today, was interpreted wholly in the light of the discrimination between 'poetry' and 'fact'. As his first English translator insisted, 'A strict representation of facts, be it ever so narrow and unpoetical is, beyond doubt, the first law.'[24] Called upon further to explicate the positive characteristics of Ranke's style, the second translator made a valiant attempt to represent the *zero degree*: 'If Ranke's style was as transparent as water, it was said, it was also as tasteless.'[25] And then of course, there is the most elliptical and celebrated of all judgements on Ranke, which will require much further discussion at a later stage: Lord Acton's tribute to the historian who taught the age 'to be critical, to be colourless, and to be new'.[26]

Within the terms of this requirement, we may well find the 'primary meaning' of Ranke's modestly assertive phrase disappearing to a fine point of unintelligibility. *Er will bloss zeigen, wie es eigentlich gewesen.* Is there any way of disentangling the message from the loading which it has had to support? Certainly not, in my opinion, if we hold to the desperate project of trying to recover a meaning intended by Ranke, as if additional material from letters and published statements would enable us to recover the plenitude of the enigmatic terms. And yet, a possibility of further inquiry does exist if we wholly reframe the questions which are asked about the Rankean text. Instead of asking: what did Ranke mean? we can pose the very different question: how was it possible for what Ranke says to be said at the time? What were the pre-conditions which made possible the emergence of this meta-historical claim at this particular period? In other words, it is not a question of vindicating a subject's 'originality' by crediting him with a 'new' formulation of the historian's task, but of asking how, within the overall economy of types of discourse, such a claim, as it happens on behalf of historiography, came to be put forward. More precisely, it is a question about the history of representation, and the singular place which 'historical' representation held within the web of representational possibilities open to the men of Ranke's time. And yet how singular a place was this? My concern is precisely to show that the apparent singularity, measured against classic notions of representation, conceals a close kinship with a stream of new, heterodox, non-mimetic forms of discourse which is already swelling by the 1820s and will have become a torrent by the end of the century.

A final point must be made, however, about the 'newness' of Ranke, or rather about the novel epistemological configuration within which his statement acquires its meaning. This study takes as its hypothesis the assumption that there is indeed a 'new history', but that its novelty cannot be assessed simply by contrast with the 'old history' of the eighteenth century. Michel Foucault has memorably argued, in *Les Mots et les choses*, that the early nineteenth century witnessed 'le grand bouleversement de l'*épistémè* occidentale',[27] and he has outlined the crucial position of historical consciousness in the radical re-composition of the map of knowledge. Above all, he has insisted that 'the lyrical halo which surrounded, at that epoch, the awareness of history, the lively curiosity for the documents of traces which time had left behind' was a reaction to an overpowering sense of loss: 'tout ceci manifeste en surface le fait nu que l'homme s'est trouvé vidé d'histoire, mais qu'il était déjà à la tâche de retrouver au fond de lui-même . . . une historicité qui lui fut liée essentiellement'[28] ('all of this makes manifest on the surface the bare fact that man has found himself to be emptied of history, but that he was already at the task of re-discovering in the depths of himself . . . a historicity which was linked to him essentially'). It is the dialectic of this loss, and this retrieval, that the next section will seek to trace.

The question which arises could be put in the following form. At what stage, and in what domains, does the ideal of *life-like representation* achieve expression both in theoretical and in practical terms? The student of the eighteenth century will instantly point out that the very notion of 'life-like representation' is a contradiction in terms. Representation is assumed, within the classicist aesthetic, to be a process of *mimesis* or imitation, in which we pass from the real to the simulated. *Vraisemblance* rather than *vérité* is the moderating criterion of this process. Nonetheless, if we examine the later eighteenth century, we find the tell-tale signs of a movement away from the paradigm of the *vraisemblable*. Etienne de Silhouette, prefacing his translations of Pope's 'Essay on Criticism' and 'Essay on Man' in 1737, expresses the aspiration 'to render faithfully the thoughts of M. Pope'.[29] By his death in 1767, his name had become famous throughout Europe to designate the cut-out black profiles, reduced mechanically from projected shadows, which had come into vogue. Both the ideal of 'fidelity' in translation and the technique of representation through a system which involves no mediating level of signs have this in common. They assume, at least as an ideal, the transparency of the signifier.

Of course in neither of these cases does the 'life-like' come into play.The translator's concern with a 'faithful' rendering, as opposed to the transposition from one set of conventions to another, must be largely a personal matter. Only the bi-lingual reader can judge the degree of 'fidelity' and acknowledge it with a remark like: 'This reads just like Pope.' Equally, the black cut-out of the silhouette is not likely to convince anyone of its life-like qualities, being so clearly devoid of all the characteristic features which we associate with a living person's image. But having made this point, we may well turn back and consider once again whether it is entirely convincing. Such a remark as 'This reads like Pope' – which is set within the terms of the *vraisemblable* – depends on our recognising a functional homology between texts: the original and the translated. What if it were a question of a narrated action? In that case, the remark 'This reads like Pope' could well be replaced by the statement: 'I could really see it happening.' In the case of the silhouette, the reservation must be even stronger. We may grant that the remark 'This looks just like X' is equally applicable to the technique of the silhouette and to any other form of iconic representation, including the traditional drawing or portrait. But there is a further stage of credence which might be represented by the phrase: 'That really is X.' The example of the photograph is there to remind us that the dissimilarity between the image and 'real life' is not an obstacle to our perceiving it as more than merely *vraisemblable*: on the contrary, it is precisely the degree of abstraction in photographic reproduction, coupled with the automatic, non-mediated process involved, that establishes the image as more than a *simulacrum*. As far as the silhouette goes, it is useful to note that the physiognomic calculations of Lavater were made from the basis of silhouettes, which were thus recognised as having an epistemological status quite different from that of the conventional portrait.[30]

In both of these cases, therefore, the movement is tentatively towards a transgressive mode of representation. 'Fidelity', whether to the thoughts of an author or to the lineaments of a profile, implies a negation of the sign as sign. What is restored is not language but life, not the symbolic but the real. But it is worth asking at this stage why such a restoration is rendered necessary. What, on the anthropological level, necessitates the abandonment of the rule of mimesis, or mediated representation, so that this transgressive mode can be received? It would appear that Foucault's explanation, confronting 'le grand bouleversement de l'épistémè occidentale', is at least a plausible one. The restoration of the life-like is itself postulated as a response to a sense of loss. In other words, the Utopia of life-like reproduction depends upon, and reacts to, the fact of death. It is a strenuous attempt to recover, by means which must exceed those of convention, a state which is (and must be) recognised as lost.

A specific case from early-nineteenth-century historiography will be chosen to illustrate, in an unusually graphic way, the dynamic of this double movement.

But first of all, and as a symmetrical pair to the example from historiography, there is an even more striking example from another, quite different sphere. As Foucault suggests, man's sense of being 'dispossessed' of history is a response to the growing awareness that there is no unified, anthropocentric history, but rather a number of 'histories' – of language, of the natural world etc. – which do not place him at their centre. The attempt to recreate the 'life-like' in the natural world is therefore strictly analogous to the impulse towards historical recreation in the narrower sense. Both form part of the same programme, as it were, and disclose common structures of theory and practice.

In 1825, the Yorkshire Catholic squire Charles Waterton published his autobiographical account of *Wanderings in South America, the North-West of the United States and the Antilles, in the Years 1812, 1816, 1820 and 1824*; it bore the sub-title: 'With original instructions for the perfect preservation of birds etc., for cabinets of natural history'. Despite the dates given, Waterton's reminiscences go back to an earlier visit to South America, around 1808, when his system 'for the perfect preservation of birds' was first partially put into practice. Having secured, and wishing to preserve, a specimen of the toucan, he decided to take precautions against the fact that all specimens which he had previously seen had lost the brilliant blue bill which was the bird's most decorative feature in the natural state. He therefore attempted a dissection which would not merely remove the perishable parts of the bird's anatomy but would also perpetuate the brilliance of its bill. This followed two stages, which were reproduced as instructions in the text of 1825: 'You have rendered the bill transparent by the operation [of paring away the lower mandible], and that transparency must be done away to make it appear perfectly natural ... [The lower mandible] must be painted blue inside. When all this is completed, the bill will please you; it will appear in its original colours.'[31] Waterton's recreation of the toucan's beak in 1808 was, as his 1825 publication suggests, merely a prelude to the sustained and (as far as one can judge) entirely original investigation of the science of taxidermy, which indeed Waterton may be said to have pioneered. In his combative and admittedly eccentric way, he put before the early-nineteenth-century English reader the claim that all previous methods of preserving birds, insects and animals had resulted in grotesque travesties of the living original. In a fascinating paper, 'On Museums', which he published together with other essays in 1838, he asserted boldly: 'It may be said with great truth that, from Rome to Russia, and from Orkney to Africa, there is not to be found, in any cabinet of natural history, one single quadruped which has been stuffed, or prepared, or mounted (as the French term it), upon scientific principles.'[32]

Of Waterton's scientific principles, the essentials may be stated quite simply. Instead of mounting the dissected carcase on an internal frame, which would impede the natural shrinking of the skin and thus produce hideous distortions, he regularly soaked it in a solution of corrosive sublimate in alcohol. After this soaking, it was entirely manipulable, and his thorough knowledge of anatomy could be employed to reconstruct the carcase in its original state – no longer subject to shrinkage or deterioration but preserved by the invisible chemical. Yet even more fascinating than his technique, for our purposes, is the end to which this technique was directed. This was, quite simply, the end of life-like represen- tation, the reconstitution of the beast or bird 'as it really was'. Other taxidermists had conspicuously failed at this (one wonders how incredulously they would have greeted the suggestion that they might attempt it!):

> Now should I call upon any one of these, who have given to the public a mode of preserving specimens for museums, to step forward and show me how to restore majesty to the face of a lion's skin, ferocity to the tiger's countenance, innocence to that of the lamb, or sulkiness to that of the bull, he would not know which way to set to work: he would have no resources at hand to help him in that operation . . . He could produce nothing beyond a mere dried specimen, shrunk too much in this part, or too bloated in that; a mummy, a distortion, an hideous spectacle, a failure in every sense of the word.[33]

By contrast, the new taxidermist could confidently attempt a hugely more impressive aspiration: 'It now depends upon the skill and anatomical knowledge of the operator (perhaps I ought to call him artist at this stage of the process), to do such complete justice to the skin before him, that, when a visitor shall gaze upon it afterwards, he will exclaim, "That animal is alive!"'[34]

Waterton's self-confidence is astounding, but his self-awareness is hardly less remarkable. Where other 'operators' have perpetuated sad *simulacra* of the natural world, Waterton claims to perpetuate the impression of life. But he can do so precisely because he has accepted the fact of death: the carcase has had to be recognised as mere malleable material for the taxidermist to work upon, and the natural colour replaced by the artificial. In this process, the guiding principle has necessarily been that of science: 'anatomical knowledge of the operator'. But it has been overtaken, with equal necessity, by the exigencies of art: 'perhaps I ought to call him artist at this stage of the process'. Waterton recognises, how- ever obliquely, that there is no inevitable link between the science of anatomy and the rhetoric of life-like recreation. They are bound together simply by the professional integrity of the man who is both scientist and artist. And in certain circumstances, where that integrity is outweighed by the temptation to cause mischief, the artist can have his head. He can create a monster.

While Charles Waterton was wandering in the forests of South America, and reconstituting the brilliant colouring of the toucan's bill, the young Napoleonic *sous-préfet* Prosper de Barante was making his home in the small town of Bressuire, in the depths of the Vendée. During his childhood, the events of the Vendée wars had made a strong impression on him and his arrival at Bressuire rekindled this enthusiasm. The inhabitants struck him by their conformity to 'the ancient French character'.[35] In their stories, the various campaigns took on a chivalric flavour that made them seem closer to the period described by Froissart and his fellow chroniclers than to the contemporary devastation which Barante had witnessed as an imperial *intendant* in Germany. This interest was greatly intensified when he made the acquaintance of his country neighbour

Mme de La Rochejaquelein, who had a double stake in the Vendée legend, both as the widow of Lescure and as the subsequent sister-in-law of his companion in arms, Henri de La Rochejaquelein. Writing to Mme de Staël on 29 June 1808, Barante emphasised the pleasure which he experienced in hearing his neighbour's first-hand accounts of the campaigns. He added: 'Si je suis destiné à passer encore un an ici, je crois que j'écrirai l'histoire de la Vendée. C'est un projet qui me plaît assez; celle qu'on a faite ne manque pas de vérité; mais elle n'a ni simplicité ni coloris local.'[36] ('If I am destined to pass another year here, I think that I shall write the history of the Vendée. It is a project which I find quite agreeable; the one that has been done is not lacking in truth; but it has neither simplicity nor local colour.')

Whether Barante would ever have attempted a full-scale history of the Vendée wars is doubtful. At any rate, the opportunity soon presented itself for supplementing the existing history, published in 1806 by Alphonse de Beauchamp, with a narrative in which 'simplicity and local colour' abounded. Mme de La Rochejaquelein had contrived to escape to Spain after the defeat of her companions. There she had begun to write an account of the wars, but had left it unfinished. When she finally returned to France and married the brother of Henri, she resumed work on these *Mémoires*, taking advantage of the more settled conditions to request information and corrections from other survivors of the campaigns. As a result, the initial character of the *Mémoires* was transformed. It had begun as a strictly personal account, but the accumulating material gave it the potential to be a more accurate and comprehensive contribution to the history of the Vendée wars. Prosper de Barante, with his revived enthusiasm for the subject, presented himself as the ideal person to review the manuscript, incorporate the supplementary notes into the body of the work and generally undertake the conversion of an important primary source into a coherent historical account. But he did so while seeking to preserve the personal character of the manuscript. The qualities which Mme de La Rochejaquelein supplied were not to be cancelled out in the search for objectivity; on the contrary, they were to be enhanced. As he wrote to Mme Récamier on 24 December 1808:

Je vous ai mandé que j'avais commencé à copier ces mémoires de la Vendée. C'est une excellente occupation; assez mécanique sauf qu'elle m'intéresse. Je n'y change rien. Je craindrais d'altérer en quelque chose la parfaite candeur et l'élévation toute simple qui y règnent. Ce n'est pas un ouvrage, c'est des sentimens et des faits, que ces mémoires. Il n'y a pas trace d'art, de but, de considération du public.[37]

[I informed you that I had begun to copy out these memoirs of the Vendée. It is an excellent occupation; quite mechanical except that it interests me. I change nothing there. I would be afraid of somehow compromising the perfect candour and entirely simple elevation that reign there. This is not a literary work, it is sentiments and facts – these memoirs. There is no trace of art, no motive, no consideration for the public.]

In effect, Barante's modesty belies the importance of the task which he had undertaken. Work on the text of the *Mémoires* was to occupy a large part of his spare time for almost a year, and the painstaking review of additional testimonies was especially time-consuming. In one sense, he had done nothing more than to counterfeit, with elaborate care, the memoir which Mme de La Rochejaquelein would have written if she had been preserved from the fallibility of an ordinary eye-witness. But in another sense – the only valid one from his point of view – he had aided the engenderment of a valid history. He had enabled the through passage of 'des sentimens et des faits', rather than overlaying them with the falsifying devices of historiographic convention. He was bearing constantly in mind the erroneous model which both he and his source of information identified in the history of Alphonse de Beauchamp, as the following letter from Mme de La Rochejaquelein makes clear:

[Beauchamp] n'a point changé sa troisième édition. Je doute que la quatrième puisse jamais être bonne dans le genre que vous préférez. Il ne descendra pas de son échafaudage. Il a fait le portrait d'Henri en médaille antique coiffé à la Titus, et, ne sachant comment la vêtir; il lui a coupé le col.[38]

Beauchamp has not changed his third edition. I doubt whether the fourth could ever be good in the genre that you prefer. He will not come down from his scaffolding. He has done the portrait of Henri in the style of an antique medal, with coiffure *à la Titus*, and, not knowing how to dress him, he has cut him off at the neck.

Reference to the particular issue of the characterisation of Henri de La Rochejaquelein makes it possible for us to consider, in more detailed terms, the issue which preoccupied both Barante and his correspondent. We may compare the 'entry', and brief description, of the Vendée hero in three distinct sources: the history of Alphonse de Beauchamp, the original, uncorrected account of Mme de La Rochejaquelein and the final text of the *Mémoires* after Barante's attentions:

Beauchamp
Un chef célèbre dans le parti royaliste parut alors sur ce théâtre de carnage.
    La Rochejaquelein, fils de l'ancien colonel du régiment royal Pologne, demeurant à Saint-Aubin de Baubigné, près Châtillon, s'était mis à la tête des insurgés de son territoire. Jeune, d'un tempérament vigoureux, l'oeil vif, le né [*sic*] aquilin, la mine guerrière, il semblait né pour les combats. Destiné à jouer un rôle brillant dans l'ancien régime, il crut pouvoir défendre le trône dans la garde constitutionelle de Louis XVI. Le 10 Août renversa ses espérances. Ce fut alors qu'au moment de quitter Paris, il dit: 'Un royaliste n'a plus rien à faire ici, j'irai dans ma province, où bientôt on entendra parler de moi.' Il émigra, rentra peu après dans le Poitou, et enfin prit part à l'insurrection. Son coup d'essai fut une victoire.[39]

[A famous chief in the Royalist party then appeared in this theatre of carnage.
    La Rochejaquelein, son of the former colonel of the royal Polish regiment, living at Saint-Aubin de Baubigné, near Châtillon, put himself at the head of the insurgents of his territory. Young, with a vigorous temperament, a bright eye, an aquiline nose, a warlike demeanour, he seemed to be born for battle. Destined to play a brilliant role in the Ancien Régime, he thought it possible to defend the throne in the constitutional guard of Louis XVI. The 10th August overcame his hopes. It was then, at the moment

of leaving Paris, that he said: 'A royalist has nothing more to do here, I will go to my province, where they will soon hear of me.' He emigrated, returned soon after to Poitou, and finally took part in the insurrection. His first blow was a victory.]

Mme de La Rochejaquelein

Je veux commencer par tracer le portrait d'Henri de La Rochejaquelein, que j'augmenterai dans la suite, son caractère s'étant singulièrement développé par la guerre. Il avait cinq pieds sept pouces; extrêmement mince et blond, une figure allongée, il paraissait plutôt Anglais que Français. Il n'avait pas de jolis traits, mais la physiognomie douce et noble. Dans ce temps-là il avait l'air fort timide; on remarquait cependant des yeux très vifs, qui depuis sont devenus si fiers et si ardents qu'on disait qu'il avait un regard d'aigle. Il était excessivement adroit et leste, montait à cheval à merveille. C'était un bon sujet, sévère sur ses devoirs.[40]

[I want to begin by tracing the portrait of Henri de La Rochejaquelein, which I shall fill out at a later stage, his character having been singularly developed by the war. He was about 5ft 7ins tall; extremely blond and slender, with a long face, he appeared more English than French. He was not good-looking, but his physiognomy was gentle and noble. In those days he had a very timid air; however people noticed his very bright eyes, which subsequently became so proud and fiery that it was said that he had a gaze like an eagle. He was extraordinarily adroit and nimble, rode on horseback with remarkable skill. He was a good subject, with a severe regard for duty.]

Mme de La Rochejaquelein/Barante

M. Henri de La Rochejaquelein était enfin parvenu à s'échapper de Paris; tout sa famille avait émigré; il se trouvait seul au château de la Durbelière ... Henri de La Rochejaquelein avait alors vingt ans. C'était un jeune homme assez timide, et qui avait peu vécu dans le monde; ses manières et son langage laconique étaient remarquables par la simplicité et le naturel; il avait une physiognomie douce et noble; ses yeux, malgré son air timide, paraissaient vifs et animés; depuis, son regard devint fier et ardent. Il avait une taille élevée et svelte, des cheveux blonds, un visage un peu allongé, et une tournure plutôt anglaise que française. Il excellait dans tous les exercices du corps, surtout à monter à cheval.[41]

[M. Henri de La Rochejaquelein had finally succeeded in escaping from Paris; the whole of his family had emigrated; he found himself alone in the Château de La Durbelière ... Henri de La Rochejaquelein was then twenty years old. He was quite a timid young man, who had little experience of the world; his manners and his laconic way of speaking were remarkable for their simplicity and naturalness; he had a gentle and noble physiognomy; his eyes, despite his timid air, appeared bright and animated; subsequently his gaze became proud and fiery. He was tall and slender, with blond hair, a rather long face, and an appearance more English than French. He excelled in all bodily exercises, and above all in riding on horseback.]

It will be clear from this comparison that much more is at stake, for Barante, than the implicit correction of an inaccurate source. He does, indeed, correct Beauchamp's inaccurate statement that La Rochejaquelein briefly joined the emigration. But his most evident concern is to preserve and enhance the invaluable personal reminiscence of Mme de La Rochejaquelein. As she perceptively described it, Beauchamp had constructed an Henri all of one piece, in a classical mould: 'médaille antique coiffé à la Titus'. Her own account, by contrast, stresses the crucial fact that Henri was changed by his very experience of the wars; his appearance and character, moreover, were made up of conflicting, even incongruous elements. Barante has taken care to extract the 'scaffolding' of this primary testimony: the *incipit* 'Je veux commencer par tracer' is missing, as is the equivocal and superfluous last sentence. But the nuances of his source are all there, and the composite 'portrait' finely and economically drawn.

It is not difficult to sketch in the immediate intellectual context of Barante's historiographic enterprise. In 1808, his close friend Benjamin Constant had been wrestling with the problem of translating Schiller's *Wallenstein* for the French theâtre, and lamenting the intolerable pressures of classicist convention: 'Je ne connais pas de naturel en tout que les nuances, mais, en France, il y a pour le théâtre un certain nombre de moules à caractères ... Les couleurs locales ne leur plaisent pas du tout, et les moeurs de tous les siècles doivent être celles convenues au théâtre.'[42] ('I know of no other form of naturalness but what is there in nuances, but, in France, there are a certain number of character moulds for the theatre ... Local colours do not please them at all, and the manners of every period have to be those which are conventionally accepted in the theatre.') In the reaction of Barante, Constant and other members of the circle of Mme de Staël against the stereotypes of classicism, history had already come to have a particular value. It served, in the simplest terms, as a principle of *difference*, a panacea against the totalitarian oscillation 'from the same to the same'. Barante, the imperial official reconstructing the testimony of a die-hard royalist, put into the apparently self-abnegating role of the re-writer of the *Mémoires* the lessons of a thorough training in the Romantic school of 'le naturel'. But he also expressed there a deep sense of the necessity to conserve the otherness of the past. We have already considered the specifications for the ideal historian laid down by Mme de Staël's friend and intellectual ally, Wilhelm von Humboldt: 'A simple presentation is at the same time the primary, indispensable condition of his work and the highest achievement he will be able to attain. Regarded in this way, he seems to be merely receptive and reproductive, not himself active and creative.' Whether or not Humboldt was aware of the *Mémoires*, it seems obvious that these words could have been applied directly to Barante's achievement. He had not only delighted his source by producing a new version which she still recognised as her own, but he had established the conditions under which he was finally to disappear completely from the authorial scene. As his friend Charles de Rémusat put it later in the century, 'Rien ne sent moins l'auteur que ces Mémoires.'[43] ('There is nothing which puts you less in mind of an author than these Memoirs.') By this time, Barante's name had disappeared from the title-page and indeed ceased to be associated with the work.

The adventitious nature of my juxtaposition of the historian and the taxi-dermist will doubtless have already made its point. Waterton repudiates a method of reconstruction which has filled museums of natural history with travesties of natural life. Mme de La Rochejaquelein, and Barante, sense the incongruity of a historical style which constructs its heroes according to a preconceived pattern of what a hero should be. To Waterton's 'mere dried specimen, shrunk too much in this part, or too bloated in that' corresponds Mme de La Rochejaquelein's 'médaille antique coiffé à la Titus' whose throat has been cut for want of any principle of animation. Waterton's radical approach provides for the dissection and reduction of the living thing to a shapeless skin, and its reconstruction, through science and corrosive sublimate, to the point where the visitor will exclaim: 'That animal is alive!' Barante's technique is to animate from within, as it were, the fragmented text of Mme de La Rochejaquelein and to give it a life in which his own science is totally obliterated. Thus the critic Alfred Nettement writes in 1858 of the constantly republished work: 'Ces mémoires feront vivre éternellement l'époque et le pays qui y sont peints avec des couleurs si vives et des traits si naturels qu'on croit voir respirer les personnages, les moeurs, la Vendée toute entière ... C'est la nature prise sur le fait, c'est la vérité dite sans réticence, sans ambages, sans ornement.'[44] ('These memoirs will give eternal life to the period and the country which are painted in them with such lively colours and such natural strokes that you think you can see the people breathing, their way of life and the whole of the Vendée being no less vivid ... This is Nature seized in the act, this is truth told without reticence, without circumlocution, without ornamentation.') The naked Clio, once again, and with a vengeance.

Let us, however, be circumspect about making too close an equation between Waterton and Barante. The taxidermist who parenthetically admitted the role of 'artist' to be more applicable to the process of reconstruction than that of simple 'operator' is indeed capable of engendering monsters. As a frontispiece to the *Wanderings*, he illustrates the most celebrated and bizarre of these: the so-called 'Nondescript' which consists of a monkey's carcase cunningly manipulated to ape the expression on the face of a learned judge. For Waterton, the exacerbation of his social and political life was at times too acute for the scientific conscience. Having possessed himself of the appropriate technique for making the dead live again, he could use this power to confute a political opponent or satirise the degeneracy of Hanoverian England. Indeed it is arguable that Waterton's veritable obsession with life-like representation has its pathological correlative in a fascination with monsters – with the composite, incongruous beast which yet simulated the seamless integrity of organic life. In this connection, it is worth pointing out that his most bitter polemic, which dogged his entire scientific career, was in defence of the claim that he had ridden on the back of a cayman: or more precisely, in defence of the authenticity of an illustration representing this feat, in which the naturalist and the reptile are incongruously clasped together.

No further reference is necessary to indicate Waterton's kinship with the pervasive Romantic fantasy of the human creator, who usurps the divine prerogative. The period which saw the publication of Mary Shelley's *Frankenstein* was well qualified to sense the ambiguities in any human preoccupation with the recreation of life. But we may well ask at this stage how the monstrous *double face* of the new taxidermy relates to the new history. How does the risk of monstrosity occur to the historian, if at all? Once the question is posed in this way, an obvious answer suggests itself. Let us grant that the historian, like the taxidermist, is conscious of the power which his technique offers him over the dissected carcase of the historic past: the pre-condition of his new concern with recreation is precisely the sense of being 'dispossessed' of history to which Foucault alludes. He will therefore have to situate somewhere, even if not in the historian's practice, the possibility of using the rhetoric of recreation to dubious ends. And a notorious culprit is there to be arraigned: the author of *Waverley*, Sir Walter Scott.

   Considered in this way, the evident perturbation caused by Scott within a whole generation of historians acquires a full significance. Ranke relates in his autobiography that, after reading *Quentin Durward*, he 'took the resolution to avoid, in [his] works, all imagination and all invention and to restrict myself severely to the facts'.[45] The very anxiety to establish this distinction between 'all' imagination and invention, on the one hand, and on the other the facts, is of course the evidence of a desire to repress the rhetorical status of historical writing – a desire which Ranke so effectively transmitted to his successors. For Macaulay, on the other hand, the monstrosity is already an intertextual fact; contemporary readers are already obliged to look 'for one half of King James in Hume and for the other half in the Fortunes of Nigel'[46] (Scott's Jacobean novel). The historian's business is therefore to aspire, at least, to recovering the mythic wholeness of the historical *disjecta membra*. If the German and the English historians express their reserve in general terms, it is left to a French historian to meet Scott promptly on his own ground. Prosper de Barante, whose success in divesting Henri de La Rochejaquelein of his classical garb has already been mentioned, was already at work on his *Histoire des Ducs de Bourgogne* when he read the French translation of *Quentin Durward*. An exchange of letters with his fellow historian François Guizot resulted in unqualified agreement on Scott's misrepresentation of the character of Louis XI. As Guizot expressed it, Scott had committed the same fault as Beauchamp with the hero of the Vendée: 'Walter Scott a conçu un type plutôt qu'il n'a peint un individu.'[47] ('Walter Scott has conceived a type, rather than painting an individual.') By contrast, Guizot's response to the successive volumes of Barante's history showed a ready acknowledgement of his success: 'Votre Louis XI m'a charmé; pour la première fois je l'ai vu tel que je l'avois un peu entrevu.'[48] ('Your Louis XI charmed me; for the first time I saw him in the way that I had just glimpsed him a little.') The critic of the *Journal des Débats* went even further in proclaiming his achievement: 'Sous la plume de M. de Barante, la narration devient une action visible. Son Louis XI parle et agit comme sur le théâtre même où s'est accomplie sa haute destinée.'[49] ('Under the pen of M. de Barante, narration becomes a visible action. His Louis XI speaks and acts as if he were on the very theatre where his lofty destiny was accomplished.')

Our comparative pursuit of taxidermy and historiography therefore returns us to a more thorough investigation of the problem of life-like representation, whether enunciated by a historian or proclaimed in the press. To single out, as comparable cases, the 'mounted' specimen of natural history and the 'narrated' specimen of the illustrious past, is to pose in more insistent terms the question of the text in which the latter is inserted. For Waterton, after all, there is an institutional boundary. The museum of natural history (and indeed, in another way, the nature reserve which Waterton himself pioneered) defines the field within which the specimen must appear 'life-like'. For the collector of historical objects, as I shall demonstrate later, the problem is strictly analogous. The creator of the Musée de Cluny, Alexandre du Sommerard, rehabilitated the diverse historical objects of his collection through arranging them in separate rooms which evoked a complex picture of 'medieval life'.[50] But for the historian proper, the extrapolation is not possible. It is therefore a question of searching more diligently for the terms of representation as they are conveyed within the text: that is to say, within the intertextuality composed of the history, the 'meta-historical' essay and the article of critical response. As anticipated in the first section of this chapter, it is a question of scrutinising the modes of representation to which the nineteenth-century historian declares his affinity, and rediscovering the undisclosed affinities which eluded his awareness.

Having begun this chapter with an allusion to 'the most famous statement in all historiography', let me open its concluding section with a return to the almost equally famous statement which characterises Ranke's mythic status as the pioneer of modern historiography. In his 'Inaugural Lecture on the Study of History', delivered in June 1895, Lord Acton pronounced: 'Ranke is the representative of the age which instituted the modern study of History. He taught it to be critical, to be colourless, and to be new.'[51] A few years later, introducing his new translation of the *Latin and Teutonic Nations* to the British public, E. Armstrong gave what was no doubt intended to be a gloss on the 'colourless' aspect of the Master's teaching: 'Ranke probably never aimed at being a colourist; his natural gift was that of an artist in black and white, or at most in tinted line. Nevertheless, when he takes up the palette, he shows a fine and delicate sense for atmosphere and texture, the result less of technical skill than of imaginative indwelling in his subject.'[52] The translator's note is, at first sight, curiously incoherent. What exactly would be 'an artist in black and white'? How does this notion, or that of 'tinted line', square with the classical image of the painter taking up the palette, on which the full range of oil colours is conventionally arrayed? Again, what is the force of the antithesis between 'technical skill' and 'imaginative indwelling', if it is something more than the mere depreciation of technique and style which we have already witnessed as a cliché of the Romantic period? These questions can be answered indirectly, at least, if we assume that the apparent incoherence is a sign of endemic disturbance within the field of representation to which reference is being made. In short, the translator is taking his metaphors from a domain which has been rendered problematic by the intrusion of photography into the traditional spectrum of the visual arts. 'An artist in black and white' – did not the great painter Degas proclaim towards the end of his life, in 1906: 'If I could live my life again, I should do nothing but black and white.'?[53] 'Colour' and 'tinted line' – it is worth bearing in mind that, until 1907 precisely, when the Lumière brothers pioneered a primitive form of colour photography known as the 'autochrome', photography could only acquire colour through tinting. 'Atmosphere and texture', 'less of technical skill than of imaginative indwelling in his subject' – are not the criteria close to those which defined the new method of capturing and perpetuating the image of the real world on a light-responsive plate?

What I would argue is that Armstrong's metaphors, and indeed Acton's adjective – applied as they are around the turn of the century – plunge us back once again into the ferment in representation which characterised the Europe of the 1820s: the decade of Niepce's first photographic image (1822) and Daguerre's historical diorama (1823) as well as of Ranke's Preface. But the connection between these disparate form of representation cannot, of course, be appreciated simply from the synchronic study of phenomena which appear to occupy the same epistemological space. We need to go back further into the history of representation if we are to understand in what sense to take the 'colour' references, whether admitted or repressed, in the historical or meta-historical text. As classic a formulation as we are likely to find, and one which is germane to the whole context which has been developed here, is the definition of types of perspective offered by Leonardo:

There are three sorts of perspective: the first is related to the causes of diminution or, as it is known, the diminishing perspective of objects according to their distance from the eye. The second is the way in which colours are modified as they get further from the eye. The third and last consists in the definition of how objects must be depicted with less and less precision as they get further and further away.[54]

What must be stressed about the relation of colour to perspective implied in Leonardo's scheme is the fact that colour is necessarily conceived as subordinate. It is a property of bodies, which alters according to their respective placing within the perspectival recession. Yet, as Jean-Louis Schefer has argued, the history of painting since the eighteenth century has been that of the gradual emancipation of colour both from figuration and from perspective. Already in the eighteenth century, with Goya and Watteau, 'the quantum invested in colour displaces and tends to continually annul the quantum in implicitness, the system of figures'.[55] From playing a merely distinctive and differential role within the Renaissance system of representation, colour has itself come to characterise the modern reversal of that system: a reversal which is exactly conveyed in the contrast between Leonardo's repression of colour as such and the crucial value attached by Cézanne to his 'petite sensation colorante'.[56]

Yet what may appear at first sight as a specific trait of the history of painting turns out to have a much more pervasive influence within the development of representation in the more general sense. Post-Renaissance painting is, as Schefer has again argued, a scenography:[57] it therefore shares with theatrical representation the system of geometrical construction according to a unique vanishing point. Moreover, the vocabulary proper to painting plays, within the theoretical writings of classicism, a colonising role. Consequently we find that the term 'colour' is a constellation which brings together the threads of the aesthetic conflict which, in the middle of the eighteenth century, already anticipated the battle of Classicism and Romanticism. Marmontel, seeking to identify the difference between Greek tragedy and that of his countrymen Racine and Voltaire, chooses his metaphors directly from painting: 'dans le grec, on verra des couleurs fortes, mais entières, sans reflets et sans demi-teintes; dans le français, mille nuances qui, loin d'affaiblir la peinture, ne la rendent que plus vivante, plus variée et plus sensible'[58] ('in the Greek, you will see strong but unmixed colours, without reflections and half-tones; in the French, a thousand nuances which, far from weakening the picture, only go towards making it more lively, more varied and more sensitive'). Marmontel is, of course, speaking at this point of the literary text. But the priority of painting as an aesthetic pacesetter is also fully demonstrated in his concern with costume and *mise-en-scène*. Pursuing his mock dialogue with the exponent of classicist convention, he asks:

Comment les habillerait un grand peintre? Il faut donner, dit-on, quelque chose aux moeurs de son temps. Il fallait donc aussi que Lebrun frisât Porus et mit des gants à Alexandre. C'est au spectateur à se déplacer, non au spectacle; et c'est la réflexion que tous les acteurs devraient faire à chaque rôle qu'ils vont jouer: on ne verrait point paraître César en perruque carrée, ni Ulysse sortir tout poudré du milieu des flots.[59]

[How would a great painter dress them? It is necessary, so they say, to concede something to the manners of one's time. So it was also necessary for Lebrun to have Porus in curls and Alexander in gloves. It is for the spectator to be displaced, and not the spectacle; and that is what all actors ought to reflect upon, with each role that they are to play: then we would no longer see Caesar appear in a square wig, nor Ulysses emerge all in powder from the midst of the waves.]

In making a catachresis out of Caesar and his wig, Marmontel pours ridicule precisely on the historical anomaly of conventional costume. And, through whatever vicissitudes of 'fidelity' Talma and his successors might lead it, the principle to be known as 'couleur locale' gained ground irreversibly throughout the revolutionary and imperial epochs. But it is important to note the force of Marmontel's succinct statement: 'it is for the spectator to be displaced, and not the spectacle'. Such an implication does not merely involve the search for authentic costume and *mise-en-scène* – which, after all, can only be judged by the ill-informed spectator in terms of their absolute divergence from his own experience of everyday life or of the stage. It also indicates, as a project, the possibility of exceeding the norms of *vraisemblance*, of literally taking the spectator out of his place through overpowering illusion. Confronted with Daguerre's diorama, the young spectator of the late 1820s can only exclaim his incredulity:

'I thought it was to be only a picture,' said Edward; 'but they must be real rocks and mountains, made on purpose!'

'*It is only a picture,*' replied Mr Finsbury. 'To convince yourself of this, you have only to change your position in the room, and you will see the objects are seen in exactly the same way, go where you will. For instance, there is a projection *represented* of a piece of rock in front. If a real projection, by moving across the apartment, you will see a little this way or that of the object behind it; but you find that it is in vain that you rise from your seat, or stoop, or go from side to side; nothing different can be seen. It must, therefore, be a plain surface.'[60]

Edward is hardly convinced, for the scene shifts finally and he protests: 'Oh, this *must be* a real town!' His insistence, and the advice of Mr Finsbury on how to reassure oneself of the representational status of the image, recalls us to the ambiguities and indeed contradictions in the sequence of developments which has been traced. For Daguerre's diorama, so far from epitomising the 'spilling' of colour within the representational system, is in effect the direct descendant of Leonardo's perspectival scheme. It is strictly dependent, as Mr Finsbury's advice demonstrates, on the establishment of a single viewpoint. It makes it a matter of intellectual proof for the image to be diagnosed as 'paper and colours' rather than 'posts, boards, tiles, stones, utensils, a roadway'. Through an extraordinarily ingenious combination of front and back illumination, it floods the image with an overall luminosity which contradicts the very principle of 'couleur locale' in its proper sense: '*Couleur locale*, en peinture, est la couleur propre à chaque objet, indépendamment de la distribution particulière de la lumière et des ombres.'[61] ('*Local colour*, in painting, is the colour proper to each object, independently of the particular distribution of light and shade.')

We therefore arrive at a conclusion which appears, at any rate, to contradict the tentative conclusions of my first section. What may seem to be the 'heterodox' representation of the diorama turns out to be the reinforcement of traditional schemata through new techniques. And yet there is still the problem of colour, 'local colour' or 'spilling' colour, in the system. Obviously the definition just quoted represents an antithetical term: the object, in painting, will never have its own colour entirely to the exclusion of 'the distribution of light and shade', but will always be more or less 'local' in its colouring. But the use of the term as a slogan by the Romantics does at least involve a transgressive intention: to proceed as far as possible in the direction of the individual and the particular at the expense of the general. Equally, Schefer's concept, which of course anticipates the 'emancipation' of colour from figure and perspective in the present century, embodies the Utopia of a colour not merely local in the object, but asserting its own materiality irrespective of all systematic constraint. Is there any significant parallel to this sense within the field of representation which has been under discussion? More particularly, can we now return to the immediate province of historiography and find comparable distinctions which will enable us to place more exactly both the 'colourless' virtue of Ranke, and the epistemological configuration within which it has its place?

The prelude to any resolution of this question is, of course, a reference to the way in which historical representation was conceived in the eighteenth century. Here, again, the *encyclopédiste* Marmontel is revealingly explicit. Despite the conventional definition of the historian's role in the terms of Herodotus, he devotes most of his attention to spatialising the historical field according to the metaphor of pictorial perspective. Invoking 'les points de perspective que les écrivains se proposent' ('the points of perspective which writers adopt for themselves'), he conceptualises the relation to the past in terms which echo Leonardo's definition: 'Plus la postérité pour laquelle on écrit est reculée, plus l'intérêt des détails diminue ... Il n'y a que les peuples célèbres et les hommes vraiment illustres, dont les particularités domestiques soient intéressantes encore à une certaine distance.'[62] ('The further away the posterity for which one writes, the more the interest of the details is diminished ... There remain only famous peoples and truly illustrious men, whose domestic particularities are still interesting at a certain distance.') An immediate consequence of this model is the repression of colour, conceived as the positive and personal element of the historian's style, and the metaphor of transparency comes to hand: 'Quelqu'un a dit que pour *l'historien*, le meilleur style étoit celui qui ressembloit à une eau limpide. Mais s'il n'a point de couleur à soi, il prendra naturellement celle de son sujet, comme le ruisseau prend la teinture du sable qui forme son lit.'[63] ('Someone has said that for the *historian*, the best style was that which resembled limpid water. But if it has no colour in itself, it will naturally take on that of its subject, as the stream takes on the tint of the sand which forms its bed.')

Prefiguring of historical space in terms of receding perspective, repression of colour as the trace of the author's style – what is the third element which, in Leonardo's terms, gives this conception its coherence? Clearly, it is the eye of the painter which, in a quasi-theological sense, ordains the perspectival system and enables the spectator to take his place there vicariously. Hence the subject who was expelled in the name of colourlessness returns to guarantee the system from his unique point of view. Marmontel can speak of the way in which the historical writer 's'impose la tâche pénible d'embrasser d'un coup d'oeil tout ce qu'un siècle lui présente d'intéressant pour l'avenir'[64] ('takes upon himself the arduous task of embracing with a glance all that a century offers him which is of interest for the future'). Note that the criterion of 'interest for the future' sets the seal upon the coherence of the system. The receding perspective departs from, and returns to, the ordaining eye: the 'vanishing point' in the picture is no more than a necessary theoretical consequence of the external, ideal subjectivity.

It is indeed striking how tenaciously the young Macaulay, in his 1828 essay on 'History', holds to this traditional view of historical representation. Not only does he defend it, but he explicitly rejects the temptation to claim for historiography a more secure epistemological grounding. For him, history is not concerned with the naked Clio, truth as 'one' and admitting of 'no degrees'. It can observe only 'the truth of imitation in the fine arts'.[65] To illustrate this point, Macaulay chooses to compare the portrait of 'a handsome peeress' by Sir

Thomas Lawrence with the same lady as revealed by 'a powerful microscope' which would disclose 'the pores of the skin, the blood-vessels of the eye'. Of course the example is disconcertingly revealing in its avoidance of the scientific paradigm. The subject (the peeress) is given, and the requirement is not for a critical instrument which will disturb this imaginary coherence in the interests of knowledge, but simply for a confirmation of a conventional status. Significantly, Macaulay develops his parallel in terms which juxtapose, as metaphors of historical representation, the avoidance of colour and the establishment of perspective:

A bust of white marble may give an excellent idea of a blooming face. Colour the lips and cheeks of the bust, leaving the hair and eyes unaltered, and the similarity, instead of being more striking, will be less so. History has its foreground and its background; *history* and it is principally in the management of its perspective that one artist differs from *conceived* another. Some events must be represented on a large scale, others diminished; the great *in* majority will be lost in the dimness of the horizon; and a general idea of their joint effect *pictorial* will be given by a few slight touches.[66] *terms*

Of course, the necessary implication of this problematic of 'diminishment' and 'dimness' is the reinforcement of the single point of view as the guarantee of perspective: in Leonardo's words, 'Perspective comes to our aid where our judgement is at fault with regard to things which recede and diminish.' Such a remark may illuminate obliquely the significance of the 'Whig view of history'. By contrast, the problematic which Augustin Thierry develops in the Preface to his *Histoire de la Conquête de l'Angleterre par les Normands* (1825) seems to be designed specifically to confute the traditional conception which Macaulay defends. The single-point perspective is superseded by the requirement of local colour:

In the present day, however, it is no longer permissible to write history for the profit of one single idea; our age will not sanction it; it requires to be told everything, to have portrayed and explained to it the existence of nations at various epochs; and that each past century shall have assigned to it its true place, its colour, and its signification.[67]

Thierry remains implicitly within the pictorial metaphor at this stage, causing a direct reversal of the perspectival scheme. But his concluding remarks go far beyond this rhetorical level. Simultaneously Thierry asserts the 'scientific' commitment which Macaulay disclaimed, and the need to place the problem of 'colour' on the level of the signifier, in the very names and linguistic forms which find their place in the historical narrative:

I have only now to mention one other historical innovation, of no less importance than the rest; the retaining the orthography of the Saxon, Norman, and other names, so as to keep constantly marked out the distinction of races, and to secure the local colouring which is one of the conditions, not merely of historic interest, but of historic truth. I have, in like manner, taken care not to apply to one period the language, forms, or titles of another. In a word, I have essayed thoroughly to reintegrate political facts, details of manners, official forms, languages, and names; so as, by restoring to each period comprised in my narrative its external aspect, its original features, its reality, to communicate to this portion of history the certitude and fixity which are the distinguishing characteristics of the positive sciences.[68].

Where then does Ranke belong within the polarity of Macaulay and Thierry? On the one hand, there is no doubt that he represses, as strongly as Macaulay, the question of 'colour'. Indeed this *lapsus*, which Thierry would legitimately lead us to associate with an attention to the historical name as signifier, causes him to repeat, towards the end of his life, the fantasy of evacuating the text of Scott which Macaulay disclosed in 1828. 'But a truly great historian', writes Macaulay, 'would reclaim those materials which the novelist has appropriated.'[69] Only a few weeks before his death (according to his first English translator) Ranke was regretting that Scott 'was not more available for the purposes of a historian than he is . . . What valuable lessons were not to be drawn from facts to which the great English novelist had the key; yet, by reason of the fault to which I have referred, I have been unable to illustrate many of my assertions by reference to him.'[70] The notion of a Scott with footnotes, sedulously split again in the apparatus of Ranke's own footnotes and references, is a comic but an intensely revealing one. The designation 'colourless' does indeed conceal an absolute dedication to the binary division between 'facts' and 'style', and a consistent repression of the signifying level of the historian's discourse.

Yet Ranke is not, quite evidently, espousing the categories of imitation and the metaphor of perspective as Macaulay does. The elliptical statement which with this essay began testifies beyond doubt to that fact. The 'high office' abjured is, at one level, the perspectival viewpoint.[71] The aim to 'show what actually happened' is breathtakingly free of the circumspection of *mimesis*. Indeed my references to the ideal of 'life-like' representation, in taxidermy, in the diorama and in the daguerreotype, have been largely devoted to establishing a representational space in which Ranke's claim could be seen to have meaning: a space in which new techniques were explicitly devoted to securing an overpowering illusion of presence. But I would wish to repeat my reservation about the 'novelty' of this aim, which can appropriately be seen as the intensification, through technique, of the conditions of representation implicit in Renaissance perspective. In this light, the 'colourless' virtue of Ranke can be regarded as a disavowal of language, of the historical *signifier*, and Ranke's nineteenth-century reputation (which still persists) as the mythic perpetuation of this disavowal. By comparison, the relative undervaluation of Thierry, despite his strict contemporaneity with Ranke, should be understood in the light of his determination to assert simultaneously the claims of language and of science.

This study will continue, therefore, along the path which Thierry invites us to take. It will trace, in the next chapter, a sequence of three historians who have an incontestable centrality in early-nineteenth-century French historiography: Prosper de Barante, whose early ghosting of the memoirs of Mme de La Rochejaquelein has already been considered here; Michelet, who raises in its most acute form the problem of the boundary between history and literature;

and Thierry himself. It will be suggested that these three historians, taken in relation to each other, offer an invaluable insight into the way in which the rhetoric of historiography was developed during the early nineteenth century. Analysis of their work prepares us for the more comprehensive review of the strategies used to recreate the past in this period – for the formulation of a 'historical poetics'.

Such an initial choice of direction perhaps implies a contemporary *parti pris*, which will become more evident in my conclusion. In the preceding argument, my concern has not been so much to depreciate the achievement of Ranke, as to draw the outline of the Rankean myth. 'To show how, essentially, things happened' was a noble undertaking, which anchored Ranke within the epistemological space of his times, and still continues to merit study and respect. But the phrase itself is liable to become, in its mythic fixity, a Head of Medusa, petrifying the impulse to meta-historical inquiry. If we want to counteract this tendency, we need only look to the lineal successors of Barante, Thierry and Michelet – to the contemporary French *Annales* school. They remind us, if any reminder is required, that a creative modern historiography need not immolate its poetics upon the altar of scientific method.

Question ability to depict objective history
- argues for creative presence of author in order to resurrect indexical trace of presence.
- based on scientific method with object to present 'as it really was' → without alternate agenda
- but accept importance of language (creativity) in process.

A cycle in historical discourse:
Barante, Thierry, Michelet

A great difficulty in evaluating the work of Michelet is the fact that he seems to call for a wholly new variety of critical attention. Or rather, his historical writings make us feel the need for a new type of critical animal by revealing themselves only partially to scholars of the traditional type. There exist, of course, exhaustive studies of Michelet the stylist. But, in these, the specific problems of historical recreation are apt to be swamped by the general considerations of rhetoric analysis. There are also many studies of Michelet the historian: yet the most honest of these are liable to conclude with an apology. 'I will in the end take Michelet, and I must take him', writes Peter Geyl, 'as he was.'[1] Roland Barthes, whose sympathy for Michelet is evident in the brilliant selection from his writings for the series 'Ecrivains de toujours', resolves the critical dilemma precisely by dissolving it. Michelet did not exercise a profession (that of historian), or a priesthood (that of poet), according to Barthes. His calling was a 'magistrature', as he himself insisted. And it was precisely through becoming a discredited historian (by scientific standards) that he was able to become by the same process sociologist, ethnologist and psycho-analyst: in short, the precursor of a 'general science of Man'.[2]

Barthes' viewpoint offers a new perspective on Michelet. But it does not wholly dispel the original dilemma. Perhaps this can be seen in its most acute form in Gustave Rudler's study of the famous section on Joan of Arc, from the *Histoire de France*. Rudler, as one might expect of a renowned historian of literature, is no less sensitive to the aesthetic issues of style than to the scientific problems of historical reconstruction. Yet this very duality of approach obliges him to do a perpetual balancing act between approval and reprobation. 'In principle', writes Rudler, 'his method was inadmissible. There could be no excuse for not basing his narrative on fresh reading and meditation.' Michelet is thus arraigned for his reliance on secondary sources. But, if he has not succeeded in presenting us with the definitive history of Joan of Arc, he can nonetheless be acclaimed as the author of a 'pathetic, dramatic, patriotic and religious legend, an epic, a work of philosophy and art'.[3]

Rudler brings to the foreground, as indeed does Barthes, the fundamental point of difference between Michelet and the German school of historians. He 'had not learnt the trade ... he had had to form himself all on his own'.[4] Michelet's relationship to his predecessors among French historians was not strictly a professional one, like that of the pupils of Ranke's seminar to their master. He had no opportunity of deriving from his academic seniors a critical method for assessing and reviewing original sources. Indeed the relationship which he established now seems perilously close to plagiarism on occasions, since not only the 'fact', but parts of the written narrative are liable to be transferred from the secondary work into Michelet's own discourse. One might have expected that in these circumstances Michelet would have been anxious to conceal the guilty secret of his 'borrowings'. Yet this does not seem to be the case. How are we to account for his apparently flagrant disregard for the protocols of historical scholarship?

The questions prompted by Rudler's reading of the 'Joan of Arc' section have more recently been reinforced by the discoveries of the editor of Michelet's journals.[5] Although a critical edition of the proceedings of the trial of Joan of Arc was available at the very moment when he was composing the relevant sections of the *Histoire de France*, Michelet made very few emendations to his manuscript in response to this original source. Whenever he 'retouched' his narrative, he did so for what appear to have been stylistic reasons. Are we to conclude that, both in his relation to his predecessors and in his treatment of source material, Michelet placed convenience before science, style before historicity? The case looks black. But there is at least a partial answer to the indictment implied in a mysterious hint which Michelet offered in a letter to Sainte-Beuve. The hint has not received much attention up to now. But, as the title of this chapter indicates, it forms the kernel of my present argument. Michelet writes:

If you examine the historians of this age, you will take into account, I imagine, both *the point at which I found history, and the step which I have made*. Barante, Thierry and I form a kind of cycle. You can only make a fair judgement of each one of us through seeing him in his relationship to the others.[6]

I suggest that it is worth lifting for a moment the heavy prohibition which hangs over the notion of plagiarism – and plagiarism among historians in particular – in order to comprehend the full significance of Michelet's remark. Evidently the basis for the condemnation of plagiarism in any context is the mythic notion of 'originality'. But this notion seems to work rather differently in the spheres of art and science. For the literary artist to be 'original' is for him to be, in some irreducible sense, the proprietor of his own language – although we are well aware that at one level he is simply combining and recombining linguistic units which are the property of all. For the would-be scientific historian, 'originality' means more precisely the free play of critical thought upon the existing materials, and a consequent integrity of approach which has cognitive rather than merely stylistic significance. Yet both of these definitions, with their personalist emphasis, neglect the possibility that the relationship between forms of discourse might be assessed according to more objective criteria. It might after all be possible to make important discoveries about the succession of different types of discourse in time, without having recourse to moralistic notions of priority and illicit borrowing. Such, at any rate, is the opening which Michelet seems to be offering in his letter to Sainte-Beuve.

Appropriate tools for following up Michelet's hint can be found in the linguist Roman Jakobson's well-established distinction between the different 'functions' of discourse, and in the anthropologist Claude Lévi-Strauss's ingenious application of three of these functions to the evolution of classical and modern music. Jakobson includes among the different functions of discourse the 'meta-linguistic', the 'referential' and the 'poetic'.[7] Lévi-Strauss singles out these three functions, renames them, and suggests that they help to account for the cyclical recurrence, among composers, of certain specific forms of musical discourse:

> It is only through recognising that there are several different kinds of music that we can overcome what is apparently contradictory in our predilections for very different composers. All becomes clear as soon as we realise that it would be pointless to want to arrange them by order of preference (seeking, for example, to understand whether they are more or less 'great'); in effect, they belong to distinct categories according to the nature of the information of which they make themselves the carriers. In this respect, we could distribute composers *grosso modo* into three groups, within which every type of passage and combination is included. Bach and Stravinsky would thus appear as musicians of the 'code', Beethoven – and indeed Ravel – as musicians of the 'message', Wagner and Debussy as musicians of the 'myth'.[8]

Despite the fact that the context of Lévi-Strauss's remarks is a little unusual – they occur in the Introduction to his anthropological study *Le cru et le cuit* – the suggestion need not be seen as a mere *jeu d'esprit*. It would appear moreover that this three-fold cycle has a possible relevance to the 'cycle' which Michelet invites us to consider. In the chapter which follows, Lévi-Strauss's cyclical model will serve as a working hypothesis in the examination of Michelet's sequence of early nineteenth-century historical texts.

Lévi-Strauss draws his illustrations from the world of music. Jakobson refers to a generalised 'discourse'. Before we can make any precise use of their models, we must obviously determine what are the characteristics of a specifically *historical* discourse. One point comes to mind straight away. The discourse of the historian does not consist, like that of the poet or novelist, in an integrated text which is the beginning and end of all critical investigation. It consists of a text, and most characteristically a narrative, which stands *in relation to* other texts (or *sources*). Indeed the credence which we attach to the text in front of us depends radically on what we suppose to be its relationship to these absent sources. There is of course a sense in which fiction also presumes a relationship to absent texts, as Gérard Genette has argued in his aptly named study, *Palimpsestes*.[9] Adherence to a genre would be one example, while the extensive category of parody is another. More directly relevant to historical narrative, perhaps, is the case of a novel like Fielding's *The History of Jonathan Wild the Great*, which takes for granted our acquaintance with a pre-existent historiographical model: the history of the life of the 'great man', which Jonathan's tempestuous career both imitates and subverts. But in all of these cases, all that is implied is a general structural correspondence between the work and its 'model', or models. The historical text is obliged to correspond to its sources in a particular, rather than a general fashion. What is more, it signals this correspondence to the reader through the textual device of 'notes' or 'references'.

In qualifying the historical text in this way, I am of course singling out a convention which is comparatively new. Paul Veyne has lately drawn attention to the fact that, in sixteenth-century France, the historian Etienne Pasquier attracted complaints of scholastic pedantry from his friends when he circulated the manuscript of his *Recherches de la France*: the view was expressed that a system of references to the work of previous authors was entirely superfluous, since time alone would endow his account with authority, and no short cuts to credibility were permissible.[10] As a supplement to this point, Veyne has indeed argued that the citing of authorities in the body of the text is a convention which belongs in the first place to the literature of legal controversy, and is transferred from there to the historical context when historiography, in its turn, becomes controversial. Whatever we may make of this argument, it is surely clear that the historical text acquires a distinctive and unprecedented authority from the stage at which sources are acknowledged and specified as a matter of course. The *Vindication* with which Gibbon replied to the various detractors of his *Decline and Fall* demonstrates to what a degree historical controversy had developed by the end of the eighteenth century, and how closely the scientific dispute turned at that stage upon the correct or incorrect acknowledgement of sources. Even the task of replying to such inadequate and self-serving critics is of considerable benefit to Gibbon, as it enables him to reveal how thorough his scholarship has been. He has no inkling of the crucial epistemological principle which we identify with Ranke's distinctive contribution to historiography: that is, the radical discrimination between what can be made of primary and what of secondary sources. But he has at least made a significant technical advance in the conventions of quotation, and he is quite ready to point it out:

As I had often felt the inconvenience of the loose and general method of quoting which is so falsely imputed to me, I have carefully distinguished the *books*, the *chapters*, the *sections*, the *pages* of the authors to whom I referred, with a degree of accuracy and attention, which might claim some gratitude, as it has seldom been so regularly practised by any historical writers.[11]

We can take it for granted that the French historians with whom we are concerned, writing more than a generation after Gibbon, were no less mindful of the specific resources available to them, and no less capable of deploying a system of references to enhance the authority of their texts. But, in order to appreciate the significance of their usage, we must try to move away from the realm of subjective intentions, and examine more closely the conventions of discourse which their texts make manifest. It is here that some of the basic tools of Saussure's structural linguistics become relevant. They enable us to see how different applications of the principle of referencing can be distinguished from one another, and how this range of distinctions is directly relevant to Michelet's notion of the 'cycle' of historians.

Saussure made a fundamental distinction between 'two forms of our mental activity: both indispensable to the life of language'.[12] On the one hand, words are related to one another in a linear fashion within discourse: they are, as he puts it, 'chained together' in the speech-acts that we make, and in the texts that we write. On the other hand, words are related to one another in an 'associative' way: a word like 'enseigner' (teach) calls to mind the word 'renseigner' (acquaint). Whereas the first type of relationship is actualised in discourse, the second takes place within the mental 'storehouse' of the individual language speaker: the first, or 'syntagmatic', series is a combination of terms *in praesentia*, whilst the second, 'associative' series is *in absentia*, available to be summoned up by the speaker. As Saussure's original insights have been extended and developed by the exponents of semiology, this distinction has been formalised as an opposition between *syntagm* (the linear order of terms 'in presence') and *system* (the associative order of potential terms 'in absence'). In Roland Barthes' *Elements of Semiology*, detailed attention is given to the potentiality of this syntagm/system opposition for the analysis of very diverse areas of signification.[13]

What then is its relevance to historiography? Equation of the historical narrative with a *syntagm* needs little justification, in view of the frequent use of the term to analyse the linear order of the 'récit', or fictional narrative. But there is also the point that historical narrative is able to encompass, at least by the end of the eighteenth century, that special relationship of the syntagmatic series to a number of additional, absent historical texts, which we term the historian's 'sources'. This second register can be called the historical *system*; it fulfils Saussure's criterion of being a 'series of associative fields', each of which affords a 'store of potential terms (since only one of them is actualised in the present discourse)'.[14] The distinctive role of historical notes, or references, is to act as a kind of shifter between syntagm and system. References serve to remind us of the immense storehouse of parallel and overlapping texts which the historian has drawn upon in the construction of his present narrative.

This schema is in itself comparatively simple, and even banal. But its function here is to facilitate our approach to Michelet's notion of a cycle of historians. If we can isolate a special feature of the historical text and describe it in these exact terms, then we can perhaps begin to perceive significant differences in the practice of Michelet's two predecessors, and open up the implications of the concepts which we have borrowed from Jakobson and Lévi-Strauss. Certainly we might expect that the distinction between Barante as a historian of the 'code', and Thierry as a historian of the 'message' would be reflected in their attitudes to the balance of syntagm and system in the historical narrative. We might expect that the historian of the code would be concerned to emphasise the primacy of the syntagm over the system: this is because his discourse is, in Jakobson's terms, 'meta-linguistic', and so draws attention to the intrinsic properties of the signifying chain. Barante's epigraph from Quintilian ('scribitur ad narrandum non ad probandum '), aptly signals his intention to do just this: he will take 'narration' rather than 'proof' as the aim of his writing. Equally, we might expect that the historian of the message, whose discourse is 'referential', would emphasise the primacy of system over syntagm. Rather than foregrounding the narrative process in this way, he would be concerned to emphasise as effectively as possible the range and importance of the sources upon which he has drawn.

If we start by examining the relationship of text to references (and hence to the 'system') in the works of these two historians, we do indeed find an immediate difference between their usages. This becomes evident if we make a comparison between two works which were almost contemporary: Barante's magnum opus, the *Histoire des Ducs de Bourgogne de la Maison de Valois* (1824–26), and Thierry's *Histoire de la Conquête de l'Angleterre par les Normands* (1825). In the case of Barante, the reference is confined in the vast majority of cases to the simplest possible indication of provenance. It may take the form of one word – 'Commines' – or several juxtaposed words – 'Hollinshed–Rapin Thoyras–Hume–Commines'. Thus the reference serves to tie the text to a source, whether primary or secondary. But this identification does not in fact permit the precise conjunction of a unit of narrative isolated from the syntagm and a unit of narrative isolated from the system. In effect, Barante's references return us to his own text. Since there is no exact reference to volume, page, etc., the link with the system is of the most schematic, not to say dubious kind.

Thierry's practice is quite different, as the following extract makes clear:

Text: 'Mais les Franks n'avaient alors de foi qu'en leurs haches d'armes, et cela suffit pour que le coeur des évêques gaulois se tournât vers eux, pour que tous, suivant l'expression d'un auteur presque contemporain, souhaitassent la domination des Franks avec un désir d'amour.'

Reference: 'Cum omnes eos amore desiderabili cuperent regnare.' (Gregor. Turonensis, cap. 23)[15]

[Text: 'But the Franks at that time had faith only in their battle-axes and that was sufficient for the hearts of the Gallic bishops to turn towards them, so that all of them, to use the expression of an almost contemporary author, wished for the domination of the Franks with a loving desire.'

Reference: 'As all wished them to rule with a desirous love.' (Gregor. Turonensis, cap. 23)]

In this case, and in many other cases, the relevant source is not only given in its original language and with a precise reference. It is anticipated in the text by a preparatory phrase: 'suivant l'expression d'un auteur contemporain'. Thus Thierry, far from throwing the weight of our attention on his text, prepares us to see the relevant phrase both as syntagm, in isolation from the narrative sequence, and as system (a term actualised from the store of potential terms). The preparatory words, on the one hand, and the reference number, on the other, serve to seal off the unit of discourse: a firm link is forged between syntagm and system.

The significance of both Barante's and Thierry's usage in this area becomes much more clear if we compare their respective methods with that of an adherent of the classical tradition in French historiography: J.-F. Michaud, the historian of the Crusades. When Michaud refers for the first time to the war-cry of the crusading army, he thinks it necessary to append the following footnote: '"*God wishes it!*" was pronounced, in the language of the time, "*Dieu li volt!*" or "*Diex le volt!*"'. ('*Dieu le veut*! était prononcé, dans le langage du temps, *Dieu li volt*! ou *Diex le volt*!').[16] Such a notation may at first sight appear to demonstrate the same concern for authenticity as Thierry's habit of replacing Latinate appellations with genuine Merovingian names:

Text: '. . . des enfants de Mere-wig . . .'
Reference: 'Par corruption, Mérovée, en latin, Merovicus, Merovoeus. Mère, moere, mehre, grand, célèbre. Wig, guerrier. (Gloss. Wachteri).'[17]

[Text: '. . . children of Mere-wig . . .'
Reference: 'Through corruption, Mérovée, in Latin, Merovicus, Merovoeus. Mère, moere, mehre, great, famous. Wig, warrior. (Gloss. Wachteri).']

There is, however, a vital difference between these two usages. Michaud situates the authentic detail in the footnote, thereby suggesting that the achievement of such auditory realism is merely incidental. Thierry, on the other hand, makes a specific point of incorporating the Merovingian name into his narrative. In his Introduction to the *Histoire de la Conquête*, he claimed with pride:

I have now only one other historical innovation to mention, of no less importance than the rest: the retention of the orthography of the Saxon, Norman and other names, so as to keep the differences between the races constantly in the foreground, and to secure the local colouring which is one of the conditions, not merely of historical interest, but of historical truth.[18]

This recourse to the intentions of the historian is a necessary step in the elucidation of our original problem: the distinction between text and reference viewed in relation to the opposition syntagm/system. In particular, the introduction of the concept of local colour is highly germane to this problem. What may be generally regarded as a woolly Romantic notion has in effect a very precise significance, not least in relation to Thierry, and to Barante, who may indeed have been the first to apply this concept to literature.[19]

'Local colour' is a concept originally derived from the art of painting, where it signifies the colour which is proper to each object, independent of the distribution of light and shade over the entire pictorial field. As Barante used the term in a series of articles of drama criticism for *Le Publiciste* in 1806, the literary exploitation of local colour meant essentially the restitution, on the level of the text, of such authentic turns of phrase as would lead the reader (or spectator) to envisage a historical milieu, rather than the milieu of the writer's own day. 'Look how in Richard', he writes approvingly of Sedaine, 'simply with the words of *crusade, the wicked Saracens, the good King Richard*, Sedaine draws us in and charms us.'[20]

It would be justifiable to see Barante's critical attitude as the direct ancestor of Thierry's principle of retaining original orthography. But it must not be inferred that local colour held exactly the same implications for both. In his unfavourable review of Bouilly and Dupaty's *Agnès Sorel*,[21] Barante concludes by quoting the verses supposedly written by Agnès Sorel to Charles VII, and contrasts them with the stilted language of the play. 'Is there a couplet, in the play,' he asks, 'which has as much grace as this?' Yet he is not arguing in favour of a style of dramatic writing which would be capable of assimilating such vivid and authentic texts. As the comments on Sedaine show, he requires simply that the language should be consistent, both in its avoidance of such modern subtleties as the pun, and in its frequent recourse to naive and simple expressions. We might extend the analogy with painting by saying that for Barante the individual parts of the picture must have just enough distinctive colouring to show that they are not simply reflecting an overall pattern of light and shade, yet not so much colouring that they break up the unity of the composition.

Before the comparison with Thierry is drawn, it seems worthwhile to extend the parallel with Michaud. In the work of Michaud, as has been shown, the authentic detail may occur in a footnote. But the text has complete primacy, because Michaud's commitment is still to the sequences of balanced phrases, amply furnished with felicitous antitheses, that were his heritage as a classical stylist. In the Preface to his work on the Crusades, he quaintly deplores his own situation by comparison with that of the modern historian of Greece and Rome. Whereas the classical historian might have provided him with 'models to follow', the historians of the Middle Ages could be said to have 'rarely sustained' him 'by the charm of their style and the elegance of their narrative'.[22]

Michaud's position is therefore symmetrically opposed to that of Barante. Michaud, finding little 'charm' in the medieval sources and preferring the classical models, expels the authentic detail to a footnote and so gives his text stylistic consistency. Barante, rejecting puns and other modern stylistic devices, discovers 'grace' in the authentic sources and allows his text to be stylistically determined by the use of language in these sources. Yet he is equally obliged to suppress the too vivid note of authenticity which would destroy the unity of his text. In the *Ducs de Bourgogne*, he adopts throughout his narrative the naive and simple phraseology for which he had praised Sedaine: '*les sages et riches bourgeois*', '*le chevalier le plus vaillant et le plus aimable*', '*au beau Château de Male*'.

Thierry's position is quite different from that of either Michaud or Barante. While both the latter tend to throw the chief weight of attention on the text, Michaud in the interests of classical and Barante in the interests of Gothic models, Thierry attempts precisely to create a balance of text and footnote, syntagm and system. Whereas Barante views local colour in terms of the predominance of a syntagmatic chain, Thierry sees it as a correspondence of syntagm and system. Thus he writes in the Preface to his *Histoire de la Conquête*: 'I have consulted none but original texts and documents, either for the details of the various circumstances narrated, or for the characters of the persons and populations that figure in them. I have drawn so largely upon these texts, that, I flatter myself, little is left in them for other writers.'[23] The last sentence is particularly significant, since it underlines the singularity of Thierry's position. He is not repelled by the barbarity of the medieval texts, like Michaud, nor does he attempt, like Barante, to create a substitute text. His aim, and, as he claims, his achievement, is to exhaust the sources in the text, while leaving for the reader the visible evidence that this process is taking place. For Thierry, the system is therefore co-extensive with the syntagm.

Up to this point, my analysis has concentrated upon the significance of the text/reference relation as an indication of the relation between syntagm and system in the work of these historians. And it is surely evident that the various usages which I have described are of central relevance to the varying conceptions of historical truth held by them. Yet my contention is that the text/reference relation, however important, is merely one aspect of an overall pattern discernible in their varying approaches to historical discourse. The distinction between Barante as a historian of the 'code' and Thierry as a historian of the 'message' becomes even more evident if we consider the overall organisation of the two works under consideration: their 'horizontal' as opposed to 'vertical' (text/ reference) discontinuities.

An initial pointer is provided once again by the expressed intentions of these historians. Just as Thierry establishes a strict correspondence between syntagm and system, so he is anxious to allow an ulterior meaning, or 'message', to emerge from his narrative. Here again, however, it is useful to take account of the sequence Michaud/Barante/Thierry. Michaud raises the central issue, when he writes in the Introduction to the fourth edition of the *Histoire des Croisades*:

I have been reproached for not having had a uniform and fixed system which serves to regulate all my judgements, and preside over the development and the very spirit of my narrative. I congratulate myself, by contrast, on not having had a limited system and viewpoint. It is easy to see in this connection that people have judged me as if I had composed a poem or a novel. The educated know very well that history is made, but that we do not make it; that we can write it, but we cannot compose it.[24]

This fascinating passage shows that Michaud was indeed aware, however paradoxical it may seem with reference to his style, of the necessity for history to be freed from the constricting pressures of classical 'composition'. Yet it is only with Barante that the full consequences of this insight become apparent. Barante also makes the point that historical writing is, in its very essence, opposed to literature: that the structure of a historical work can never be intrinsic, like that of a literary work, since it must always be measured against the extrinsic structures of history as a whole. Thus he writes, not with reference to classical models but to the historical novels of Scott: 'The beauty of history is to be the link in an uninterrupted chain. The literary composition closes its conclusion upon itself.'[25]

[Handwritten margin note at top: Barante: let the structure emerge from the work to facilitate illusion of transportation]

This view of the individual work as a link within the overall chain of history is reflected in the internal divisions of Barante's *Ducs de Bourgogne*. Lévi-Strauss provided as his definition of the 'musician of the code' that he should 'make explicit and comment upon . . . the rules of a musical discourse'. In the same way, Barante fulfils the condition of being a historian of the code to the extent that the structure of his work is calculated to emphasise, on every level, the process of history as an uninterrupted chain. Here lies the explanation of his insistence on the syntagm, which is itself most characteristically presented in the form of a chain.[26] On quite a different level, here is the reason why his *Ducs de Bourgogne* is a near approach to a continuous narrative, with divisions only of the most neutral kind. The smallest unit of division in this work is the individual 'book', which is never shorter than 35,000 words. The only larger units of division are the 'given' periods of time provided by the reigns of the four Dukes and Marie de Bourgogne. And never at any of these points of transition does Barante attempt to 'sum up', or create a convergence of themes. In fact he takes great care to minimise the break in continuity, as when a description of the funeral procession of Jean-sans-Peur is confined to a subsidiary clause, and the main clause opens the reign of Philippe-le-Bon with an account of the resumption of the war with France.

Indeed Barante's concern to exclude any hint of an overall system existing beyond the 'enchainment' of the narrative lays him open to the charge of mystification. The broad division of the history according to the reigns of the Dukes of Burgundy becomes ultimately, with the reign of Marie de Bourgogne, the merest subterfuge. By this stage, the central character of the work is, without a shadow of a doubt, Louis XI, King of France. Yet even this result may be seen as a vindication of Barante's consistency. So far from 'closing its conclusion upon itself', this work progresses towards the historically given stage at which its subject, the Duchy of Burgundy, ceases to exist as a separate unit. Barante chooses for his ending the precise point where one 'link' in the chain is joined to another.

If we return to Thierry, it is clear that the section of history which has been chosen represents not a link in the chain, but a definable historical problem. In other terms, the unity of the work is a function of a particular system which rapidly becomes evident. The title reads in full: 'Histoire de la Conquête de l'Angleterre par les Normands, de ses causes, et de ses suites jusqu'à nos jours, en Angleterre, en Ecosse, en Irlande et sur le Continent'. Whereas Barante establishes his 'meta-linguistic' emphasis through using the epigraph from Quintilian – 'scribitur ad narrandum, non ad probandum' – Thierry begins his work with a quotation from the Chronicle of Robert of Gloucester:

> The folk of Normandie
> Among us woneth yet, and shalleth evermore.
> Of Normans beth these high men that beth in this land,
> And the lowmen of Saxons . . .

The character of the system which earned for Thierry Marx's appellation of 'father of the doctrine of class struggle' is thus evident from the outset. Even

[Handwritten note at bottom: Thierry – sources organized & presented to facilitate arg/thesis = message]

the division of books in his work, which may seem at first sight to be more or less neutral, can be shown to reflect this overall system. Such a heading as 'From the formation of the refugee camp in the Isle of Ely up to the execution of the last Saxon chief' ('Depuis la formation du camp de refuge dans l'île d'Ely jusqu'au supplice du dernier chef Saxon') presumes not merely a chronological but also a conceptual division. And indeed Thierry's narrative, in direct contrast to that of Barante, involves a certain amount of general discussion on the themes raised within a particular section.

It therefore appears that the broad distinction between Barante as an adherent of the syntagm and Thierry as an adherent of the system can be perceived on many levels. Barante, reacting violently against the classicist tradition in historiography, exploits the syntactic principle of 'enchainment' in a most extreme form: to this end, he abandons not only precise references to sources but also divisions within the narrative that might suggest conceptual patterns over and beyond the syntagm. Thierry, by contrast, implies both in his title and in his epigraph that he is dealing with the problematic of English history in the relevant period. Thus, although he states in his Introduction that the age will not sanction the writing of history 'for the profit of a single idea', and proclaims that his method is essentially that of narrative, he is aware at the same time that his work is a construct as well as a linear flow:

Under this philosophical point of view, and independent of the picturesque interest which I have endeavoured to create, I hoped to aid the progress of science by constructing, if I may use the expression, the history of the Welsh, of the Irish of pure race, of the Scots . . .[27]

Since we have examined the opposition between Barante and Thierry on a number of levels, we might indeed complete the line of polarities by incorporating what might be described as the ultimate level of intentionality: the two historians' choice of subject, and the precise relation of these subjects to the notion of history, more precisely European history, as a whole. Here, in accordance with Jakobson's insight,[28] we might extend the opposition of syntagm and system to an opposition of metonymy and metaphor. In the case of Thierry, the *Histoire de la Conquête* is presented as a metaphor of the underlying conflicts of early medieval Europe. To borrow a graphic phrase from the prospectus to his first volume: 'The conquest of England by the Normans is the *image* [my italics] of those great Germanic invasions which are the primitive basis of the principal European nations . . .' In the case of Barante, there is no such identification. The history of Burgundy is simply a part of the greater history of France and Europe. One might develop the point a little further by claiming that, for Thierry, the History of England becomes the History of Europe by substitution and identification (metaphor), while for Barante the History of Burgundy becomes the History of France by contiguity and assimilation (metonymy). The former results from the decision of the historian to view his material in such terms, while the latter arises from the natural and inevitable progress of historical events.

[handwritten margin note: Thierry – subject matter (message) is metaphor for larger message. Barante – subject matter is historical link in contextual chain. (metonymy).]

This opposition between metonymy and metaphor recurs in an unusually striking way if we consider not simply the respective narratives of Barante and Thierry, but also the extensive visual materials which were published in conjunction with the texts. Yet we need to look first of all at the implications of bringing this kind of material within the field of historical discourse. It is by no means clear that all of this illustrative material (maps, portraits, vignettes, etc.) was collected together with the historians' co-operation, and substantial differences exist between the ranges of material found in different editions of the same work. We can in fact be fairly sure that, in some cases, illustrations were not formally 'passed' by the historian, since no other hypothesis could account for the appearance in a late edition of Thierry's *Histoire de la Conquête* of a plate celebrating an event which the text announced to be fictitious.[29] A note had to be included to point out that the incident was 'not historical', but had been 'taken inadvertently by the draughtsman from a legend which is cited as being a mere fable'. In view of these reservations, some might argue that materials of this kind are strictly irrelevant to our purpose, however interesting they may be in their own right – as cartography, or minor Romantic art.

In spite of these difficulties, it can be maintained that the method which has been adopted in this chapter inevitably entails a consideration of the visual apparatus of the historical text. Already, in examining the implications of the different usages of the reference or footnote in Barante and Thierry, we have made the assumption that the text mobilises a system of references which exists outside itself, and that this dimension is an integral aspect of its meaning. We might well expect that not only footnotes, but line drawings, engravings and maps, and whatever other types of illustration are employed, participate in the unified effect of historical discourse, and are involved in the general problem of balancing the historical narrative (syntagm) against the historical system.

Indeed the conclusion of this line of inquiry may well be a frankly 'transsubjective' view of the communication implicit in historical discourse. Once we move from the simple consideration of 'words on the page' to the examination of signifying procedures like the relation of text to source, we are obliged to take into account a much wider field of analysis. It is no longer so much a question of the individual historian and his proprietary text, as of 'history' being communicated throughout a particular society according to a special set of rules and protocols. Once this is conceded, we are bound to diverge to a certain extent from the terms of this investigation prompted by Michelet and undertaken with the aid of semiological method. It may not in fact be a question of the 'historian of the code' or the 'historian of the message', but of 'history of the code' and 'history of the message'. At any rate, this seems probable from a comparative survey of the illustrations in their respective works. If we look at the successive editions of the *Ducs de Bourgogne* and the *Histoire de la Conquête*, we find that illustrations of the metonymic and the metaphoric order are indeed linked in the first instance with the different textual strategies of the two historians. But it is also clear that metaphoric representations tended, with the passage of time, to

metaphoric illus = integrated w text in coherent system
vs metonymic = distinct but to augment argument
44   The Clothing of Clio contiguous (metonymic) = part of whole.

supplement and even to displace the metonymic. By the stage of Barante's sixth edition (1842), most of the illustrations are of the same type as those which had originally appeared in earlier editions of Thierry.

The claim that the initial illustrations to the *Ducs de Bourgogne* belong to the metonymic rather than the metaphoric order needs no special pleading. Illustrative material occurs for the first time in the third edition of the work (1825–26), and is published in the form of a self-contained 'Atlas' which was announced in the eleventh volume of this edition.[30] No doubt the spectacular success of the *Ducs de Bourgogne* had alerted the publisher Ladvocat to the opportunity of providing something more elaborate and imaginative than the simple narrative text, and had induced him to approach, among others, the rising young Romantic painter, Deveria. It was Deveria who had provided drawings for the engraving of the portraits of the Dukes of Burgundy, which could be inserted as frontispieces to the relevant volumes of the edition. Each consists simply of the bust of the particular Duke, with face and clothing strongly individualised, against a background no more precise than a stormy sky. Withdrawn from the 'action', they form a simple series, destined to be placed in contiguity with the volumes of the work which bear their respective names. They do not relate to the narrative in any more specific way. Nor do they *illustrate* it, at least in the sense in which the term is used at present.

No doubt because of the pressure to make all available capital out of a bestseller, the Atlas contains another series of portraits which follow a different convention of presentation. Instead of confining himself to the bust, Deveria shows his subject in full figure, suggesting an appearance on a stage rather than the traditional pose of portrait painting. But there is still the irresistible impression that these figures have been abstracted from the action, like costumed characters appearing on the stage after the curtain has gone down. Only in one instance does Deveria vary this formula. The caption to the engraving reads: 'An officer of arms announcing the death of Charles VI to his son the Duke of Touraine (1422)'. But the vivid specificity of the caption is hardly borne out by the image, which merely shows the messenger in appropriate dress, and provides neither background nor interlocutor for the scene which is evoked. If this image stands out, it is precisely because it fails to satisfy the expectations that a significant action will be recreated, in all its circumstantial detail.

It would be hazardous to explore the significance of these visual addenda, if the prospectus to the Atlas had not offered a number of clues to their intended function. Thus we read that: 'the journal of a siege or the description of a battle will speak more clearly to our thought when the draughtsman interprets the historian, and when the compass can verify the calculations of the pen'. This formulation leaves us a little in the dark. Precisely *how* will the draughtsman 'interpret' the historian? A subsequent passage offers us a more substantial clue: 'the imagination conceives a more vivid idea of an action, *when it is able to place it on the scene where it has taken place*' [my italics]. The phrase must be taken in its most literal sense, however odd the consequences for our own notion of 'historical-mindedness'. The point is that 'scene' and 'action' must remain separate, each belonging to quite a different syntagmatic chain from the other. Thus, when a plate of the 'Grand Place de Bruges' is provided, it is shown entirely devoid of action, and dated 1740, which is of course several centuries later than the tumultuous events recounted in the *Ducs de Bourgogne*. When a plate of a late medieval building is provided, it bears the caption: 'This house, forming a part of the fortifications of Paris constructed by Philip Augustus, can be found on the site between the Rue Mauconseil and the Rue du Petit Lion'. In both cases, the reader must himself supply the historical context, whether from information supplied by the preceding narrative or from more general knowledge of the late Middle Ages in France and Flanders.

As can be seen, the illustrations to the third edition of Barante's *Ducs de Bourgogne* form a limited and incoherent system. Whether or not they are taken out of the Atlas and distributed throughout the text, they succeed one another in a merely rudimentary type of classification, signalled by such headings as 'Personages and costumes of the time', 'Monuments' and 'Plans'. Any conjunction between the narrative text and the illustrations occurs not on the level of the narrated action, but as a kind of interweaving of separate syntagmatic chains. We could say that the illustration is not substituted for an episode in the narration (metaphor); it relates to the narration simply through contiguity (metonymy). 'On reading of the seditions in the main square at Ghent', suggests the prospectus, 'one feels the need to see the gothic facade *before which* [my italics] all of these furious people pressed themselves'. No attempt is made to illustrate the turbulent action which is here evoked.

If we turn from the *Ducs de Bourgogne* to the 1838 edition of Thierry's *Histoire de la Conquête*, it can be seen that the relationship of narrative to illustrative matter has changed quite radically. There are a few images which are reminiscent of the earlier usage. For example, Thierry's frontispiece displays a juxtaposed 'Saxon warrior and Danish pirate', who are no less clearly abstracted from the action than Barante's Dukes. Yet even here it could be argued that Thierry's figures have a different significance. They are, after all, symbolically representative of the overall system, the dialectical 'message' of the whole work. Apart from these rare instances, Thierry's illustrations consist to an overwhelming degree of episodes selected from the narrative. The spectrum of incidents extends from the virtually static scene – 'The monk Augustine preaching before King Ethelbert' – to the highly dynamic action – 'Massacre of the monks of Croyland by the Danes'. And, as a matter of course, the plate is inserted in the book opposite the precise point in the text where the relevant incident occurs. The visual elements do not exist *in relation to* the text, as is the case with Barante's Atlas. On the contrary, each plate *is*, by metaphorical substitution, an action related in the narrative.

In the 1842 edition of the *Ducs de Bourgogne*, 'metaphoric' illustrations of this type are used to supplement the 'metonymic' images which belonged to the earlier editions. We not only have, for example, the splendidly caparisoned

2. *Costumed characters appearing on the stage after the curtain has gone down:* Jean-sans-Peur (John the Fearless, Duke of Burgundy), from Barante, *Histoire des Ducs de Bourgogne* (1842 edition)

3. *Shown at the very moment preceding his assassination:* Meurtre du duc Jean (Murder of Duke John), from Barante, *Histoire des Ducs de Bourgogne* (1842 edition)

Dukes of Burgundy, in full-figure illustrations which seem to be based on Deveria's original drawings (or their contemporary sources); we also have Tony Johannot's vivid and exciting sketches, engraved by Thompson, of significant turning points and colourful episodes in the narration. Jean-sans-Peur poses before us in the most sumptuous of robes, against a lightly indicated and vaguely Gothic background. A few pages away, however, he is shown at the very moment preceding his assassination, with his bonnet fallen to the ground and the assassin's axe uplifted. The visual artist has exploited a device which the historical narrator cannot lay claim to. He has used the simultaneity of the image to arrest our attention with the prospect of imminent catastrophe.

To the extent to which this comparison between Barante and Thierry has involved the incorporation of illustrative material as an integral part of the historical discourse, it also opens up a much more general question of the limits of this particular analysis. Clearly the differences between types of illustration, and their development through time, cannot be regarded simply as exclusive to the system of historical discourse, in the strict sense of historical narrative. Deveria may be Barante's illustrator, but he is also a historical painter, of the Romantic school, with links to, say, Bonington and Delacroix. Are we to assume that there is a more general 'historical-mindedness', of which historical painting and the historical narratives discussed above are separate but, as it were, convergent aspects? If so, what part is played by the specific properties of the medium in determining the character of the historical representation which is achieved? We certainly do not, as a matter of convention, test historical paintings by the same criteria of authenticity as we employ to test a historical narrative. Yet the very fact that visual representations of different kinds are used – as in the preceding examples – to supplement or complement the narrative suggests that we are not just dealing with a categorical distinction between the 'true' and the 'fictional'. These questions cannot be fully discussed at this stage, but the next chapter will attempt to set out some detailed lines of procedure for assessing the visual representation of historical events throughout this period. Initially we must return to Michelet, for whose *Histoire de France* the earlier sections of this chapter have been a kind of prolegomenon. What originally formed a plan of considering Michelet according to his own concept of a 'cycle' of historians, has turned out to have a more precise applicability to the historical texts, once we admit the relevance of semiological and rhetorical analysis. Just as Barante and Thierry have been shown to adhere, on several different levels, to the protocols of two separate (and opposed) modes of discourse, so Michelet can be shown to adopt yet a third mode of historical discourse, defined in Jakobson's terms as the 'poetic'. Lévi-Strauss, who calls this the discourse of 'the myth', suggests that its defining mark is that it should be coded 'from the basis of elements which are already in the order of the *récit*'.[31] And here perhaps lies an initial reason for the apparently paradoxical attitude of Michelet to his predecessors. 'My book ...', he explains in the Introduction to the first volume of the *Histoire de France*, 'is wholly taken from original sources. However I owe a great deal to some of our contemporaries.'[32] The previously noted fact that Michelet does use, and indeed transcribe on occasions, the *récit* of his contemporaries should not simply be seen as a disreputable filching of material, but as an indication of Michelet's position in a cycle of historical discourse – a position whose implications he was in no way concerned to hide.

Of course this analysis carries conviction only if we are prepared to concede two things: first of all, that the meta-language of these historians – the stated intentions of their prefaces – is an adequate guide to the character of their discourse; secondly, that the linguistic and rhetorical concepts which I have been using do indeed help to elicit systematic differences which are implicit both in the text and in the historian's commentary. My study began with the working hypothesis that there was a convergence between Michelet's notion of a cycle and Lévi-Strauss's application of the same term to successions of musical composers. Having concentrated up to this point on the opposition between Barante and Thierry, it is necessary to look at the place which Michelet himself occupies at the end of the cycle. A good text with which to begin the inquiry is a statement from the introduction to the *Histoire de France*, which comes a few pages after the one which has been previously quoted:

This [work] is nothing less than a *récit* and a system, a formula of France, considered on the one hand in its diversity of races and provinces, in its geographical extension, on the other hand in its chronological development, in the growing unity of the national drama. It is a cloth whose frame is space and matter, and whose shuttle is time and thought.[33]

We can therefore see Michelet's history not simply as the successor of those of Barante and Thierry, but as a genuine third stage in the cycle: as an attempt at a synthesis between syntagm (*récit*) and system. Mention has already been made of Thierry's desire that his *Histoire de la Conquête* should be a *construct* as well as a linear flow. Obviously there is an analogy with Michelet here. But Michelet far surpasses Thierry in the rigour and tenacity with which he pursues this objective. It was suggested previously that Thierry emphasises the correspondence of syntagm and system through a firm linkage between text and references, with the references embodying quotations from original sources and therefore being a step nearer to historical 'reality'. Michelet does not favour this situation of correspondence or balance between two levels of discourse. He uses footnotes and references, but, as Rudler reminds us in a most significant passage, 'they are very often subsequent, often external, to the text and without serious connection with it'.[34] For Michelet, the relation between syntagm and system does not depend upon a formal division of this kind between levels of discourse: it remains an intrinsic dimension of the narrative.

It is appropriate to draw a comparison between this creation of levels within the narrative itself, and some of the most perceptive comments that have been passed on Michelet by his contemporaries and successors. Roland Barthes has pointed out the aptness of Sainte-Beuve's reference to the 'vertical' style of Michelet, with its 'frequent short plunges', as opposed to the 'sliding', horizontal style of Chateaubriand.[35] Thomas de Quincey, in his lively essay on Michelet's 'Joan of Arc', remarks with characteristic hyperbole upon the same feature, showing us the historian performing upon the facts as if they were a kind of trampoline:

Facts, and the consequences of facts, draw the writer back to the falconer's lure from the giddiest heights of speculation. Here, therefore – in his *France* – if not always free from flightiness, if now and then off like a rocket for an airy wheel in the clouds, M. Michelet, with natural politeness, never forgets that he has left a large audience waiting for him on earth, and gazing upwards in anxiety for his return: return, therefore, he does.[36]

De Quincey is right to bring out the element of sheer performance in Michelet's style. For an audience acquainted both with Barante's quasi-medieval account of the story of Joan of Arc, and with the original sources for the trial, Michelet must simply do more. He must involve the nineteenth-century reader in an imaginative recreation of the past which is not just an abdication of his nineteenth-century viewpoint, but a thorough involvement in the perilous oscillation between present and past. Hence his typical use of the rhetorical question – what did Joan feel when she heard the five hundred bells of Rouen ring out on that Easter Sunday morning? Note that even in the speculative, flighty appeal of that question, there is contained the approximate factual detail of the five hundred bells. Michelet is the master of what Barthes has fittingly called the 'reality effect':[37] that imaginative supplementation of the historical account with details which may be factually based or may be probable extrapolations, but have the role of confirming its historicity through the very vividness and, as it were, unmotivated immediacy of their effect. It comes perhaps as a surprise to us today to recognise how recently a distinguished historian could recognise this kind of effect as giving history its 'highest truth'. I refer to Nevins's discussion of a paragraph from Parkman in his *Gateway to History*: Parkman's colourful characterisation of a column of soldiers marching through the forests of New England is held to have come close to this 'highest truth', and to have made comprehensible Michelet's aim that history should be a 'resurrection'.[38]

Of course Michelet's concern to make the nineteenth-century reader relive, in some sense, the medieval period is closely bound up with his awareness of the dilemma of modern man confronted with an 'age of faith'. His originality lies in fact that he does not dismiss the dilemma (like Barante), but even sharpens its horns. Hence Rudler is driven to acknowledge that the section of the *Histoire de France* concerned with Joan of Arc is the only existing work 'to combine rationalism and tradition; even better, rationalism and fideism'.[39] Such a claim can, of course, be substantiated only through a demonstration of the rhetorical strategies which Michelet employs in the construction of his narrative. They are at work, I would maintain, from the very first lines of the section devoted to the story of Joan of Arc.

Ce qui fait de Jeanne d'Arc une figure éminemment originale, ce qui la sépare de la foule des enthousiastes qui dans les âges d'ignorance entraînèrent les masses populaires, c'est que ceux-ci pour la plupart durent leur puissance à une force contagieuse de vertige. Elle, au contraire, eut action par la vive lumière qu'elle jeta sur une situation obscure, par une force singulière de bon sens et de bon coeur.[40]

[Joan's eminent originality was her common sense. This sets her apart from the multitude of enthusiasts who, in ages of ignorance, have swayed the masses. In most cases, they derived their power from some dark contagious force of unreason. Her influence, on the contrary, was due to the clear light she was able to throw upon an obscure situation, through the unique virtue of her good sense and of her loving heart.]

What is fascinating about this particular passage is the scrupulous care with which Michelet explores the 'semantic space'[41] proper to historical discourse: the way in which he makes us conscious of this space through stating, or implying, a series of polarities – modern/medieval, rational/irrational, singularity (Jeanne)/plurality (foule). One might indeed reconstruct his meaning according to the following basic schema of oppositions:

Joan of Arc	influenced	the masses by	common sense (light)
enthusiasts	swayed		unreason (obscure situation)

As might be expected at this stage in his work, Michelet is concerned primarily to render present, or to actualise, on the plane of historical narrative, the (absent) historical figure of Joan of Arc. Part of his procedure can be ascribed to this purely technical necessity: against the terms which qualify Joan (*originality, set apart, clear light, unique virtue*) the contrary terms (*multitude, ages of ignorance, swayed, contagious force*) provide a kind of grey and cohesive background. But this procedure of placing Joan in sharp relief against the medieval background is by no means devoid of implications on the historical level. For, by the very fact that he withdraws her from this background, Michelet tends to bring her closer to the reader: Joan's 'light' not only enlightens the 'obscure situation', but also has the effect of drawing her towards our own 'age of enlightenment'.

One might therefore define one of the central features of Michelet's historical discourse as a kind of 'chiasmus', that is to say, a link between terms that belong to different sides in a recurrent series of associated polarities. The point is substantiated in a passage shortly following the one previously quoted. Michelet writes that Joan's originality 'was not in her visions': he then proceeds to quote numerous cases of visions, ending with one from his own time ('la béate du Tyrol').[42] The chiasmus might be represented as follows, with the example of modern obscurantism symmetrically corresponding to Joan's medieval enlightenment:

$$\frac{\text{medieval}}{\text{modern}} \times \frac{\text{visions}}{\text{good sense}}$$

I hope that I have adduced enough examples to establish that Michelet's 'vertical' style, with its 'frequent short plunges', takes its character from a consistent use (and abuse) of polarities, and that these polarities revert constantly to the central historical opposition of past and present (unknowable and knowable, irrational and rational). Michelet's grandiose aim was to write 'a book of this time and of that time',[43] if we may borrow the phrase which he himself applied to Barante's *Ducs de Bourgogne*. But Barante's success was limited to a short period of time: as soon as the original texts of Froissart and Commines were published, and as soon as the public had learnt to recognise, if not to read them, the system so rigorously excluded from the *Ducs de Bourgogne* began to appear behind the carefully constructed syntagm. Barante's attempt to create a substitute text, to annihilate the system of sources which lay between the syntagm of narrative and historical reality, thus resulted in failure: Michelet himself eventually dismissed the *Ducs de Bourgogne* as 'nothingness' ('néant').[44] Where Barante had tried to create the illusion of authenticity through suppressing any overt hint of the gap between past and present, Michelet by contrast chose to recreate, and reiterate, this gap within the very texture of his narrative.

Consistency requires that I should make reference to two further aspects of Michelet's work, both of which have been taken into account in the case of Barante and Thierry. In the first place, there is the question of the relation of the particular history to a wider field, or to history as a whole. I suggested that the distinction between Barante and Thierry in this respect lay in the fact that, for Thierry, the History of England becomes the History of Europe by substitution and identification (metaphor), while for Barante the History of Burgundy becomes the History of France by contiguity and assimilation (metonymy). With Michelet there is, once again, a refusal to allow programmatic division of syntagm and system, metaphor and metonymy. The History of France becomes the History of France: that is to say, France as a mere union of provinces finally becomes France as a unity, a chemical concretion, of provinces.[45] The final stage of this process is the Revolution, but the initial stage, of no less importance, is the mission of Joan of Arc. Michelet writes:

Pour la première fois, on le sent, la France est aimée comme une personne. Et elle devient telle, du jour qu'elle est aimée.

C'était jusque là une réunion de provinces, un vaste chaos de fiefs, grand pays, d'idée vague. Mais, dès ce jour, par la force du coeur, elle est une Patrie.[46]

[For the first time, we sense it, France is loved like a person. And she becomes such, from the day that she is loved.]

[Up to then there was a collection of provinces, a vast chaos of fiefs, a large country, with a vague idea. But, from that day, through the force of the heart, France is a Fatherland.]

Here, perhaps, is the most dramatic example of Michelet's connections between syntagm and system. The great theme of French unity, the dominant 'message' of the entire work, is brought down to the level of one unit of syntax, one link in the chain. France herself is 'born from the heart of a woman'.

It remains merely to mention Michelet's attitude to the problem of illustrations, which we previously identified both on a metonymic and on a metaphoric level. Here the answer is quite simply that illustrative material, when it occurs, is as lacking in 'serious connection' with the text as are Michelet's footnotes. For the truth is that here, as in the other cases which have been discussed, Michelet attempts to articulate the division between syntagm and system within the narrative itself. Illustrations are neither necessary nor helpful, because Michelet is his own illustrator and portraitist. As Roland Barthes remarks, 'each body' in history is to Michelet 'a secret' which must be explored and understood.[47] Hence his characterisations – 'Robespierre–Chat', 'Marat–Crapaud' – which bring before us not the external, picturesque lineaments, but the inward personality, according to a complex psychology of materials and humours. The only possible visual gloss on these verbal characterisations (as Barthes himself leads us to conclude) is material drawn from the stock of contemporary portraits of the subjects in question.

In conclusion to this chapter, it seems necessary to anticipate one major objection, and to sound one note of warning. The objection would be that this section concentrates, to an excessive degree, upon particular works by three French historians, and therefore forfeits the possibility of reaching any general conclusions about historical discourse in early nineteenth-century Europe. Two separate issues are involved here: whether the works, or sections of works, are typical of their authors, and how these three French historians relate to their age.

As far as the first point goes, there seems to be little genuine cause for objection. The two works by Barante and Thierry are, in the former case unquestionably, and in the latter case arguably, the central creations of their careers as historians. The references made to the *Mémoires de Madame de la Rochejaquelein* in the previous chapter will have shown how consistent was Barante's concern to efface himself behind his source. In the case of Thierry, even a work so different in structure from the *Histoire de la Conquête* as his *Lettres sur l'histoire de France* exemplifies the same local features. As for Michelet, there can be no disputing the central place in his career occupied by the *Histoire de France*, and the 'Joan of Arc' episode must surely be regarded as one of the acid tests of his 'resurrectionist' method.

In answer to the second point, I should like to state immediately that, in my view, no 'cycle' of such plausibility could be found among English, or German, historians. Ultimately this must be because of the unique historical experience of France, which involved rupture and discontinuity of an order much greater than in the other two countries during the period in question. Engels wrote in his Preface to *The Eighteenth Brumaire* that Marx had a 'particular predilection'[48] for French history, because it demonstrated in an almost classical form the structural changes in European society which formed the basis of his historical analysis, from feudalism to the Bourgeois Revolution. For our purposes, no doubt, French historiography has the same exemplary role. Conscious of the break with the eighteenth century and working within no defined institutional framework, like their German contemporaries, they offer a pattern of development which seems to be integrally related to the new 'historical-mindedness' of the period. They show how different rhetorical strategies, different ways of representing the past to an increasingly sophisticated public, succeed one another in a regular, and not an arbitrary fashion. I would not wish to imply that 'history of the code', 'history of the message', and 'history of the myth' are explanatory concepts which will suffice for the very extensive review of historical representation contained in this study. At the same time, I would hold that this particular 'cycle' demonstrates the dividends of a semiological or rhetorical analysis of historiography, and helps us to determine the place of historiography within the colourful spectrum of ways of representing the past which forms the focus of this study.

3   Image and letter in the rediscovery of the
      past: Daguerre, Charles Alfred Stothard,
      Landseer, Delaroche

In the previous chapter, attention was directed to the three narrative histories of
Barante, Thierry and Michelet. Here, it might be argued, was the primary
material for any investigation of 'historical-mindedness' in the period: a series
of texts which directly and unequivocally proclaimed themselves to be history.
Yet my investigation did not take for granted the generic label of 'history', as if
it conferred a distinct and privileged status upon this collection of texts. On the
contrary, it tried to establish certain distinct procedures of the *new* historiography of the early nineteenth century, and used Lévi-Strauss's cycle of code,
message and myth to indicate how these procedures developed in a series of
concrete examples. Yet, as a direct result of this analysis, an interesting problem
emerged with regard to the illustrative material included in successive editions of
these histories. The predominant type of illustration appeared to change, with
the transition from earlier edition to later edition, from metonymic to metaphoric: from inclusion of plans, maps, historical monuments and individual
historical personages, to the portrayal of actual moments in the narration. In
other words, illustrative material followed a similar pattern of development as
the historical text itself – though as an independent variable, since even Barante's
impeccably metonymic history had acquired, by the 1840s, its complement of
lively historical scenes.

This question of the illustration, which is used in conjunction with the
written text but is related at the same time to a wide range of other modes of
visual representation, poses the more general issue of the role of the visual image
in recreating the historical past. Upon what basis is it possible to compare the
relative roles of the image and the letter in establishing a new vision of history?
The whole issue is complicated, of course, by the embedding of metaphors of
vision in our descriptive language. If, as was argued in the first chapter, the
notion of perspective has been an indispensable figurative aid to conceptualising
the historical field, then we must beware of confusing this metaphorical 'vision'
with the literally visual image of the historical painter, or the historical set
designer. We must also, as in the case of the historical text, look for the identi-
fiably new elements, of technique or subject matter, which distinguish certain
forms of visual representation from others, and so establish which forms had the
distinctive property of acting as carriers for the new awareness of the past.

This chapter makes no claim to be a comprehensive review of the myriad

visual representations of history in early nineteenth-century Europe; it simply
seeks to clarify the conditions under which the visual image became part of the
general movement towards rediscovering and recreating the past. A useful short
cut can be made if we concentrate first of all on the wide-ranging and provocative study of historical painting in the nineteenth century which was published
by Roy Strong in 1978: *And when did you last see your father?* In his passage on
'Historic architecture' from Batty Langley to Hunt, Strong touches upon the
crucial issue. Referring to earlier studies like Lord Clark's *The Gothic Revival*, he
points out that the considerable research undertaken into the work of Victorian
revivalist architects has not spilled over into adjacent areas of study. 'In other
words, the work of the early investigators has been looked at vertically, in terms
of its influence on later generations, but never horizontally, in the broad context
of its overall relationship to the rediscovery of the past.'[1] Precisely so. And it is
with the 'broad context' of relationships to the 'rediscovery of the past' that
this study is specifically concerned. But this apparent convergence of aims
obliges us to look more closely at the implicit and explicit assumptions of Strong's
survey. He has, without any doubt, brought together types of visual material
which complement and extend the material that has been used up to this point.
But it could be argued that he has failed to appreciate all that is involved in the
'rediscovery of the past'.

The main reason for this defect becomes clear from the opening of Strong's
account. Inextricably interwoven with the survey of British historical painting
in the later eighteenth and nineteenth centuries is a sharp polemic against some
of the entrenched tendencies of present-day art history. Strong is opposed to the
'Berensonian belief that art is really little more than the evolution of style', and
he holds that the persistence of this belief has distorted our sense of the relative
importance of Victorian painters:

We cultivate third-rate Pre-Raphaelite artists because we approve of their milieu – a
world of images echoing the obsession of our own painters with private as against public
mythologies – but we ignore the sheer quality and brilliance of C. W. Cope's or E. M.
Ward's great historical set pieces in the Houses of Parliament.[2]

This may well be so, and Strong may be justified in taking up the cudgels on
behalf of heroic High Victorianism. But this is a very different matter from
determining the contribution of historical painting to the rediscovery of the
past. Strong makes a revealing admission when he asserts that such paintings
'are often maligned and underestimated as works of art in their own right'.[3]
Again, the judgement is sustainable according to aesthetic (Berensonian?)
criteria. But it has little to do with the status of historical painting as a representation of history – not 'in its own right' but in the right of the past, so to speak.
These objections are not merely quibbles. For they testify to the fact that Strong
has taken historical painting as an *a priori* category, without testing the assumption that the 'work of art' is a privileged vehicle in the process which he is
describing. By 'work of art', he means in effect the academy picture, the full-
dress oil painting, or the major architectural commission: such works follow one

Roy Strong And when did you last see
your father

4. *The* ne plus ultra *of scenic illusionism:* L.-J.-M. Daguerre, Ruins of the Chapel of Holyrood (1824), after a diorama shown in London in 1825–6

another in majestic succession in his valuable index of 'Subjects from British history from the Ancient Britons to the outbreak of the Napoleonic Wars exhibited at the Royal Academy, 1769–1904'. But it is by no means self-evident that such a cavalcade of historical paintings played a central role in the 're-discovery of the past'. And even if it is conceded that they must have made *some* contribution, it is not immediately obvious how this contribution might be measured or related to others. Here, of course, the 'broad context' must be reasserted.

One example may help to clarify this point, since it poses the question of the hierarchy of types of visual communication in a particularly acute way. A visitor to an art gallery featuring French nineteenth-century painting comes across a small oil which is entitled 'Ruines de la chapelle de Holyrood' ('Ruins of the Chapel of Holyrood') by Louis-Jacques-Mandé Daguerre, dated 1824. He will certainly start to form certain conclusions about Daguerre's interest in medieval architecture, and the possible role of topographical painting in the 'rediscovery of the past'. But such speculation will be rudely interrupted when he learns that this picture is in fact hardly more than a by-product of Daguerre's scenographic spectacle, the diorama: that it reproduces, in miniature form, the composition of the diorama spectacle 'Ruins of Holyrood' which was on show in London together with the 'Cathedral of Chartres' between March 1825 and February 1826. The picture is still in circulation. The spectacle of the diorama can only be reconstructed with the use of our imagination, from surviving technical details, from contemporary testimony, and from visual evidence such as this. But the inference to be drawn is nonetheless clear. The fact that a portable oil painting has survived, while a complex system of scenographic representation has not, should not lead us to give a disproportionate weight to the former in assessing the historical mentality of the 1820s. In fact, the present example suggests that the degrees of importance might be reversed. We might now regard the picture as a mere souvenir, a pale memento, of the brilliant diorama, well established both in Paris and in London by the mid-1820s, and (as was suggested in the first chapter) offering a *ne plus ultra* of scenic illusionism. We would be able to imagine, within the overall context of visual communications, the magnetic attraction exerted by this novel apparatus. We would surely conclude that if new types of visual representation had anything to do with the 'rediscovery of the past', then Daguerre's diorama must have had a privileged place in the process.[4]

On the basis of this example, some initial ideas about the part played by visual representation in creating the new historical-mindedness may be formulated. I suggest that we should look for two distinct yet complementary functions. On the one hand, there is the localised and particular *effect*. This is comparable to, but by no means identical with, the 'effet de réel' or 'reality effect' which has already been mentioned in connection with Michelet. Barthes uses as one of his examples of the 'effet de réel' the brief sentence which Michelet inserts towards the close of his description of Charlotte Corday's imprisonment: 'after an hour and a half, someone knocked softly at a little door behind her'.[5] Judged in the context of Charlotte Corday's brief respite from execution, and the final arrival of the ominous summons, this 'little door' has no special narrative function: it simply assures us of the 'reality' of the process which is being re-enacted. In the case of visual representations, the 'effect' is also in a sense one of redundancy: it is precisely the authentic detail which appears *almost* gratuitous – which passes *almost* unnoticed – that will confirm and enhance the historical realism of the image. But since there is no precise equivalent in visual representation for the binding coherence of narrative, the danger is that such authentic details will appear *completely* gratuitous – that they will make their impression brutally, and disrupt the historical milieu.

In other words, the 'effect' may be no more than a temporary enhancement of our perceptions – what we could call a *technical surprise*. Precisely because it draws attention to itself, and does not obliterate itself in the interests of 'reality', it may succeed in disconfirming rather than authenticating the pictured scene. An amusing example comes to mind from a domain which lies mid-way between the historical painting and the historical narrative, that of historical drama in the last years of the eighteenth century. The great tragic actor Talma, who survived to become Napoleon's chosen model for regal and imperial roles, decides to suit his costume to the Roman role which he is playing and appears in a toga. But his leading lady, not fancying herself in the female equivalent of the toga, persists in wearing the conventional eighteenth-century costume of wig and gown.[6] The technical surprise is fleetingly achieved, but the effect is lost in the ironic contrast between authenticity and convention. In other words, we require not only the technical surprise, but the insertion of the effect within a *historical series*. We require the persistence of the effect, or at least its non-contradiction; and that implies the persistence of a discourse in which such an effect can echo and reverberate . Another way of expressing this need for a historical series is to say that only if the effect is located, syntagmatically, within a chain of terms which establishes 'history' as an orderly system can we speak of something so momentous as a 'rediscovery of the past'.

The place of theatrical costume in the development of historical realism is worthy of further investigation. Yet it must be conceded straight away that the unfortunate case of Talma may have been, in one respect, misleading. It is well known that, in the English theatre, scruples about appearing in authentic, rather than conventional, dress were not so stubbornly maintained. By the mid-eighteenth century, David Garrick was pioneering the adaptation of costume to the particular historical period, and by the 1820s Edmund Kean was popularising his intense histrionic style through the medium of prints which showed him in celebrated roles like Shakespeare's Richard III. But such authenticity of costume and, to an increasing extent, of theatrical accessories necessitated the support of assiduous scholars who were willing to research into the visual environment of former periods. Where Talma was able to rely on the minute, if selective, study of Roman remains carried out by the painter David and his students, the English theatre could benefit from the informative publications of antiquarians like Joseph Strutt, of whom Strong persuasively writes:

Burrowing, as no one else had ever done, through a morass of visual and written evidence together with early printed source material, he pieced together for the very first time a picture of everyday life in England from the Anglo-Saxon down to the Tudor age. The consequences were revolutionary for the art of historical reconstruction, and it was Strutt more than any other person who gave the painters of the new Artist–Antiquarian phase the sources that they so desperately needed.[7]

Strong's tribute to Strutt's antiquarian publications is quite justifiable, but it leaves us in some doubt about where, precisely, the 'revolutionary' element in this 'art of historical reconstruction' resides. If we can assume – as is undeniable – that stage designers benefited as much as painters from the repertoire which Strutt assembled, then we can put the question in a form which clarifies the issue considerably from our own point of view. Does the 'revolutionary' element reside simply in Strutt's accumulation and publication of antiquarian materials? Surely not. Does it then reside in the successful incorporation of Strutt's research into the costume and accessories of a dramatic production (or a history picture)? Up to a point – but, as far as the drama is concerned, it is surely clear that such external trappings can have formed only the basis, or pre-condition, of a successful reconstruction. The quality of the acting must have been of paramount importance: in Kean's case, the effect of breaking away from the artificial, declamatory style of Kemble and creating what has been called 'the illusion of *being* rather than *playing*, a character'.[8]

The example just given reinforces the point that we must look not simply for novel effects, or 'technical surprises', but for the degree of success with which these are integrated within the specific conditions provided by a particular medium. Kean's illusionistic acting and his luxurious historical costumes must be thought of as working together, if we are to recapture the full effect, in this domain, of the art of historical reconstruction. Nevertheless, for our purposes, the art of the theatre must remain on the periphery, since so vital a part is played by the integration of different factors which remain imponderable or at least problematic to the historian: vocal technique, gesture, movement and stage-setting being among them. Although it is possible to recover information about the introduction of technical innovations closely relevant to our theme – such as the arrival of gas lighting in the 1820s – it is hard to talk with confidence about the integrated effect of theatrical productions in this period. Indeed it seems probable that the novelty and transgressive quality of such new spectacles as the diorama resided precisely in the fact that, jettisoning the element of histrionic performance, they were able to compose from more limited elements a more overwhelming and undivided illusion.

If we return to the particular problem of historical painting, and the still visual image, this excursus into the theatre brings at least one important factor to the foreground. When history painting passes from what Strong calls the 'Gothic Picturesque' into the 'Artist–Antiquarian' phase, it does not simply shift from reliance on a make-believe historical milieu to a milieu whose details have been carefully researched. It also passes from a particular style to another, recognisably novel style. Frederick Cummings brings out the point succinctly when he discusses the evolution of French historical painting over the last quarter of the eighteenth century and the first quarter of the nineteenth century.[9] If we consider the series of works based on medieval subjects which were painted for the French Chapelle Royale in 1773, we find them to be indistinguishable in style and facture from other pictures of the period of Louis XVI. By contrast, if we follow this type of subject matter through to the artists of the 'Style Troubadour', which reached its apogee in the French Restoration with Revoil, Richard and the early Ingres, we find a reliance on the medieval period for style and facture as well as for subject. Brilliant colours and a small format recall, and are designed to recall, the medieval illuminated manuscript. In the case of Ingres' 'Paola and Francesca' composition, of which no fewer than seven variants were completed between 1814 and *c.* 1845, one particularly splendid version is enhanced by the provision of an elaborate 'medieval' frame, with a text in Gothic script and carving in a suitably flamboyant idiom.[10]

The artists of the 'Style Troubadour' did not select exclusively medieval subjects: seventeenth-century figures like Henri IV and Louise de la Vallière were also featured in their work. But, in their medieval themes at least, they could claim a degree of authenticity. Like Barante composing a substitute Chronicle, they used as their model – to some extent – the visual sensibility of the period whose subject they had chosen to represent. We must not, however, make the error of supposing that this 'archaeological' element was all that was required to authenticate the new historical painting of the early nineteenth century. Freshness and immediacy of impact were the pre-conditions of the technical surprise, no less than fidelity to a pre-existent model. The point is well demonstrated by the justly famed series of water-colours on historical subjects completed by the English artist, Richard Bonington. As Strong indicates, such a painting as 'The Earl of Surrey and the Fair Geraldine' (1825–26) is based upon careful research into the portraiture of the Tudor period. But it also relies upon the vividness and limpid freshness (untrammelled by any Tudor connections) of the water-colour medium which was previously associated (in Bonington's work as in that of others) predominantly with the genre of landscape. The ambiguity of the technical surprise, as this example indicates, is that it must depend primarily on the novelty of an effect, and only secondarily on its authenticity. Or rather the authentic reference or mode will only create its effect – that is, convince its audience – to the extent that its medium is novel.

Perhaps the most striking instance of the premium placed upon a genuinely new medium in the popularisation of history at this time can be found in the remarkable development of lithography. Invented by the Bavarian Senefelder towards the end of the eighteenth century, the medium of lithography made little headway, in France at any rate, until the period of the Restoration, when presses for the production of the new prints were established at Paris and Mulhouse. In 1818, Charles Nodier, on an archaeological expedition to Normandy, conceived the idea of utilising the new medium for a systematic record of architectural antiquities. Not only was it cheaper than traditional methods of engraving on metal plates, but it offered a new aesthetic effect: as Nodier himself emphasised, 'the bold pencil of the lithograph seems to have been invented to fix the free, original and rapid inspirations of the traveller who gives an account of his sensations'.[11] From Nodier's original conception, and from the technical refinements of Godefroy Engelmann's studio, was derived the immensely successful project of the *Voyages pittoresques et romantiques dans l'ancienne France*, which harnessed the talents of numerous French artists during the 1820s.

It is only necessary to compare the *Voyages pittoresques* with more traditional engravings of the same period, such as Cotman's *Architectural Antiquities of Normandy* (1820), to note the radical difference in aesthetic effect. Cotman's engravings have astonishing finesse, but the work of the engraver's tool –

assiduously chiselling its texture of parallel lines – is always evident. By contrast
the lithographic medium allows broader and softer effects to be obtained. What
it sacrifices in detail, it makes up for in its unprecedented capacity to register
subtle effects of light. Eliane Vergnolle has aptly characterised the spirit of these
plates of ancient buildings – interiors and exteriors – which formed the *Voyages
pittoresques*:

The atmosphere of the place is just as important as the edifice itself, an atmosphere
which is often dramatic, dark and tormented, but sometimes transparent and clear; it
is light which brings the image to life.[12]

It should hardly come as a surprise to us that one of the many contributors to the
Voyages pittoresques was Daguerre. Indeed one of the most obvious and intriguing points in this general review of visual representation is the fact that the
'technical surprise' which we have found to be inextricably connected with the
choice of historical subjects is so consistently allied with an effect of luminosity.
In the case of the lithograph, this effect must have been a relatively short-lived
one, as the spontaneity and 'atmosphere' of the new prints presumably wore off
to some degree as the medium was popularised. In the diorama, the effect was a
much more powerful one, exposing the spectator to luminous stimuli of great
intensity as he sat in the darkened house. But the diorama was by no means the
end of the process of experimentation which sought to present both French and
English audiences with ever more intense illusory experiences during these
years. We can only speculate on the quality of effect produced by the so-called
'Panstereomachia of the Battle of Poitiers', which was available to the citizens
of London in 1826.[13] But we can imagine that, as the spectacle was composed of
actual three-dimensional objects in a deep field, a remarkable ingenuity of
lighting must have been necessary to dissolve the harsh edges and achieve an
overall atmosphere.

In his wide-ranging study, *Discipline and Punish*, Michel Foucault has drawn
attention to the close connection between devices for organising a particular
visual effect and the predominant political and penal strategies within a given
society.[14] In particular, he has drawn a direct antithesis between the structure of
the amphitheatre (a vast crowd on the perimeter view a single event in the centre)
and that involved in Bentham's ideal prison, or *panopticon* (a single observation
tower in the centre commands the view of a vast number of individual cells,
where individual prisoners quail before the all-seeing eye, but cannot observe
each other). Whatever ideological construction we may put upon them, these
new viewing devices invented in the nineteenth century testify to an extraordinary appetite for commanding vision: as a form of spectacle enjoying
consistent popularity from the late eighteenth century onwards, the panorama
effectively sets up a structure analogous to Bentham's *panopticon*, in which the
centrally placed spectator can experience a clever simulation of all-round vision.
Historical recreation is certainly not the only purpose of these diverse forms of
spectacle. Representation of the exotic, or picturesque, and recreation of unusual

atmospheric conditions – as when Daguerre contrived an eruption of Vesuvius with real rocks showering upon the stage – are no less important. But there can be little doubt that the historical dimension provided an additional distancing, to add to, and in a real sense subsume, the picturesque and atmospheric dimensions. Daguerre's elaborate representation of the ruins of the Chapel at Holyrood, for example, combined the flavour of the Scottish picturesque with remote and suggestive Gothic associations. Like the venerable monuments of the *Voyages pittoresques*, in their own more modest register, it must have impressed its audience as the empty and deserted scene of historical action.

This brief survey of types of 'technical surprise' – from the trappings of the 'Style Troubadour' to lithography and the diorama – makes it all the more imperative for us to confront the problem of the 'historical series'. How was it possible to obtain persistence of effect? How was it possible to simulate not the empty scene, but the seamless continuity of history? The diorama was indeed a spectacle which altered in time, as new subterfuges of lighting were used to highlight specific features of the composition, and suggest different times of the day, or the transition from quiescence to eruption. But such a continuous and repetitive process of temporal disclosure should not be confused with a structured articulation in time. Again, the series of the *Voyages pittoresques* (as, indeed, Cotman's *Architectural Antiquities*) was an accumulation of distinct views, and so achieved an effect considerably greater than that of the individual plates considered separately. But this effect of redundance cannot have amounted, in itself, to a consistent and convincing representation of the past. As we shall see in the next chapter, it required the specific situation of the museum – and in particular, the innovatory organisation of the Musée de Cluny – to convert a mere accumulation of distinct historical elements into an orderly representation of past epochs. But this important development is a special case, which brings in considerations irrelevant to the visual materials considered in this section.

How then should we approach the concept of the 'historical series'? The historical series is, in its strong and culturally sanctioned form, the historical narrative. We can take it for granted that the traditional strategies of narrative exposition have been (at all periods of western civilisation up to, though possibly not including, our own) the predominant methods of signifying the reality of the past. Yet, within the sphere of historiography proper, the concept of narrative shades off – as Hayden White has demonstrated – into types of historical account which dispense almost entirely with the props of discursive continuity.[15] Annals, for example, may list the years in succession without even specifying a significant event in some of them. Yet, as White correctly points out, it is too hasty to assume that such a vestigial series is an imperfect, or incoherent representation of history: it has its own coherence, even though that may not be the coherence associated with the chronicle or the fully fledged narrative history. By analogy with this example, we can look at certain forms of visual communication – more exactly, 'mixed' forms, involving both image and text – as establishing a historical series, within our own period. The fact that they do so without being able to rely, except indirectly, on narrative strategies does not preclude them from having some role to play in the rediscovery of the past.

Our starting point is a distinctive development of late eighteenth-century art and showmanship: the so-called 'Gallery' of specially commissioned pictures, which exists both as a standing exhibition and as a repertoire of images for illustrated history books. Relevant examples are Alderman Boydell's Shakespeare Gallery, inaugurated in 1785, and Robert Bowyer's Historic Gallery in Pall Mall: 'a collection of paintings of scenes from British history commissioned for a large folio edition of Hume issued between 1795 and 1806'.[16] The formation of the latter collection is of particular interest if we reflect that it is almost exactly contemporary with the gathering of the historical monuments for Lenoir's Musée des Petits-Augustins, which will be discussed in the next chapter. But such a comparison, as will become very clear, is all to the disadvantage of the 'Historic Gallery', if we judge it in the context of the rediscovery of the past. Bowyer's collection, made up of over a hundred pictures, and involving commissions from a wide range of artists, was largely given over to incidents of a sentimental and romantic type: Queen Margaret of Anjou and the robber, Lady Elizabeth Grey entreating Edward IV to protect her children, Lady Jane Grey's reluctance to accept the crown, her subsequent execution and so on. Its stated purpose was 'to raise the passions, to fire the mind with emulation of heroic deeds, or to inspire it with criminal deeds'.[17] In other words, the dominant associative principle was not the historicity of the incidents, but their hortatory or sensationalist effect. In isolation from Hume's history, upon which they were undisguisedly parasitic, the works of the 'Historic Gallery' must have offered a rather febrile and disorderly vision of the past.

A much more interesting example comes to light, however, if we follow the course of English history painting a little further. One of the contributors to Bowyer's Gallery was the Academician Thomas Stothard (1755–1834). Although this artist's early historical paintings are securely within the 'Gothic picturesque' mode, thematically allied to and technically indistinguishable from the works of his colleagues, there is a distinctively new note in his work when he produces his painting of the 'Canterbury Pilgrims' in 1806–7. This is scrupulously researched, deriving its medieval costumes from Strutt's *Dress and Habits of the People of England*. But it is also innovatory in form and technique, setting the pilgrims in 'a processional frieze based on the paintings on *cassone* chests'.[18] Whatever might have been the historical connection between *cassone* chests (the finely painted receptacles for dowries which are associated with the Italian Renaissance) and the age of Chaucer is, of course, irrelevant to Stothard's success. He had produced, in the 'Canterbury Pilgrims', an image that was to become – after its engraving by Cromek in 1817 – one of the most celebrated of all nineteenth-century emblems of the Middle Ages in Britain. A suitably framed copy of the engraving hung, and still hangs, over the fire-place of Scott's study at Abbotsford.

However it is Charles Alfred Stothard, second son of Thomas, whose work pays the greatest dividends from the point of view of the historical series. Born in 1786, Charles Alfred initially followed in his father's footsteps. At the 1811 Academy he exhibited a picture of the death of Richard II which observed a scrupulous detail in historical costume. And in the same year he also began to publish the early stages of a more lengthy enterprise, which was to occupy him until his early death in 1821, and to preoccupy his heirs for some years after that. This was to be, in the grandiloquent terms of the title-page: *The Monumental Effigies of Great Britain, selected from our cathedrals and churches, for the purpose of bringing together, and preserving correct representations of the best historical illustrations extant, from the Norman Conquest to the reign of Henry the Eighth.* With this great work, monumental in more senses than one, we reach a test case of the capacity of the image to stimulate the rediscovery of the past. Yet it is not a simple matter to judge its effect retrospectively. In rhetorical terms, we might say that it is a discourse which hovers between the metonymic and the metaphoric: between relations of discrete terms ordered in simple chronological sequence, and aspirations towards integration in a comprehensive view of history. This ambiguity is also mirrored in the texts which accompany the visual material, and can be taken as a clear indication of the shifting attitudes to the recreation of the past which took place within the decade of Charles Alfred's dedicated documentation.

A comment on Stothard's way of working helps to clarify this question. The complete *Monumental Effigies* was designed to consist of twelve 'numbers', or sets of engravings, each totalling twelve separate plates. Stothard began publication in 1811, but he did not always follow the order which was to be laid down in the complete publication: in this edition, for example, the first plate (of Roger of Salisbury) is identified as having been 'drawn and etched Nov. 1812' and 'published 1813', while the second (of Geoffrey Plantagenet) is given as 'drawn and etched July 1817' and 'published 1819'. Stothard was assembling material, and publishing occasional plates, as he went along. Only in the final edition would the 144 plates be assembled in order: that is, in a strict chronological sequence according to the date of death of each historical figure who was included. To this extent, of course, Stothard was compiling a simple metonymic series: one which involved the reduction of the historical figure to his date of death, just as it reduced the study of costume to the limited repertoire of the appurtenances of the monumental effigy. But having made this reduction the principle of the series, he now begins to invert the process: the accompanying text starts to rehabilitate the scattered fragments.

This two-fold process is fascinating to follow. On the one hand, the engraved plates deliberately accentuate the element of reduction and fragmentation. Three-dimensionality is rarely emphasised, and the effigy is often portrayed from above, with the effect that its flatness is accentuated. Characteristically, small details and enlargements of clothing, armour and decorative motifs are placed in juxtaposition with the image of the effigy as a whole. These are picked out in colour, on occasions, and so accentuate the schematic, non-naturalistic character of the representation. But in the juxtaposed texts, Stothard moves from simple itemisation of elements to evocations of the life and work of the subject of the effigy. We begin with phrases like: 'This is a coffin lid', or 'He wears a steel cap, in form like the Phrygian, enamelled with a leopard of gold.' But shortly afterwards, we are being invited to dramatise, through narrative, the subject of the enunciation. We are being offered not the effigy, but the historical actor, rehabilitated from the presumed container of his mortal remains.

This movement towards rehabilitation, indeed resurrection, is epitomised by the frontispiece to the whole collection: 'The Monumental Effigies rescued from Time'. In this plate, drawn by Thomas Stothard and etched by Charles Alfred, a stern Father Time complete with scythe is powerless to restrain the upward movement, urged on by *putti*, of the ungainly effigies. A female figure – surely she must be Clio? – assists the process by standing on Father Time's grey locks and brandishing aloft a scroll labelled 'Records'. Charles Alfred's introduction to the publication follows. Though still unpublished at the time of his death in 1821, it was later included in a more extensive introduction by his brother-in-law. It provides a striking justification for the new interest in history, which glosses the allegorical frontispiece:

By these means [the documentation and publication of effigies] we live in other ages than our own, and become nearly as well acquainted with them. In some measure we arrest the fleeting steps of Time, and again review those things his arm has passed over, and subdued, but not destroyed. The researches of the Antiquary are worthless if they do not impart to us this power, or give us other advantages; it is not to admire any thing for its age or rust that constitutes the interest of the object, but as it is conducive to knowledge, the enlargement of human intellect, and general improvement.[19]

It is curious to observe the tensions in Charles Alfred Stothard's declaration. After memorably expressing the new, keen sense of the rediscovery of the past, he concludes with a reversion to the most flat and banal utilitarianism. Was it really for the sake of 'general improvement' that Stothard braved the rickety ladders of innumerable country churches, including the last one which was to be the cause of his untimely death in 1821? Clearly, the dilemma of this passage is that it oscillates, like Stothard's work as a whole, between a traditional scientific objective – that of recording, assembling and detailing for the sake of 'knowledge' – and a passionate commitment whose aim cannot so easily be expressed – that of rehabilitating the 'object' and thus resurrecting the past. Stothard places beyond doubt his concern with history as a lived reality, when he uses a telling organic metaphor in his justification for the collection of 'monumental effigies': 'To history they give a body and a substance, by placing before us those things which language is deficient in describing.'[20]

Yet Stothard's last remark creates a further paradox, in posing the general problem of the relation of image to language in the rediscovery of the past. The monumental effigies do not come across as representations of death, or of individual dead men and women; on the contrary, they give 'a body and a substance

5. *Resurrecting the past:* Thomas and Charles Alfred Stothard, The Monumental Effigies rescued from Time (frontispiece to *Monumental Effigies*, 1811–33)

to history', trading their incomplete status as effigies for the fuller enhancement of the reality of the past. But, even if they succeed in representing ('placing before us') what 'language is deficient in describing', they are still dependent on the narrative effect which language, and language alone, is qualified to achieve. Charles Alfred's descriptive writing, his enumeration of 'coffin lids' and 'Phrygian caps', is indeed deficient, because it is simply redundant. But when he slips into a passage of extended narrative, listing even summarily the career of Roger of Salisbury or Geoffrey Plantagenet, he makes us aware of the capacity of narrative to create an integrated series which we accept (in Hayden White's

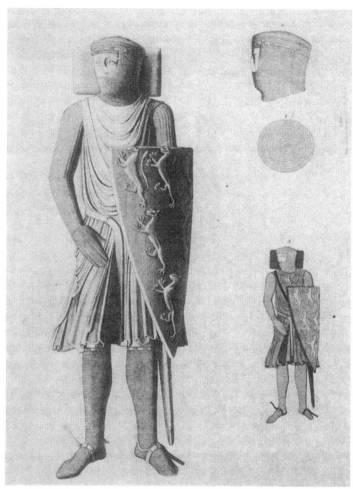

6. *Reduction and fragmentation:* effigy of William Longespée, Earl of Salisbury (from Charles Alfred Stothard, *Monumental Effigies*)

terms) as an 'icon' of the past. To put the issue another way, Charles Alfred's effigies cannot be 'rescued from Time' by the gesturing of allegorical figures, or by the new accessibility of the 'Records' which Clio brandishes in her hand. They can be rescued from Time only by being inserted in a discourse which mimes the process of chronological sequence. They can be rescued from Time only by narration.

Charles Alfred Stothard's *Monumental Effigies* therefore belongs mid-way between the illustrated histories mentioned in the last chapter, and the new historical museums which will be the particular field of investigation in the next chapter. His images are not mere illustrations, ancillary to the text and subject (like those of Barante and Thierry) to the vicissitudes of the publishing process. They themselves, in their finesse and detail, are the vehicle of the imaginative recreation which Stothard urges upon his public. And yet they require the support of the narrative text. Only in the context of the historical museum, where the relation of objects to one another could be made clear with the minimum of textual information, would Stothard's urge to give 'body and substance' to history outside the domain of language be effectually realised. And only in this context will it be possible to test the full implications of my initial distinction between the metonymic and the metaphoric (or synecdochic) modes of organisation.

Yet the fascinating example of Charles Alfred Stothard should not entirely divert us from the review of historical painting undertaken in this chapter. I began by postulating the two factors of the 'technical surprise' and the 'historical series' as pre-conditions of the contribution of visual representation to re-discovery of the past. This distinction led to the exploration of a wide range of new techniques for creating visual illusions current at the time, and to an examination of the pictorial series in the strict sense of the term, from Bowyer's 'Historic Gallery' to the *Monumental Effigies*. I argued that not only a novel technical effect, but also a degree of persistence and articulation in time was essential for the creation of a vision of the past. We must not forget, however, that the individual oil painting was itself, from the public point of view, part of a series: it was characteristically viewed at the Academy, in the company of other examples of the sub-set of historical painting, and juxtaposed with the other prevalent genres: portraits, landscapes, etc. Although we are no longer talking strictly of a historical series, it is worth looking more carefully at some selected examples of early nineteenth-century salon or academy painting, to appreciate both the relevant qualities and the special problems of this mode of representation.

One important point can be stressed immediately. Whereas, in most of the examples discussed up to now, we have been concerned with writers or artists whose main concern is historical representation within the conditions of a particular discipline or medium, the salon painter is very rarely committed, to this exclusive degree, to the practice of historical painting. Although the opportunities provided by historical subjects were taken by a large number of nineteenth-century artists, it is unusual to find – at least in the period which concerns us most – a career whose chief emphasis is on historical painting. Indeed the difficulties of establishing precisely where the boundaries of historical painting lie are considerable: to the retrospective classifier, they pose almost insuperable problems. In the 1982 exhibition of the work of Sir Edwin Landseer, at the Tate Gallery, a section was set aside for 'historical' paintings. But, both inside and outside this section, it was possible to infer quite different meanings for the term 'historical', which presupposed quite different orientations to the past. For example, Landseer painted notable contemporary figures in historical characterisations: either specific, as with 'Queen Victoria and Prince Albert as Queen Philippa and King Edward' (1842) or more general, as with 'The 7th Duke of Beaufort at the Eglinton Tournament', caparisoned in full armour, his casque standing proudly in the foreground. Landseer also painted the figure most intimately associated, in Britain, with the rediscovery of the past: 'Sir Walter Scott', on his home ground at Abbotsford. The portrait probably dates from Landseer's first visit in 1824, but there is a further work – an evocative genre picture called 'A Scene at Abbotsford' – which dates from a subsequent visit made in 1827.[21]

All these works imply that a specific use is being made of the historic past. In the case of the royal portrait, the medieval impersonation is little more than a polite conceit; with the record of the Eglinton Tournament, the subject is more complex, as we are dealing with an actual attempt, by Victorian aristocrats, to re-enact the chivalric ceremony of the later Middle Ages. With the two Abbotsford pictures, there is of course no historical role to be assumed. But, in 1824, Scott's figure is juxtaposed with an important and emblematic historical property: the lower half of a suit of armour said at that time (but erroneously) to have been worn by the tallest man at the Battle of Bosworth Field. In Landseer's later picture, 'A Scene at Abbotsford', priority is also given in the composition to various items of armour, including a casque with raised visor. However this eloquent, but empty, evidence of Scott's neo-medieval decor is relieved by the presence of live dogs and hawks, as if to give the spectator a flavour of the pleasures of the baronial hunt. Characteristic of Landseer, and a result of his facility for sketching animals and birds, is this displacement from the historical on to the hunting scene: from objects or situations having a real connection with historical events, to the creation of a fictive world in which the real subject is the timeless drama of the chase. Thus one of his first full-dress historical compositions, 'The Battle of Chevy Chase' (1825–26), has a companion piece of the same date, demonstrating even greater vigour of execution, which is entitled 'The Hunting of Chevy Chase'. Of his two major historical compositions of the 1830s, 'Hawking in the Olden Time' (c. 1832) casts the human participants into distant obscurity, foregrounding the incredible tussle of a heron and a hawk; 'Scene in the Olden Time at Bolton Abbey' (painted for the Duke of Devonshire before 1834) fills the stage with appropriately robed monks and peasants, but cunningly reinstates the immediacy of the natural world through taking as its subject the offering of the Abbey's rent in kind – a cornucopia of birds, fish and game.

It seems as if almost the only 'historical' paintings which Landseer does not twist unashamedly to suit his special skill are the scenes which take Scott's fiction as their intermediate source: small and unimportant compositions recording 'The Bride of Lammermoor' and the 'Death of Elspeth Mucklebackit' from *The Antiquary* (both painted by 1830). And these works, as we might

expect, are characterised by their sentimental appeal rather than by any real
concern to emulate Scott's antiquarian commitment. Landseer is therefore a
good example, for our purpose, of the highly ambiguous status of historical
painting, or at least of the type of painting which masquerades under the colours
of the genre, while it is actually observing quite different criteria of fidelity. But
we should beware of concluding that this sort of distinction passed unnoticed at
the time, since critics were in fact extraordinarily sensitive to nuances of
authenticity. In 1840, for example, Thackeray remarked in his review of the
Royal Academy exhibition: 'A painter should be as careful about his costumes
as a historian about his dates.'[22] This judgement did not, however, imply a mere
archaeological accuracy. Landseer was reproached, in the same review, for
giving the impression that historical dress had been 'put on for the first time';
four years later, Herbert's 'Trial of the Seven Bishops' was enthusiastically
applauded according to the same criteria, because 'men are quite at home in their
quaint coats'.[23]

We can follow the way in which this particular test was applied right through
to the end of the century, when quite explicit recognition is given to the devasta-
ting standard of comparison which would explode the pretensions even of the
most sedulous accuracy and the most striking recreation. This was simply the
test of the actual paintings which had survived from a particular period, at
least from the Renaissance onwards. The painter G. A. Storey confesses his
embarrassment with regard to Velasquez:

In the work of Velasquez I knew that not only were the costumes correct, but the actual
men of the time were there before me, the period stamped, not only on the dress, but on
every face, in the very attitudes even of the figures; the whole belonging so completely
to its own day, even as the hand that wrought it, that I felt I had a true page of history
before me, and not a theatrical make-up of a scene dimly realised in the pages of some
book written many years after the event.[23]

Storey's comment may seem to us an apt indictment of most, if not all history
paintings of the nineteenth century. But it is crucial to realise that such a
comparison, made right at the end of the period, has very little relevance in the
context of the earlier 'rediscovery of the past'. Just as Barante wrote a substitute
Chronicle, and Michelet was encouraged to even greater flights of imagination
by the knowledge that the documents of Joan of Arc's trial were about to be
published, so the historical painter exploited not simply the documentary
evidence of the past, but the act of recreative imagination which could fuse it
into a new poetic vision. To repeat De Quincey's witty judgement on Michelet,
'facts' could be treated like the falconer's lure. An indispensable point of reference
for the artist, they did not necessarily prevent him from soaring higher and
higher in flight before his captive audience.

It is appropriate to conclude this brief examination of historical painting and
other visual means of representation with a glance at one of the most accomplished
and successful performers in the historical genre. There is probably no painter

more clearly identified with the success of historical painting in its first flowering than the French artist Paul Delaroche, who was born in Paris in 1797 and died there in 1856. After entering the Ecole des Beaux-Arts in 1816 and competing unsuccessfully for the Prix de Rome in landscape in the succeeding year, Delaroche entered the studio of Baron Gros in 1818. By 1824, he was contributing examples of the 'Style Troubadour' to the Salon: 'Filippo Lippi devient amoureux de la religieuse qui lui servait de modèle' (1822) and two subsequent pieces showing a distinct evolution of subject and manner – 'Saint Vincent de Paul prêchant devant la cour de Louis XIII' (1823) and 'Jeanne d'Arc malade est interrogée dans sa prison par le cardinal de Winchester' (1824). Critics praised these latter works for their distinctive blending of sentimental theme and archaeological accuracy. Official recognition came fast to Delaroche, with a promotion to the Légion d'honneur in 1828, and a rising tide of official patronage, which was not cut off when Louis-Philippe supplanted Charles X in 1830. In the Salon of 1831, he achieved remarkable popular and critical success, to the point of being acclaimed as the greatest living French artist. He had succeeded in bringing together for this occasion a large group of historical paintings which covered the preceding three years: 'Le Cardinal de Richelieu' (1829), 'Cardinal Mazarin mourant' (1830), 'Edouard V et Richard, duc d'York' (1831) and 'Cromwell et Charles Ier' (1831). Although Delaroche continued to exhibit in the Salon with some success until 1837, rising to such triumphs as 'Jane Grey' (1834), he never recaptured the central position which he had held at the beginning of the July Monarchy. And it could also be argued that historical painting as such never seemed more central to French art, within the range of possible genres, than it was in Delaroche's heyday.

What was at stake in this popularity? Obviously the salon visitor of the period, acquainted with the range of representations of history from the novels of Scott and the narratives of Barante and Thierry to the stage sets of Ciceri and the dioramas of Daguerre, would have had a certain sophistication in judging 'archaeological accuracy'. But it is also worthy of note that the development of French painting was far from uneventful at this time. As Lee Johnson has written of Delacroix's 'Massacre de Chios' which was shown for the first time at the Salon of 1824:

Delacroix opened the breach between official teaching, dominated by the ideas of David, and progressive painters. This breach was continuously widened by Delacroix then by Courbet, and ended in total rupture in the Impressionist era.[24]

At the same time as Delacroix was leading the movement away from neo-classical orthodoxy, Delaroche was putting his considerable talents behind the harnessing of certain aspects of the neo-classical style to form a vehicle for historical realism. The contrast can easily be seen if we compare Delacroix's own historical paintings from the late 1820s with those of Delaroche. From Delacroix we have, anticipated by the colouristic extravaganza of the 'Death of Sardanapalus' (Salon of 1827–28), a series of works which dramatise historical conflict through the use of sonorous colour and rich glazes. The 'Murder of the Bishop of Liége' (1829) reproduces the climactic scene of Scott's *Quentin Durward* with rough, vigorous brushwork and an extraordinary intensity of diffused light which sweeps across the alarmed participants of the fatal banquet. Delaroche, by contrast, has eliminated any such expressive plasticity from his style by 1830. 'Edouard V et Richard, duc d'York' (his picture of the Princes in the Tower) has, in the words of a French critic, 'a cold and perfect finish'; it 'betrays hardly any trace of brushwork: exempt from any baroque rhetoric, it indeed marks the end of Delaroche's romantic phase at the approach of the 1830's'.[25]

The conclusion is not hard to draw. In our terms, we can say that there has been a definite cleavage between two aspects of the 'technical surprise' that had been held in an uneasy balance: the archaeological element and the novelty of idiom. By 1830, Delacroix has visibly committed himself to renewing the medium of painting, through a reversion to the broad colour effects and vigorous brushwork of the Baroque, and an ever more conscious exploitation of the phenomenon of complementaries. This applies as much, of course, to his great historical compositions of later years, like the 'Prise de Constantinople' (1840) as to his exotic, biblical and mythological pieces. It makes little sense to single out from this undivided stream the current of Delacroix the historical painter. On the other hand, his rival Delaroche has chosen, by 1830, to fix his mode of historical painting within a regime of neo-classic (one might almost say photographic) clarity, which will enable him to pay minute attention to the archaeologically accurate details which are the basic safeguard of the genre.

And yet, as early as Delaroche's triumphant salon of 1830, some critics had diagnosed the limitations of such an approach. Jal suggested that he might think again about the care with which he 'rendered everything in the same way, curtains, the wood of the bedstead, flesh and velvet'.[26] Another critic, Planche, detected a kind of implausibility in the very scrupulousness of Delaroche's photographic technique:

As for Edward V [The Princes in the Tower], we must admit that the two heads lack life, that it is impossible to divine the blood under this violet flesh; everything is dreadfully new, the furniture, the clothing, even the faces are new and have never been used . . . The great fault of M. Delaroche's painting is, in effect, to be too similar to the kind of painting which wants to be pretty and clean before all else.[27]

Planche thus isolates a problem which his own age was perhaps on the point of encountering, in the literal sense: that of 'reproduction furniture' which reproduces nearly all the external characteristics of 'period' furniture, except for the all-important one of looking old! Yet his complaint must have seemed a little puzzling to poor Delaroche. Did Planche suppose that there was never a time when antique furniture, and period clothes, had been new? The issue is significant because it is bound up with the wider question of how we are to read

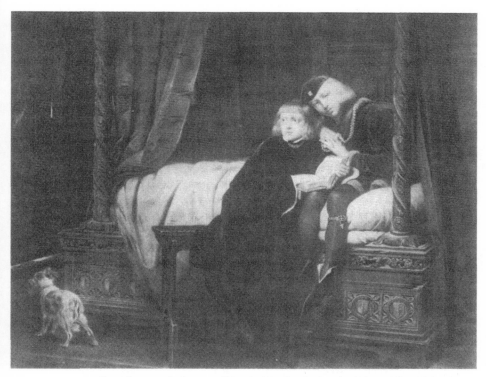

7. Gesturing towards the scene of historical fatality: Delaroche, Edouard V et Richard
Duc d'York (also called Les Enfants d'Edouard), 1831

• such a picture – of what we are to take as the proffered guarantee of its authenticity. Strong resolves the issue by postulating a kind of psychological and,
as it were, scenic realism, which outweighs the occasional implausibility of
detail:

Instead of choosing to depict the actual murder, he moves back in time to an imaginary
moment of realization. The Duke of York is reading to his brother the King, who sits on
the bed in a distant reverie. The younger child has raised his head from his book, and
his eyes are filled with fear. A spaniel moves towards the door, beneath which chinks of
light and strongly cast shadows suggest incipient action. So compelling is Delaroche's
evocation that the viewer never notices that the columns of the bed are inappropriately
carved with the Beaufort portcullis and the Tudor rose.[28]

Certainly the columns of the bed are carved with these two heraldic emblems
of the Tudor dynasty, as well as (it appears) the Prince of Wales's feathers, which
pursue them round the spiralling shaft. But Strong argues that this is a mere
anachronism, whose effect has to be counteracted by the scenic realism of the
'evocation' as a whole. If this were true, then we would be putting extreme
constraints upon the historical painter, which do not apply to the practitioners of

other genres. We would be making the assumption that historical painting is defined by the absolute synchronicity of all its elements, as if in an instantaneous photographic rendering. And yet Strong's own interpretation depends at the same time on the power of the painting to *anticipate* an event; it interprets the scene as 'the moment of realization' by the young Duke, and thereby takes for granted our own (not conclusively historical) knowledge that a murder lies in store. Why should not the emblems of the Tudor dynasty serve as a foreshadowing of the end of the preceding House of York? Is this not more likely than the conclusion that Delaroche, who searched diligently for his props and presumably knew his dynasties, has perpetrated an anachronism?

This issue is worth pursuing simply as a debating point (and even though it may imply a procedure unsupported by Delaroche's other work) because of the light which it throws upon the status of the detached historical painting. There is one kind of historical painting which does not need to present its titles of justification. That is, as Storey recognised, the original period picture, which exists as a document, as 'a true page of history'. We take for granted, unless we have overwhelming reasons for not doing so, that the period details of a Velasquez are accurate. With a Delaroche, by contrast, we require to be positively convinced that all the details are correctly transcribed, and we are ready to seize on apparent anomalies like the Tudor rose to cast doubt upon the whole painting – or we concede that such faults of detail are only outweighed by the potency of the overall evocation. It is as if we were asking the artist to supply his picture with invisible footnotes, which detailed the references for such and such a costume, or such and such an article of furniture. But the individual painting, by its very nature, cannot provide such a system of verification.

To put the problem in its most radical form, Delaroche's painting can be analysed as the sum of a number of distinct declarations, all of which have historical import. This is the Order of the Garter; this is an illuminated book; this is a fifteenth-century carved bed, etc. We are on the whole quite willing to accept that these declarations are veracious, partly because we feel that Delaroche's research has been painstaking, and partly because the very minuteness of the execution seems, by a kind of metonymic sliding, to vouch for their authenticity. But we have no assurance of the way in which these individual declarations are syntactically connected, as we would have in the most banal of narrative statements: 'The Princes sat on an antique carved bed, the elder wearing the Order of the Garter and the younger reading to him from an illuminated book.' Such a sentence, despite its banality, could form part of a chain of sentences, which would be the story of the murder of the Princes. By contrast the image, even if it is authenticated by a host of accurate visual details, is barred from the continuity of narrative; its strength seems to reside rather in the capacity of gesturing towards that 'other scene' which is the historical fatality. What Strong considers to be the scenic and psychological realism of Delaroche's painting could therefore be viewed simply as a factor of its rhetorical potency. The image simultaneously asserts and obliterates itself, in anticipation of the incommunicable event. No doubt there is an echo of this effective formula in Noel Paton's gripping 'Paolo and Francesca', first exhibited at the Society of Artists, Edinburgh, in 1837. The doomed lovers, with their neglected book, occupy the centre of the scene, while on the left – vestige of an earlier figure on a larger canvas – the bony fingers of the avenging husband make their sinister and prophetic appearance.

The ambiguity of Delaroche's achievement makes him particularly relevant in assessing the contribution of historical painting to the rediscovery of the past. Having chosen to create his 'technical surprise' not through the stylistic bravura of a Delacroix but through minute archaeological detail, he moves increasingly towards a certain type of subject matter. Whether with the Princes in the Tower, or with Mazarin on the point of death, or Lady Jane Grey bandaged for the executioner, or even Charles I being mocked by the Cromwellians, he becomes the poet of impending catastrophe. Even where the catastrophe has already occurred (as when Cromwell inspects the dead body of Charles I), we are still struck by the enormity of the event whose fatal outcome has been evoked by the painter. As Barthes puts it, with reference to historical photographs, we tremble before a catastrophe which has already taken place.[29] The psychological power of such an effect is however bound to be variable: we are more moved by the impending fate of such youthful innocents as the Princes in the Tower and Lady Jane Grey than we are by the aged Mazarin expiring in his bed. And it is an unstable effect, in so far as it depends upon our predisposition to conflate the disconcerting propinquity of the fateful event with our abiding sense of the otherness of the past. What begins as historical painting is liable to become, sooner or later, timeless melodrama. In the hands of Delaroche's successors in the middle years of the century it is already melodrama, enlivened only by the sedulous historical detail of the costumes, whose accuracy Thackeray is so very confident in debating.

A footnote underlines this point. In 1856, after Delaroche's death, the Ecole des Beaux-Arts devoted a retrospective exhibition to his work. For the first time, it was possible to see virtually all the important works of this most typical of history painters in a continuous sequence. Among the visitors to Paris who took advantage of the opportunity was the young Henry James (born in 1843) who was touring Europe with his family. In his autobiography, *A small boy and others*, James confesses that only his brother William's enthusiasm was able to persuade him of the greatness of Delacroix. But about Delaroche he had no such doubts:

Yet Les Enfants d'Edouard thrilled me to a different tune, and I couldn't doubt that the long-drawn odd face of the elder prince, sad and sore and sick, with his wide crimped sidelocks of fair hair and his violet legs marked by the garter and dangling from the bed, was a reconstitution of far-off history of the subtlest and most 'last word' modern or psychologic kind . . . and I can surely have enjoyed up to then no formal exhibition of anything as I at one of those seasons enjoyed the commemorative show of Delaroche given, soon after his death, in one of the rather bleak salles of the Ecole des Beaux-Arts to which access was had from the quay. *There* was reconstituted history if one would, in the straw-littered scaffold, the distracted ladies with three-cornered coifs and those immense hanging sleeves that made them look as if they had bath-towels over their arms; in the block, the headsman, the bandaged eyes, of Lady Jane Grey . . .[30]

James's retrospect is manifestly ironic. Yet the irony is all the more pungent if we recall that in 1914, the year after the first publication of *A small boy and others*, James was to return to his own project of 'reconstituted history', the abandoned novel which we know as *The Sense of the Past*. The almost insuperable problems which James set himself in this project form a sharp contrast to these recollections of the spontaneous enthusiasm of childhood. The child who had assented so willingly to Delaroche's evocation of historical events is the father of the novelist who baulked, eventually, at the momentous assignment of reconstituting the past.

Poetics of the museum:
    Lenoir and Du Sommerard

The story is told by the art historian Lord Clark that, in the days when he used
to stay at Berenson's Florentine villa, I Tatti, he would try the experiment of
moving a small Renaissance bronze a few inches from its original position each
evening on retiring to bed. Each morning, as he came down to breakfast, he
was able to note that it had been restored with great precision to its former
location. This story illustrates, of course, more than a mere mania for domestic
order. To Berenson, no doubt – if not to Lord Clark – the bronze was not
simply an object which could be moved here and there without detriment to its
aesthetic significance. It was a term in a system, whose exact relationship to
other terms had to be maintained as, by imperceptible stages, Berenson's home
became the Berenson Museum. Yet when, with Berenson's death, that process
had become complete, we may well wonder how much of this original order was
in fact preserved for posterity. Given that the original placing of each object
within a defined series of contiguities was indeed the result of his intentions, we
might ask if these intentions are likely to have been conveyed to the new
stewards of his collection in the form of a comprehensible system. If not (and
discounting the possibility of an intuitive *rapport* beyond the grave), we would
have to envisage the inevitability of the museum collapsing into a form of
anomie. Borrowing once again the terminology of linguistics, we could say that,
the systematic plane being barred by Berenson's absence, the syntagmatic
plane (the ordering of objects in real space) would inevitably lose its coherence.
If the museum continued to communicate, it would at the same time be afflicted
with a speech disorder or *aphasia*. Connections and relationships which were
once the visible demonstration of a total view of art and the world, would have
been reduced to mere contiguities and juxtapositions.[1]

I choose this contemporary example – which is of course entirely hypothetical
– in order to stress the fragility of the type of communication which will be
described here. Mention has already been made in my introduction of the
'focalising' capacity of rhetoric, which (in line with the theory of Dan Sperber)[2]
can establish para-linguistic structures within specific assemblages of objects. It
must surely be clear that the objects assembled by a collector, whether perpetuated in a museum or not, form an ideal test case for the proof of such a
hypothesis. But it might be argued, on the other hand, that the entropy or loss
of order which affects a collection of objects with the passing of time is of so high

a degree that we can never in practice recover the integrity of the original system
or code. It might even be contended that such a recovery is not desirable, since
the objects themselves ought to be emancipated, through the creation of new
meanings, from the paranoia of an all-embracing system. We all know the
benefits, for any museum collection, of a periodic overhaul.

But what may well be necessary for the well-being of museums does not
prevent us from using this line of analysis in trying to understand the relation of
museums and collectors to the 'historical-mindedness' of their age. In choosing
the title 'Poetics of the museum', I am assuming that it is possible, in certain
special circumstances, to reconstruct the formative procedures and principles
which determined the type of a particular museum, and to relate these procedures
to the epistemological presumptions of our period. Certainly there is no law
which states that, in this or any other age, a museum or a collection will exemplify
the kind of systematic order which justifies the use of the term 'poetics'. The
lengthy pre-history of the British Museum, from the Sloane legacy of 1753 to
the opening of the present premises in 1851, would turn out to be somewhat
incoherent by this test, because of the makeshift character of the original display
in Montagu House. As the Earl of Elgin discovered while humping his inconvenient marbles around London, there is no reason why a collector's objects
should reach a point of rest within any existing conceptual, or spatial, scheme.
But the stages of the formation of the Musée de Cluny in Paris offer what must
surely be regarded as a brilliant counter-example. In the sequence of events
which led up to its official adoption by the French state in 1843, we can follow
what is both an exemplary pattern of the formation of a museum and, which is
more to our purpose, an ideal source for tracing the development of historical
discourse and the historical sense in the Romantic epoch.

The argument of the preceding chapters is, of course, taken for granted in the
analysis which follows. At the close of this chapter, I shall raise some general
considerations which emerge from taking the Museum as a special example of
the transformation in Romantic attitudes to the past. My starting point must be,
however, to question from the basis of contemporary testimony the conventional
assumption that historical discourse is essentially (or indeed exclusively) confined to the historical text in the narrow sense of the term. In *Les Arts au Moyen
Age* (which began publication in 1838) Alexandre du Sommerard – the founder
of the Musée de Cluny – challenged this very assumption as it was implied in
Augustin Thierry's much-quoted encomium of Sir Walter Scott, contained in
the *Lettres sur l'histoire de France*.[3] Du Sommerard suggests an alternative
channel through which an 'ardour' for the medieval period could be stimulated:

Loin de là, l'ardeur pour le moyen âge s'est étendue chez nous du prestige historique
aux objets matériels qui contribuèrent tant à l'inspiration du grand peintre écossais
zélé collecteur en ce genre. Les mêmes moyens, une collection méthodique des
brillants dépouilles de nos aïeux, ajouteraient un vif intérêt à la lecture de nos
chroniques.[4]

[Far from that, in our case ardour for the Middle Ages has spread from the prestige of history to the material objects which contributed so greatly to the inspiration of the great Scottish painter, a zealous collector in this genre. The same means, a methodical collection of the brilliant remains of our ancestors, would contribute a lively interest to the reading of our chronicles.]

Du Sommerard thus implies a kind of priority of the historical object over the historical text. A collection of such objects will not simply be parasitic upon the vision of the Middle Ages revealed by Scott and the chroniclers. It will enable a host of antecedent perceptions to enliven the reading of the original texts. And Du Sommerard is surely right to mention Scott's own absorption in the material vestiges of the past – a concern which is evident in Washington Irving's account of his visit to Abbotsford, and will be thoroughly analysed in the next chapter.[5] Du Sommerard well understood that it was a gesture of fidelity to Scott to go beyond the written text and demonstrate how the sense of the past could be aroused by the display of historical objects. Always provided, of course, that the objects were the fruit of a 'methodical collection'.

A brief biographical sketch of our protagonist is necessary in the first place. His life was, essentially, the life of a collector, for (as his son Edmond wrote after his death) it was to his collection that he sacrificed everything, 'fortune, health and (his very) existence'.[6] Alexandre du Sommerard was born in 1779, a member of the extensive class of provincial *noblesse de robe* which performed judiciary and financial functions under the crown. He did not emigrate, but in fact served as a volunteer in six campaigns of the revolutionary armies, culminating in Bonaparte's Italian campaign of 1800. The establishment of the Empire allowed him to take up a permanent post in the Cour des Comptes – very much the type of career which he could have expected if there had been no revolution. But even at this early point, much of Du Sommerard's energy was devoted to the patronage of the arts, which he encouraged both by forming a small collection of drawings and by holding a salon largely frequented by artists. With the coming of the Restoration, he became an active member of the reconstituted 'Société des Amis des Arts', and it was in these years (according to his obituary notices) that his collection of medieval and Renaissance objects, as opposed to classical and contemporary French arts, began to be formed.

'A methodical collection' – we can in fact trace in retrospect some of the stages through which method was progressively introduced into Du Sommerard's collector's madness. In the early years of the Restoration, the historical materials appear to have been utilised primarily as a convenience for the artists of his acquaintance, who were invited to examine and draw them. By around 1825, however, this ancillary role – which harmonised well with conventional studio practice and the classicist doctrine of imitation – had given place to something more significant. Du Sommerard was himself the subject of a painting completed in this year by the artist Renoux: he is shown seated beside an interlocutor in his 'Cabinet d'Antiquités', surrounded by items from his collection and identified by a title that could not fail to recall the influence of Scott –

8. *A chaotic assemblage of objects crammed into a small space:* Renoux, L'Antiquaire
(The Antiquary – portrait of A. du Sommerard), 1825

'L'Antiquaire' – The Antiquary. Interestingly enough it was in the succeeding
year that Du Sommerard divested himself of the earlier part of his collection,
which consisted of drawings, mainly of the modern French School. The published auction catalogue describes the anonymous collector as being a 'passionate and insatiable amateur',[7] and recounts how for some time he has had
difficulty in reconciling the possession of these drawings with the other items in
his collection, notably the proliferating group of 'national antiquities'. The
problem is represented in the auction catalogue as one of lack of space, but we
may suspect that it was also a question of the need for systematic order. The
portrait of 'L'Antiquaire' shows a chaotic assemblage of objects crammed into a
small space, with armour and fire-arms invading the carpet. Du Sommerard
finally solved the problem of space and of order when, in 1832, he succeeded in
becoming tenant of the late Gothic town-house of the Abbots of Cluny, adjacent
to the Palais des Thermes at the crossing of the Boulevards St-Germain and
St-Michel. The journalist Jules Janin explained the move in the following terms:

9. *Objects have been allotted their respective places:* collection of the Hôtel de Cluny, François Ier room, from Du Sommerard, *Les Arts au moyen âge*

Quand il eut bien agrandi sa collection, M. Du Sommerard pensa qu'il était temps de la mettre en ordre, et, comme complément à sa passion dominante, il imagina de la transporter tout simplement dans le plus vieux palais que possède la France, ruine imposante encore ... Comme il n'était pas assez riche pour acheter le palais des Thermes tout entier, ou seulement pour occuper l'hôtel de Cluny, il avait imaginé d'en louer, sa vie durant, la partie la plus pittoresque et la mieux conservée.[8]

[When he had built up his collection, M. Du Sommerard thought that it was time to put it in order, and, to suit his ruling passion, he thought of transporting it quite simply into the most ancient palace which France possesses, still an impressive ruin ... As he was not rich enough to acquire the Palais des Thermes in its entirety, or only to occupy the Hôtel de Cluny, he had had the idea of renting the most picturesque and best preserved part of it for the rest of his life.]

Janin seems to imply that Du Sommerard would ideally have wished to live in the Hôtel de Cluny, while arranging his collection in the vast halls of the Palais des Thermes. But his resources did not allow him this luxury, and this was probably a good thing. Emile Deschamps, writing in 1834, describes the carriages which thronged the small courtyard of the Hôtel de Cluny once it was opened to the public, and he leaves us in little doubt that Du Sommerard himself (as in the portrait of the Antiquary) was a necessary part of the experience of viewing the collection:

Ameublements, tentures, vitraux, vaisselle, armures, ustensiles et joyaux, tout a été miraculeusement retrouvé et conservé; vous marchez au milieu d'une civilisation disparue; vous êtes comme enveloppés de bons vieux temps chevaleresques, et la cordiale hospitalité du maître complète l'illusion.[9]

[Furnishings, hangings, stained glass, dishes, armour, utensils and jewelry – all has been miraculously recovered and preserved; you walk in the midst of a vanished civilisation; you are as if enveloped by the good old chivalric times, and the cordial hospitality of the master rounds off the illusion.]

Obviously, in that initial syntagmatic chain – furnishings, hangings, stained glass, crockery, armour, utensils, jewelry – there is more than a threat of chaos, of meaningless juxtaposition. But the rhetoric of the guide-book triumphantly asserts itself over this threat. The orderliness of the system is celebrated through the alibi of the 'good old chivalric times', and the master himself is on hand to complete the effect of illusion.

In advance of the more detailed analysis which will seek to get beyond the mythic terms of contemporary description, I would stress one crucial point which may not have been made sufficiently clear. Du Sommerard's collection, as displayed in the Hôtel de Cluny from the early 1830s, was not only a striking spectacle. It was a new experience. Its capacity to 'envelop' Du Sommerard's contemporaries in an illusion of the past was a direct function of this novelty. But since anything new can only be assessed by comparison with what went before, I must now introduce and analyse a previously existing system – one which has in fact a very direct relationship to Du Sommerard's own. The relation which I shall posit between these two types of historical discourse relies implicitly on the principle developed by Michel Foucault in *The Order of Things*: that there is such a thing as an 'épistémè', or epistemological totality, within which the various discourses of an age are structurally related to one another; and that an apparently continuous system of discourse (for example historical discourse) is in effect fractured by the *coupure* or break which signifies the shift from one 'épistémè' to another. What I shall try to demonstrate about Du Sommerard's long, passionate and exhausting progress towards 'a methodical collection of the brilliant remains of our ancestors' is that it reveals in an exemplary way that epistemological break in historical discourse which defines the novelty of the Romantic period. The 'chivalric' space in which Deschamps and the Parisian public of the 1830s are enveloped is no longer the historical space of the eighteenth century, Foucault's classic age.

My example in fact lies near to hand. When the Musée de Cluny was finally accepted as the responsibility of the French state in 1843, it consisted not only of the collection of Du Sommerard, but also of the extensive collection of French antiquities which had been assembled during the revolution by Alexandre Lenoir and installed in the pre-revolutionary Convent of the Petits-Augustins on the Left Bank.[10] It hardly needs to be emphasised that such a collection was put together in quite different circumstances, and in accordance with quite different principles, from those of Du Sommerard. In fact, Lenoir was not so much collecting as salvaging what could be salvaged from the dilapidation and even destruction of French national monuments which followed upon the confiscation of church property by the revolutionary government. The monumental objects which he successfully transported to safety included treasures of considerable value, such as the fountain ascribed to Jean Goujon from Diane de Poitiers' Château of Anet. But they were essentially fragments, often mutilated fragments, which testified eloquently to the drastic reappraisal of French history and institutions during the revolutionary epoch. But Lenoir did not simply salvage. He placed the recuperated objects on exhibition to the public within an overall chronological scheme that appears to have been without precedent. The journal of Lord John Campbell, a visitor to France during the short-lived Peace of Amiens, provides a brief but lucid description:

... we went to see The ci-devant Convent of the Augustins in which are deposited all the tombs and monuments which escaped the fury of the revolutionists, (they are arranged in different cloisters and appartments) each containing the specimens of statuary and sculpture during one century beginning with the earliest periods of the art, and receiving light through windows of coloured glass as nearly of the same antiquity as possible. Some very beautiful and curious specimens ... are among them.[11]

Lord John's testimony gives a slightly over-simplified impression of the organisation of the museum. There was an impressive 'Salle d'Introduction', with original early eighteenth-century ceiling paintings, in which a full historical range of sculptural objects were displayed, from antiquity to the seventeenth century. Nonetheless, it is surely significant that he has singled out as the most striking effect Lenoir's distribution of objects according to centuries, which extended over five separate rooms of the museum. Within this section, at any rate, the history of France was illustrated in clear, paradigmatic form from the thirteenth century until the age of Louis XIV. Lenoir was eventually forced to close the museum in 1816, partly as a result of the inveterate hostility of Quatremère de Quincy, who had been appointed 'Intendant général des arts et monuments publics' by the new Bourbon government. But up to this date, the French and foreign public had the opportunity of witnessing in the Petits-Augustins a form of historical representation which was surely unavailable in any other context. They could experience the notion of the 'century' made concrete by the successive installation of appropriate monumental fragments.

Of course the model which Lenoir had adopted also had its limitations. The unity of the 'century' is a schematic notion, and one may be tempted to conclude that the objects were only weakly bound together by such a link. Indeed Lord John's term 'specimen' seems exactly appropriate. Within each 'century' set, the 'specimen' fragment would represent metonymically the greater whole from which it had been detached, the Abbey or Château of its original location. In relation to the other 'specimens', it could have no associative link except what arose from the simple fact of contiguity or juxtaposition. Unlike the case of the Musée de Cluny, there would be no effect of illusion, no overall concept of a historically authentic milieu, in the light of which the fragments might achieve overall integration.

Yet we should beware of underlining this contrast as if Lenoir were presenting a rudimentary and imperfect precedent for Du Sommerard's later success. In fact, as my reference to Foucault implies, the question is not one of placing the two collectors at different points in a single evolutionary scheme, but of showing how their differing types of discourse relate to different epistemological totalities. The surviving evidence of the museums themselves is perhaps not enough in itself to establish this point. But there is fascinating additional testimony in the case of Lenoir, which can be found in a remarkable letter which he wrote to the 'Conservateur des monuments publics' at an early stage in the Restoration. It is a published letter which is framed by the righteous indignation of its editor, a M. Guiffrey writing in 1880, who gives every sign of having uncovered an epistemological scandal!

According to Guiffrey, Lenoir determined at an early stage in the life of his museum to supplement his collection of works by great French artists by busts of the same artists, and by busts of a number of great historical figures for whom he had been unable to obtain contemporary effigies. A fascinating point emerges. Lenoir evidently had no scruples about mixing the authentic fragment with the contemporary, archaising bust. But there is an even more surprising detail to underline this point. In order that they might be able to work on the new busts, a number of contemporary sculptors of Lenoir's acquaintance were given 'marble debris' from the historical collection. As Guiffrey remarks:

Combien de fragments précieux ont dû périr, grâce à cette transaction étrange à laquelle d'ailleurs personne ne trouvait alors à redire, et dont Lenoir fait lui-même l'aveu avec une franchise qui prouve la tranquillité de sa conscience.[12]

[How many precious fragments must have perished, as a result of this strange transaction which no one seems to have taken objection to, and which Lenoir himself avows with a frankness which proves that his conscience was clear.]

As Guiffrey implies, Lenoir's 'avowal' strongly suggests that he had no overriding notion of historical authenticity, in accordance with which the 'marble debris' would *automatically* be more important than whatever a modern sculptor might make with the aid of them. Equally, Guiffrey's own horrified reaction to the barbaric behaviour of the classic age shows that he himself implicitly adhered to such a notion. But we have not exhausted the account of Lenoir's revealing lapsus. In the letter published by Guiffrey, Lenoir actually testifies that he supplied the sculptor De Seine with the authentic skull of Heloise (so much useless debris), so that he could refer to it while preparing a bust of that unfortunate lady for the Museum. Lenoir speaks with astounding coolness about De Seine's bust of Heloise, 'which he modelled after the bones of the head of that interesting woman which I supplied him with'.[13] He concludes, with quiet pride: 'This bust is deserving of praise.'

What can we possibly make of a discourse which admits M. De Seine's bust of Heloise to a place of honour, but excludes – indeed dismisses as insignificant except for the purposes of *mimesis* – the mortal remains of 'that interesting woman'? Our own reservations about the authenticity of the remains are, of course, entirely irrelevant. Lenoir evidently believed the remains to be authentic; the significant point is that such authenticity counted for so little in his project of mobilising and displaying the objects of the past. Similarly, we should be warned by this example against supposing that Lenoir's organisation of the museum by centuries *necessarily* betokens an integrated historical milieu, a coherent *system*. That seems unlikely to be the case. Indeed the order which Lenoir established can be viewed as a quite unusually pure example of metonymy, of the reductive rhetorical strategy whereby the part does duty for the whole in a purely mechanistic way, without implying reference to any organic totality. The contemporary bust of Heloise, like every other bust commissioned by Lenoir, enters this metonymic order as a part–object contiguous to other part–objects. And in such a space, the mortal remains have, quite simply, no cognitive status.

My argument up to this stage has relied to a great extent upon the illuminating article by Hayden White, which analyses Foucault's method in tropological terms.[14] White suggests that, in the shift from what might be called the classic to the romantic 'épistémè', there is implied a movement from the predominant use of the trope of metonymy to that of synecdoche. Whilst the part–whole relation in metonymy is reductive and mechanistic, that involved in synecdoche is both integrative and organic. The two elements are 'grasped together', as aspects of a whole that is greater than the sum of its parts in isolation (as in the expression 'He is all heart').[15] And if Lenoir's procedure is relentlessly metonymic, the strategy of synecdoche seems to apply exactly to the Musée de Cluny, where the object from the past becomes the basis for an integrative construction of historical totalities. When the historian Prosper de Barante spoke in the Chamber of Peers in favour of the purchase of the collection by the French government he unambiguously stated the principle that each object was to be valued for its synecdochic charge: each object offered access to a historical milieu and to the real historical characters with whom it had once been identified, through a process that derived its imaginative cogency from the myth of the resurrection of the past:

L'épée d'un grand guerrier, les insignes d'un souverain célèbre, les joyaux d'une reine grande ou malheureuse, les livres où un écrivain traça quelques notes, sont autant de reliques qu'on aime à voir, et qui font un autre impression que la lettre morte du volume où nous lisons leur histoire.[16]

[The sword of a great warrior, the insignia of a celebrated sovereign, the jewels of a great or an unhappy queen, the books in which a writer traced a few notes, are so many relics which people like to see and which make a different impression from the dead letter of the volume where we read their history.]

From 'specimen' to 'relic' – the very shift in terms alerts us to a radical change in conceiving the relationship of the historical object to the past. And of course it is not only the relationship, but the class of object which has changed. Where Lenoir assembled monumental fragments, Du Sommerard brought together and displayed (at a stage when this was being done nowhere else) a full range of both precious and utilitarian objects which survived from the late Middle Ages and the Renaissance. He made a special point of distributing these objects into separate rooms. But his principle of differentiation was not the mechanistic division of centuries, as in the Musée des Petits-Augustins: it was a classification which respected the existing distribution of rooms in the Hôtel de Cluny, and the rich associations which they already held:

Dans la chapelle de l'hôtel furent rangés avec ordre tous les objets qui avaient eu jadis une destination religieuse, tels que les reliquaires, chasses, livres d'église, etc. Les coupes, les fayences, les poteries trouvèrent leur place dans la salle à manger, les objets d'ameublement tels que lits, sièges, tapis, candélabres, etc. du XVIe siècle servirent à orner une vaste chambre, qui, de l'époque même de ses meubles, prit le nom de François Ier. Enfin le salon et deux galeries formèrent une sorte de terrain neutre, où furent accumulés des objets d'art de toutes les époques.[17]

[In the chapel of the Hôtel, there were arranged in order all the objects which had formerly had a religious destination, such as reliquaries, shrines, church books and so on. The cups, faience and pottery found their place in the dining-room. The objects of furniture like beds, seats, carpets, candelabra and so on from the sixteenth century served to adorn a vast chamber which, from the very period of its furnishings, took the name of the 'Chambre de François Ier'. Finally the salon and two galleries formed a kind of neutral territory, where art objects of all periods were accumulated.]

It is rather refreshing to note the existence of that 'neutral territory', which recalls Foucault's mention of Borges's Chinese encyclopedia with its provision for aberrant taxonomy![18] Clearly Du Sommerard's arrangement of objects eschewed the paranoia of Lenoir's centennial system. This could be seen as relevant to the whole issue of Du Sommerard's passion for collecting, and to the links between such a consuming passion and the much discussed problem of fetishism. Du Sommerard's collecting impulse was, as his son's account testifies, not far short of pathological. Yet, in terms which will gain in relevance when we discuss Scott and Ruskin, Du Sommerard can be held to have transcended the overtly fetishistic impulse of his early life as a collector. He can be shown to have successfully integrated the detached fragment within an overall milieu, to have restored the part to the whole.

If we compare the portrait of the 'Antiquary' with a contemporary engraving of the so-called 'Chambre de François Ier', we can immediately see the transformation which has taken place.[19] In the 'Antiquary', the objects are in disorder. Conjunctions seem to be absurd: a miniature nude shares a table-top with household utensils, and the armour clutters up the floor. Perhaps the Antiquary

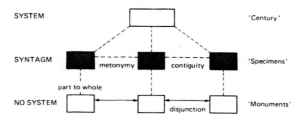

1. Musée des Petits-Augustins: Lenoir

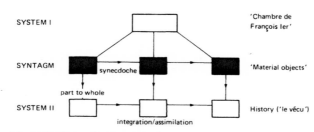

2. Musée de Cluny: Du Sommerard

himself has to intervene to sort out this chaos, by picking out an object and telling its story – as appears to be happening in the picture. In the 'Chambre de François Ier', on the other hand, objects have been allotted their respective places. Not only do all of them come from one period, but they are distributed according to a rational and intelligible economy: the central table, though well covered, is covered with objects that belong on tables, like books and gaming dice. The armour has been diligently reassembled, and it even appears that two suits of armour are playing draughts in the window embrasure. We have no need for a learned guide in this new context: the historical portrait, presumably one of François Ier himself, seems to place the whole room under the honorary, mute guardianship of the regal figure who is evoked, synecdochically, by the combined reference of all the objects assembled there.

We can in fact tabulate, in a simple diagram, the differences between the 'century' room of Lenoir and Du Sommerard's 'Chambre de François Ier', or any other of his 'thematic' rooms. If we take the objects in both examples as units in a syntagmatic chain, then we must allow for two 'systematic' constraints which govern the way in which these syntagmatic units function as discourse: first of all, the organising concept of the 'century' or 'religious' room, and secondly the wider system to which the part-objects relate, to the extent that they evoke a totality outside the walls of the museum. With these features in mind, we can surely establish that Lenoir's museum is marked by the *disjunction* which intervenes after each unit in the chain. Objects are bound together simply by the schematic 'century' link, which can find room for the modern bust that merely *replicates* the past. The connection between each tomb, or fountain, and its original context is a reductive one of part to whole, which in no way necessitates an imaginative link between the series of abbeys, châteaux, and other monuments that were Lenoir's sources of material. By contrast, Du Sommerard's museum employs the integrative notions of 'religious life', 'kitchen life' and the 'Chambre de François Ier' to gesture towards a system that is entirely homogeneous. Underlying the operation of the synecdoche, which leads us from the part-object to the revived historical user (whether named or not), there lurks the mythic system of 'lived' history, history as 'le vécu'. It is this assertion of the experiential reality of history which the rhetoric of the museum both produces and annihilates. 'History' is made real through the fiction of the transparency of the historical syntagm.

The two collections which have been reviewed therefore testify to a discernible shift in the character of historical discourse. In their sharp opposition, they suggest the operation of an 'epistemological break' of the type formulated by Foucault, and identified by Hayden White as the substitution of one dominant trope for another. It is clear that Foucault himself does not claim to explain the actual process of 'epistemological break', and White is concerned with answering the claim that Foucault's discontinuity is unsystematic, rather than with resolving the issue on his own terms. In fact, there seems little reason to question Foucault's methodological limitation to an 'archaeology' at this stage of his career, even if its necessary consequence is the detachment of discourse from 'le vécu'.[20] After all, the aim of a study such as this is precisely to show that the equation of a certain discourse with 'le vécu' is an effect of rhetoric rather than a natural correspondence which remains inaccessible to critical method. Thus our next task is to broaden the argument by setting Du Sommerard's achievement within a wider context, and relating the Musée de Cluny to the other forms of historical representation which have been discussed in this study up to now.

There can be no doubt about the distinctive place which Du Sommerard has here. Two contrasted examples will suffice to recall the spectrum which has been under review. The historian Prosper de Barante, whose stated intention of achieving a kind of stylistic transparency in historical narrative was judged successful by the French critical consensus of 1824, came to be dismissed by later generations, largely because the technical device of writing a substitute chronicle, with no authorial intervention, appeared spurious by comparison with the authentic, newly published medieval sources.[21] By contrast, the historical showman Daguerre, with the novel spectacle of the diorama, harnessed an overwhelming type of technical effect to the project of representing the otherness of the past. And he succeeded in graduating from the diorama to the invention of the daguerreotype, which (in Barthes' terms) annihilates the distance between *dasein* and *dagewesensein* (between 'being there' and 'having-been-there'). In other words, Daguerre achieved through the visual medium of photography what Barante had unsuccessfully striven for in the domain of narrative. But this achievement was a fragile one, as far as historical

— bring history to life.

representation is concerned. No one could deny that the photograph was the imprint of a past event. But that event as recorded was condemned to remain mute – and, as it were, frozen – as long as there was no way of reinserting it within a narrative chain.

As we have seen, Du Sommerard fully appreciated the difficulties which accompanied these two contrasted methods of historical representation. We can follow throughout the course of his published writings an increasing realisation of the technical resource which was necessary to steer between Scylla and Charybdis, and bring his collector's cargo to port. As early as 1822, his modest publication under the title *Vues de Provins* bears traces of his commitment to the new historical mentality; his first task, as he conceives it, is to expel the ironic, or 'satirical', discourse of the previous century:

Nous n'ignorons pas, quoique étranger à Provins, que ses habitants sont divisés depuis plus de trois cent ans, sur la question de l'antiquité plus ou moins reculée de cette ville . . . La discussion a dès-lors perdu le caractère qu'elle aurait dû conserver; et la polémique, empruntant le langage de la satire, a envenimé la discussion au lieu de l'éclairer.[22]

[We are not unaware, though strangers to Provins, that its inhabitants have been divided for over three hundred years, over the question of the greater or less antiquity of this town . . . discussion has since lost the character which it ought to have kept; and polemics, borrowing the language of satire, has poisoned the discussion instead of clarifying it.]

Du Sommerard announces the liquidation of these ancestral disputes, and puts forward simply the neutral code: 'a simple description of the monuments and ruins in their present state, presented from their picturesque side'. What might picturesque mean in this context? It means more, one imagines, than the mere selection of the pictorial format for representing the 'monuments and ruins', and the assurance that this convention will be turned to good account. As Prosper Mérimée recalled, the interest of *Vues de Provins* lies particularly in the fact that it was one of the first applications to historical topography of the new technique of lithography, contemporary with the first volumes of Nodier's *Voyages pittoresques*.[23] Du Sommerard himself insisted on stressing in his illuminating introduction 'the effect . . . which can be expected, in our view, from the invention of lithography, from these local descriptions which are at once picturesque and historical, placed by the modesty of their prices within the range of moderate fortunes'.[24]

That the new printing techniques were not valued by Du Sommerard simply for their cheapness and accessibility is clear from the fact that he continued to work with the most refined modern methods of reproduction available to him, pushing his concern with the perfect 'description' to a stage where it appears almost fanatical. When, in 1838, he finally published the first volume of his crowning documentary achievement, *Les Arts au moyen âge*, he went out of his way to stress the unprecedented combination of techniques which had been used in the reproduction of historical sites and objects: the work had come to fruition 'in spite of the difficulties which we created for ourselves in submitting, *for the first time* [Du Sommerard's italics], the execution of certain plates to four successive operations . . . (*reduction, engraving, transfer* of the engraving on to stone, colouring and modelling of the line with the lithographic pencil)'.[25] The result, even for the modern eye satiated by photographic reproduction, is quite sensational. In fact, this work, which started to appear only a year before Daguerre announced his discoveries to the world, is a further proof (if any were necessary) of the compelling will to realism which ran parallel to (but was not in any way exhausted by) the technical innovation of photography. Du Sommerard is working in that uneasy space of representation where the classical doctrine of mimesis no longer carries conviction, and truth becomes a function of the ever-increasing virtuosity whereby the gap between the original and the reproduction has to be disavowed and camouflaged in consequence.

Yet, in spite of Du Sommerard's triumphs in pictorial reproduction, it is the grouping of objects in the Musée de Cluny which shows his full originality. This new system is connected with other developments in pictorial representation during the period, but remains essentially distinct from them. A brief comparison with the 'Panstereomachia' of the Battle of Poitiers (a prodigy which was mentioned in passing in the last chapter) will clarify this issue. As we learn in the informative pamphlet which accompanied the spectacle, the Panstereomachia could be defined as 'the representation of a Battle, entirely composed of solid figures in their relative proportions'. In other words, the spectators were faced with a coherently organised visual display, divided into 'front ground', 'back ground', 'distance', etc., where groups of related figures enacted different episodes in the course of a particular battle. The figures, or at least those in the front ground, must have been themselves free-standing and complete, since the proprietor of the spectacle was anxious to point out his readiness to meet 'any persons desirous of possessing groups, or single figures'.[26] But they were, at the same time, subordinate to the perspectival ordering of the scene, just as the entire spectacle was subordinate to the narrative of the battle. Indeed the pamphlet is very largely taken up by an 'account', drawn directly from Froissart, of the successive stages in the engagement, and the 'description' of the spectacle itself can only be achieved with the help of frequent injunctions to 'See Historical Account'.[27]

The 'Panstereomachia' is therefore parasitic both on pictorial convention, and on the historical narrative. However carefully Mr Bullock may have studied the 'costume and arms of the period', his 'specimens of the artillery and battering rams' were merely solid models, which cannot have convinced anyone for long. Du Sommerard, on the other hand, found room for the actual objects which survived from the historic past. And not only did he find room for them. He assembled them in groupings which allowed them at one and the same time to retain their individual authenticity, and to participate in an overall, recreative vision of the past. At the Musée de Cluny, there was no need for visualisation according to the laws of perspective, no need for a historical narrative to underpin the presentation, no prodigious technical effect to be striven for: there was simply the inducement to prefigure an order in the synecdochic mode. But we need not, at this late stage, entirely abandon Alexandre Lenoir. For the acceptance of the collection of the Musée de Cluny by the French state foreshadowed the merging of Du Sommerard's legacy with that of Lenoir. Much of what Lenoir had brought together was distributed throughout the imposing remains of the Roman baths which (even today) are connected by a stairway to the medieval apartments of the Abbot. Du Sommerard's own son became the first director of the united collections, while Lenoir's son remained in association as the museum's officially accredited architect.

The 'poetics' of the modern museum is not Du Sommerard's system, nor is it that of Lenoir. Instead it lies in the alternation of the two strategies which have been outlined here. This is a feature which is well illustrated in the arrangement of museums like the Victoria & Albert, in London, or the Philadelphia Museum of Art. Passages and rooms devoted to the metonymic sequence of schools and centuries are interrupted by 'reconstructed' rooms, offering the synecdochic treat of a *salon* transported from the Ile Saint-Louis, or a dining-room from a departed Jacobean manor-house. Perhaps the automatic way in which the ordinary museum-goer shifts between these two modes implies a modern replacement for the synecdochic and the metonymic museums: the ironic museum, in which we oscillate between the different varieties of imaginative projection that are required.

What can hardly be doubted is the extraordinary prestige which still attaches to the notion of reconstructing the historical object or milieu within the museum setting. In the past few years, the Metropolitan Museum of New York has re-erected the Egyptian Temple of Dendur, which rises majestically above a stretch of water in a vast enclosed place set aside exclusively for it; the Metropolitan has also installed, at the expense of Mrs Brooke Russell Astor, a Chinese garden court of the Ming Dynasty which is an outstanding, indeed hyperbolic, demonstration of the search for absolute authenticity in all material details.[28] The scale of these enterprises is, of course, incomparably greater than anything Du Sommerard could have attempted. But more significant, perhaps, is the way in which the reference to history has changed. Du Sommerard worked at a time when his countrymen were rediscovering their own history. He devised a unique way of satisfying a social and cultural need which was already being revealed in innumerable different ways by novelists, historians, painters and so on. It can hardly be argued that these new achievements, ingenious and popular though they may be, achieve the same binding relationship to cultural and historical experience. Indeed it could be denied that they have historical significance of any kind, since the historical dimension is almost entirely subsumed in those of the spectacular and the exotic; it is an effect of *transumption*, or far-fetching, rather than of synecdoche, that the Temple of Dendur should stand in mummified isolation a few yards from Fifth Avenue. It is the real thing, and the Getty Museum at Malibu is, by contrast, only a surrogate Roman villa of the first century A.D. But the difference between these two monuments of museology is perhaps not so great as might at first sight appear.

The contemporary problem which emerges here cannot be pursued in this chapter. It must be deferred until the concluding section of this study. For the moment, it is worth focusing on the intriguing paradox of Du Sommerard's achievement. A passionate collector, he was nonetheless able to transmute his fascination with the objects of the past into an orderly and accessible vision of period and place. No one would claim that the present Musée de Cluny is an exact reflection of his guiding ideas and principles of arrangement. But it could be argued that he managed to devise a formula which would prove resistant to the entropy evoked at the beginning of this chapter. He showed that an original historical setting, amply furnished with authentic objects, would evoke a potent and sustaining image of the past. Even when the 'Antiquary' was no longer there to weave his story around each object, the internal consistency of the milieu would continue its recreative effect.

Of course it is true that such an effect depended (as it still depends) on the museum-goer's historical culture. To this extent, Du Sommerard was being a little disingenuous when he maintained that 'material objects', rather than texts, could have priority in stimulating the sense of the past. But, in audaciously claiming kinship with Scott – the 'great Scottish painter' – in this respect, Du Sommerard raises the fascinating issue of the possibility of a primary, unmediated relationship to the objects of the past. What psychological mechanisms could explain this? Du Sommerard's unenlightening biography bars access to any quest for explanation in psychological terms, except by way of the inadequate notion of the collector's fetishism. But Scott himself, the outstanding creative figure in the historical revival of the Romantic period, left many telling signs of the personal, subjective investment which underpinned his poetic reappropriation of the past. In the chapter which follows, Clio's allegorical defences are removed, at least for a time. As in Clodion's bas-relief, she is disclosed as a sustaining mother, rather than a stern mentor. The trick lies in substituting, for the bust of Napoleon, the figure of Scott.

5 The historical composition of place: Byron and Scott

Towards the end of August 1817, the young American author Washington Irving, armed with a letter of introduction from the poet Thomas Campbell, presented himself at the gate of Abbotsford in the hope of meeting the as yet unknighted Walter Scott. A stay of several days ensued, in the course of which Irving visited the surrounding countryside and antiquities in the company of his host, and spoke with him at length about all that was to be seen in the neighbourhood. His travelling notes, though later acknowledged to be 'scanty and vague', were nonetheless to form the basis of one of the most vivid sketches of Scott on his home ground, and were to be liberally quoted in Lockhart's *Life*. But evidently Irving did not think it suitable that the published record of his visit should stand on its own. When, in 1835, he brought it out simultaneously in London and Paris, he yoked the novelist's domain with that of his only serious competitor for popularity in the lists of European Romanticism. The account of a further visit during the 1820s to the ancestral home of Lord Byron in Nottinghamshire was coupled with the record of Scott. 'Abbotsford and Newstead Abbey' was the title of the publication.[1]

Comparing these two accounts which lie within the covers of a single book, we cannot fail to be struck by a remarkable incongruity between the two accounts which Irving provides: an incongruity which is not simply due to the differing stages at which he made his visits, and the paucity or abundance of his records. The Laird of Abbotsford is the unifying focus of the first account. His poetic reputation, his intimate knowledge of the history of the border country, his plans for the completion of the 'huge baronial pile' which Irving saw in the early stages of construction – all are deftly interwoven in a portrait which is compelling in every detail. There is ample evidence for the fruitfulness of the meeting in confirming Irving's own vocation as a writer, which at that point was hanging in the balance.[2] The sense of occasion is impossible to miss. At Newstead, by contrast, the Lord of the Manor is absent; that is to say, he has been replaced by a benevolent, but inferior, surrogate. It is the Byronic connections, naturally, that Irving has arrived to observe and record. But it is Colonel Wildman, Byron's schoolfellow and purchaser of the estate, who extends the hospitality. If Abbotsford is redolent with the poetic spirit of Scott, Newstead has to be searched assiduously for Byronic relics and associations, its architectural features canonised by quotation from *Childe Harold* and *Don Juan*. As if poignantly

aware of offering us Hamlet without the Prince, Irving concludes his hetero-
geneous journal with the lengthy story of 'The Little White Lady', who haunted
the grounds of the Abbey in single-minded devotion to the memory of the poet
whom she had encountered through his writings. Where the account of the visit
to Abbotsford is unified by Scott's presence, the visit to Newstead takes on a
bizarre and fragmented literary form, in which anecdote jostles quotation and the
closing sections are almost wilfully maudlin in their lament for the absent Lord
Byron.

   It is easy to discount this comparison by claiming that 'Abbotsford and Newstead Abbey' is, in any event, an occasional work of little value, by an author
specially addicted to the 'miscellany'. It is also quite fair to observe that the

10. *Scott's huge baronial pile:* South Court and entrance of Abbotsford

character of Irving's two accounts was, to a great degree, dictated by the character of the two houses which he was visiting. Abbotsford was, without doubt, in an extraordinarily exciting stage of transition. 'The huge baronial pile, to which this modest mansion in a manner gave birth, was just emerging into existence: part of the walls, surrounded by scaffolding, already had risen to the height of the cottage, and the court-yard in front was encumbered by masses of hewn stone.'[3] Small wonder that Scott, in the exhilaration of seeing his grandiose projects taking shape before his eyes, should have held the attention and provoked the imagination of his interlocutor! Newstead, on the other hand, was painfully recovering from the state of extreme dilapidation to which Byron's grandfather had arbitrarily condemned it, and from which Byron himself had been unable to rescue it. And of course, where Abbotsford – for all its size – was a single unified architectural conception, Newstead was the result of a forced marriage between the sacred and the secular:

> An old, old monastery once, and now
> Still older mansion, of a rich and rare
> Mix'd Gothic . . .[4]

11. '*A rich and rare Mix'd Gothic*': Peter Tillemans, view of the West Front of Newstead Abbey in the early eighteenth century

The lines, of course, are from *Don Juan*, and Washington Irving was certainly not the first to note the transparency of the Byronic text as far as references to Newstead are concerned. Nor was he the last, since the contemporary guide-book to the house quotes the same lines on its title-page.

This chapter begins, therefore, with a straight comparison between two great country-houses which Washington Irving's title quite unambiguously celebrates. But the real subject of investigation, which Irving's treatment brings irresistibly to the foreground, is the relationship between these two houses and their celebrated occupants. More generally, it is the variable relationship of architecture to text. Newstead is part of the Byronic text, as the most summary reference to the collected works of Byron will attest. Besides the passages from *Childe Harold* and *Don Juan* which may (though not unproblematically) be taken as direct references, there are such poems as 'To an Oak at Newstead' and the 'Elegy on Newstead Abbey'. Abbotsford, Scott's own personal architectural creation, obviously does not enter the poems and novels of its author in the same allusive and partial way. But I shall suggest that it has an even more intimate relationship to Scott's literary creations. Formed as a project in Scott's mind, and gradually acquiring physical definition throughout the fertile period of the first Waverley Novels, it enables us to grasp by analogy what might be called their underlying rhetoric. Abbotsford, or Scott's relationship to Abbotsford as Irving faithfully records it, enables us to trace the figure in the Waverley carpet.

Two specific examples will help me to convey, from the outset, the type of assertion which is being made here. Maynard Mack has argued with great skill and sensitivity that Pope's villa and garden at Twickenham were not merely the scene of his later writings, but in a sense their pre-condition. He writes: 'I venture to suggest that Pope's "creation" of Twickenham constituted an act of mythopoeic imagination and (to borrow a phrase from the manuals of religious meditation) a "composition of place" without which he could not have written his mature poems as we have them.'[5] The comparison to be established with Scott's own brand of 'mythopoeic imagination' is surely not a remote one. And if it is no less clear that Byron does not fit the bill in respect of any 'composition of place', it will perhaps be accepted that he offers a remarkably cogent negative example to set beside Scott's positive one. Byron's Newstead is in many respects the other side of the Abbotsford coin. And I hope to show that the opposition which resides in this comparison is not merely a facile rhetorical antithesis, but a valuable indication of the new sensitivity to historical place which was such a notable feature of the early nineteenth century.

Here it is worth adding the second relevant example, which is my own foregoing account of the foundation of the Musée de Cluny by Alexandre du Sommerard.[6] Just as Du Sommerard's originality is highlighted by comparison with his predecessor in the formation of a historical museum, Alexandre Lenoir, so Scott's distinctive role is thrown into relief by the counter-example of Byron. It is not a question, as with Lenoir and Du Sommerard, of two figures belonging to different generations. But, despite the parity of age and indeed the close personal ties between the two authors, we can speak with some justification of Byron as spokesman for the old and Scott as spokesman for the new: of a cleavage between eighteenth-century irony and nineteenth-century naiveté which may seem schematic at the outset, but will gain in conviction and cogency as we proceed.

One reservation must however be made. In looking at the collecting habits of Du Sommerard, I deliberately avoided the temptation of exploring the psychological motives for his accumulation of the objects of the past. The basis for such an investigation does not in fact exist. Or rather, to pursue the matter would be to risk the error of *petitio principii*: because Du Sommerard wasted his money and ruined his health in the accumulation of his vast and initially disorderly collection, he was a fetishist. Such a deduction is liable to masquerade as an explanation: because Du Sommerard was a fetishist, he wasted money and health in acquiring his collection. In the case of Byron and Scott, by contrast, the relationship to the architectural and domestic milieu raises the psychological problem in a way which cannot ultimately be avoided. In both cases, there is, from the start, the intervention of the motif of inheritance. Byron inherits as a child, from a grandfather who had done his utmost to exclude the intervening heirs from enjoyment of the estate. Byron then effectively disinherits his own progeny by selling the ancestral acres. Scott, it might be argued, builds Abbotsford as a substitute inheritance: he succeeds in compensating for the improvidence of his ancestors, who alienated the inheritance of Dryburgh Abbey, by building a coherent medieval substitute a few miles further up the Tweed. In both cases, possession and alienation, inheritance and disinheritance, mark the embroilment of the estate with the paternal law. But there is also the question of the perception of architectural form, and the implicit motif of relationship to the mother, as wholeheartedly accepted by Scott as it is, for the most part, repressed in Byron. These threads will form the underlying tissue in my argument.

An appropriate point of departure for more detailed study is the brief epitome of Newstead which occurs in Canto XIII of *Don Juan*. We must however restore a little more of the poetic context than the guide-book, and Washington Irving, allow:

> To Norman Abbey whirl'd the noble pair, –
> An old, old monastery once, and now
> Still older mansion, – of a rich and rare
> Mix'd Gothic, such as artists all allow
> Few specimens yet left us can compare
> Withal . . .[7]

Byron chooses to epitomise 'Norman' (alias Newstead) Abbey with a paradox: that it was 'an old, old monastery once' and now a 'still older mansion'. Presumably the explanation of the paradox is that the mansion now *includes* the monastery, and therefore subsumes its age (the other possible reading, that the time which elapsed since from the foundation of the monastery to its dissolution is still smaller than the time from the purchase of the estate by the Byrons in 1540 to the poet's own time is simply incorrect). Yet the effect of Byron's paradox is actually to cast doubt upon the historicity of the building: as with the phrase 'mix'd Gothic', we are offered an image of confusion and incoherence *in the present* rather than with an imaginative evocation of the past. Washington Irving, having quoted the above passage, carefully works to restore historicity in the following terms:

One end was fortified by a castellated tower, bespeaking the baronial and warlike days of the edifice; the other end retained its primitive monastic character. A ruined chapel, flanked by a solemn grove, still reared its front entire. It is true that the threshold of the once frequented portal was grass-grown, and the great lancet window, once glorious with painted glass, was now entwined and overhung with ivy; but the old convent cross still braved both time and tempest on the pinnacle of the chapel . . .[8]

Irving cleverly shelves, from the very first sentence, the monastery/mansion problem. Newstead is, at one end, a baronial edifice, and at the other, a monastery. But the real purpose of his commentary is to enhance the historicity of the compromised vision. Of the terms chosen in this passage, an unusually high proportion are essentially markers of time: *days, primitive, still, once frequented, once glorious, old, still*, etc. The strategy is to point to a telling contrast, between the building as it was and the building as it is now – but to establish the historical dimension through this very contrast. Byron, on the other hand, insists in his subsequent descriptive stanzas on the point already suggested by 'mix'd Gothic'; Newstead is quite simply a monster:

> Huge halls, long galleries, spacious chambers join'd
> By no quite lawful marriage of the arts,
> Might shock a connoisseur; but when combined,
> Form'd a whole which, irregular in parts,
> Yet left a grand impression on the mind,
> At least of those whose eyes are in their hearts:
> We gaze upon a giant for his stature,
> Nor judge at first if all be true to nature.[9]

Newstead, therefore, is a creature of disordered artifice: its immediate impact upon the 'mind' or 'heart' cannot be expected to conceal for long its miscegenated origins. Irving invites us to historical reverie. Byron, as the following lines from the opening canto of *Childe Harold* make quite clear, is fully prepared to demystify the past through accusing it of an unholy alliance with the present:

> Monastic dome! condemn'd to uses vile!
> Where Superstition once had made her den
> Now Paphian girls were known to sing and smile;
> And monks might deem their time was come agen,
> If ancient tales say true, nor wrong these holy men.[10]

Byron's equation of the Middle Ages with 'Superstition', and the ironic crediting of the monks with womanising tendencies, are by no means incidental flourishes in the overture to *Childe Harold*. For, as the 1813 addition to the Preface makes clear, Byron's whole conception of the poem is of a mock-heroic celebration of chivalry and the medieval pilgrimage. He answers the complaint that the Childe was '*unknightly*, as the times of the knights were times of love, honour and so forth' with the forthright statement (consciously reminiscent of Voltaire?) that: 'the good old times . . . were the most profligate of all possible centuries'.[11] Authorities such as La Curne de Ste-Palaye's *Mémoires sur l'ancienne chevalerie*, published in 1781, are cited in support of his iconoclastic views.

So it is impossible to avoid the connection between Byron's descriptions of Newstead and his ironic view of history. But I mean to suggest a deeper connection than is conveyed by such a simple juxtaposition of statements. Gibbon, to whom Byron admiringly refers in *Childe Harold* as 'The lord of irony, – that master-spell',[12] attributed the genesis of his *Decline and Fall* to a moment at which architectural contemplation was invaded by a sense of acute historical anomaly: 'as I sat musing amidst the ruins of the Capitol, while the bare-footed friars were singing vespers in the Temple of Jupiter'.[13] It is this rhetorical effect of *catachresis*, the abrupt collocation of antagonistic terms with an anomalous result, that Byron consistently employs in his descriptions of Newstead. Indeed the apostrophe, 'Monastic dome', might appear to be the supreme example of catachresis, though I shall suggest at a later stage that another, no less apt reading of the phrase can be made.

One might ask how Washington Irving copes with Byron's irony, and with the inconvenient heterogeneity of Newstead. The answer, as with the previous quoted extract, is that he seeks to recreate the historical dimension which Byron satirically dispels. Instead of the abrupt collocations ('Huge halls, long galleries, spacious chambers'), we have the comfortable phraseology of the guide-book, with a constant shifting from the object to the lived, historical past:

Everything thus far had a solemn monastic air; but on arriving at an angle of the corridor, the eye, glancing along a shadowy gallery, caught a sight of two dark figures in plate armour, with closed visors, bucklers braced, and swords drawn, standing motionless against the wall. They seemed two phantoms of the chivalrous era of the Abbey.[14]

An innocent little scenario of resurrection is being played out in these lines – reminiscent of the anthropomorphic suits of armour who appear to be playing chess in Du Sommerard's 'Chambre de François Ier'.[15] The term 'figures' involves an ambiguity as to whether the armour is, in fact, tenanted: the closed visors, the bucklers and the drawn swords incline us to sustain our aroused credulity. And we are consoled with the semblance of the 'phantoms', rather than mere empty armour, once this little fantasy of recreation has been played out.

Yet it would be wrong to imply that Irving was unaffected by Newstead's heterogeneity, and by the poetic irony of its former master. The account of the visit is, as I stated at the outset, a congeries of short, disconnected episodes. The house itself is described with less clarity than the neighbouring Annesley Hall, visited for its associations with Byron's youthful sweetheart, Mary Chaworth, and discovered to have all the comforting harmony of the typical: 'Every thing around us had the air of an old-fashioned country squire's establishment.'[16] Nevertheless, even Annesley Hall is described in terms of its rambling, indeterminate character: 'waste apartments of all shapes and sizes', 'a rambling, irregular pile, patched and pieced at various times, and in various tastes'. Irving has to choose his spot carefully before he invites the reader to a moment of vicarious historical contemplation:

> The rear of the Hall, which overlooked the garden, had the weather-stains of centuries; and its tone-shafted casements, and an old-time sundial against the wall, carried back the mind to days of yore.[17]

But of course Annesley is not the only antidote to Newstead: the major counterweight is supplied by Irving's earlier visit to Abbotsford. The historically minded author has already been schooled in the class of Scott. And it is to the description of Scott's, or rather Irving's, Abbotsford that we must now turn. First of all, it must be recalled once more that Washington Irving arrived at Abbotsford at a peculiarly appropriate juncture. Scott had purchased his 'cottage' on the site in 1811, and by August 1817 he had initiated work on the new house which was to appropriate the earlier, historic name with its monastic associations. At Newstead, there was the problem of distinguishing, in the complex architectural fabric of the 'Abbey', the two opposing terms of the 'monastic' and the 'baronial'. At Abbotsford, the 'modest mansion' is discovered in the process 'giving birth' to the 'huge baronial pile'. The difference is, on one level, a difference between opposing rhetorical strategies, which Irving both detects, and strives to apply himself in the elaboration of his twinned accounts. At Newstead, despite the repeated historical marking of aspects of the building and its surroundings, it is a question of metonymic reduction: 'Newstead Abbey' is decomposed, from a whole into component parts. At Abbotsford, by contrast, it is a question of synecdochic assimilation: Abbotsford the less is 'giving birth' to Abbotsford the great, and the earlier part is destined to be subsumed in the unity of the whole.

Washington Irving is acutely aware, as he witnesses this scene and Scott's participation in it, that the process which he is describing is a poetic or rhetorical one. Indeed he stresses the connection between the continuing creation of Abbotsford, and its architect's literary constructions: 'As yet, however, all was in embryo and perspective; and Scott pleased himself with picturing out his future residence, as he would one of the fanciful creations of his own romances. It was one of his air castles, he said, which he was reducing to solid stone and mortar.'[18] Yet Irving also intimates that a different, in a way opposing process is taking place. Scott is not merely 'reducing' the ideal conception to the literal terms of stone and mortar. He is carrying on a consistent strategy of *assimilation*, by way of which the Gothic fragment, or as Irving more significantly terms it, 'morsel', is appropriated for the enhancement and authentication of a larger, newly composed structure. As Irving records: 'About the place were strewed

various morsels from the ruins of Melrose Abbey, which were to be incorporated
in his mansion. He had already constructed, out of similar materials, a kind of
Gothic shrine over a spring, and had surmounted it by a small stone cup.'[19]

The process which Irving traces can be more exactly defined in the following
terms. Scott is not a restorer of Gothic ruins. He does not envisage the rehabilitation of Melrose Abbey on the site where its ruins still remain. On the contrary,
he rifles 'morsels' of medieval stonework from the ruins of Melrose, and constructs his 'kind of Gothic shrine' *in another place*. Note that it would be in-
appropriate to describe Scott's action as one of *reconstruction*. There is no
indication that the 'morsels' belonged together in the first place, or indeed that
they formerly had anything at all to do with a shrine. Scott has had to use his
own knowledge of Gothic structure to set up the new creation, and the authenticity which it achieves is a measure of its author's knowledge and imagination,
rather than of any traceable link with an object that existed in the past.

An analogy can surely be made here with the 'new taxidermy' of Charles
Waterton, which deliberately abandoned the former habit of retaining and en-
hancing the entire carcase of the dead bird or animal, and chose instead the
system of softening the skin and moulding it into shape from the inside. Waterton
succeeded in obtaining, not a sorry carcase which rapidly became distorted
through the desiccation of skin and bones, but a chemically prepared external
skin which recreated the liveliness of the actual specimen.[20] In a directly
analogous way, Scott's plan for the Gothic shrine, and indeed his master plan
for Abbotsford as a whole, was an audacious recreation rather than a laborious
reconstruction of any particular known type of building. But Waterton was
obliged to work, for the most part, with the remains of actual living creatures –
only as a satirical aberration would he attempt the production of a 'non-descript'
or impossible animal. Scott, on the other hand, as an architect and as a novelist,
was obliged to make 'air castles' – to multiply the poetic structures until they
appeared almost to take leave of their vestigial basis in authenticity. How indeed
could they hold on to it? The passage which follows Irving's mention of the
'Gothic shrine' gives us a valuable clue.

Among the relics from the Abbey, which lay scattered before us, was a most quaint and
antique little lion, either of red stone, or painted red, which hit my fancy. I forget whose
cognizance it was, or from whose monument it had been taken, but I shall never forget
the delightful observations concerning old Melrose to which it accidentally gave rise.
The Abbey was evidently a pile that called up all his poetic and romantic feelings; and
one to which he was enthusiastically attached by the most fanciful and delightful of his
early associations. He spoke of it, I may say, with affection. 'There is no telling', said he,
'what treasures are hid in that glorious old pile. It is a famous place for antiquarian
plunder. There are such rich bits of old-time sculpture for the architect, and old-time
story for the poet. There is as rare picking in it as in a Stilton cheese, and in the same
taste, – the mouldier the better.'[21]

At this point, Irving's account, which is never less than entertaining, becomes
quite extraordinarily revealing. In the first place, it makes absolutely plain the

intimate connection between the architectural and the poetic processes of creation, both of which are seen as being catalysed by the experience of the 'glorious old pile' of Melrose. The little red lion which has been carried off to Abbotsford is presumably to be incorporated in some part of the new structure, like the stone cup in the Gothic shrine. But it could equally well form the central motif in a poetic romance, like the relic of the heart of Robert the Bruce which Irving proceeds to discuss as the possible focus of another addition to the Waverley corpus.[22] In both cases, the structure of transference, so to speak, is identical. An object, detached from a greater whole, becomes the part which irradiates a new whole: in strictly rhetorical terms, a metonymic reduction (whole to part) gives place to a process of synecdochic integration (part to whole). But Scott's conversation, filtered through Irving, allows us to go further than this basic rhetorical analysis. The history of the poetic 'subject' is also intimately involved. Melrose is already the object of Scott's 'attachment' as a result of 'early associations'. What is removed from Melrose, for the purposes of the new creation, is the *edible* fragment: Irving's morsel made even more concrete through the image of the overripe Stilton cheese. In other words, Scott indicates the intensity of his attachment through language which quite undisguisedly betrays an oral/libidinal basis.

Scott is far from being the only nineteenth-century writer to describe his relation to architecture in terms of oral pleasure. We also have, notably, the case of Ruskin, who wrote to his father in 1852: 'I should like to draw all St. Mark's, and all this Verona stone by stone, to eat it all up into my mind, touch by touch.'[23] In a more recent period, we have the architectural writings of Adrian Stokes to remind us, with the aid of Melanie Klein's psychoanalytic categories, how directly our architectural experience is modelled on the appetites of infancy.[24] In the case of Scott, certainly, we are not dealing with the experience of architecture as such, but with the way in which architecture (Melrose and Abbotsford) can figure in the poetic appropriation of the past. The focus is not psychology and aesthetics, but historical poetics. Nonetheless, Scott's choice of terms in the previous passage is too significant to be neglected. It is worth carrying out a further investigation of their psychoanalytic import, since this will allow us to clarify the question of Scott's unique creativity, and, incidentally, to resume our interrupted comparison with Byron.

The essential features of Melanie Klein's psychoanalytic theory, for our purposes, can be found in a paper dating from 1934 and entitled 'A contribution to the psychogenesis of manic-depressive states'. Mrs Klein follows Freud and Abraham here in accepting that 'the fundamental process in melancolia is the loss of the loved object'.[25] However she gives a new significance to the concept of 'introjection', by which the infant ego, in the process of formation, identifies its self with other, substituted objects and figuratively takes them into itself. On the personal level, she envisages the child who has been weaned attempting to recover the total identification with the good object which it enjoyed at the mother's breast, but risking failure with its substitute objects, since its oral appetite embodies a strong sadistic element. In her view, the resolution of this conflict can be achieved only through a change in the position of the ego 'from a partial object-relation to the relation to a complete object'.[26] Yet this change is not so much to be thought of as a definitive and irreversible stage of maturation, but as a drama the ego re-enacts in the manic-depressive cycle. Characteristically, the anxiety which the ego experiences in manic-depressive states is bound up with the desire to introject the good object and expel the bad, and with the need to move from a relation to the partial object to an integrated relation with the complete, good object. Mrs Klein expresses it in these terms:

> To quote only a few [anxiety-situations]: there is anxiety how to put the bits together in the right way and at the right time; how to pick out the good bits and do away with the bad ones; how to bring the object to life when it has been put together; and there is the anxiety of being interfered with in this task by bad objects and by one's own hatred, etc.
>
> Anxiety-situations of this kind I have found to be at the bottom not only of depression, but of all inhibitions of work . . . In this connection I shall only mention the specific importance for sublimation of the bits to which the loved object has been reduced and the effort to put them together. It is a 'perfect' object which is in pieces; thus the effort to undo the state of disintegration to which it has been reduced presupposes the necessity to make it beautiful and 'perfect'.[27]

It is surely not essential to hold dogmatic views about the relationship between psychopathology and artistic 'sublimation' in order to see the relevance of this passage to our subject. Mrs Klein is necessarily concerned with the pathology of 'inhibitions of work', and the analytic process necessary to overcome this disability. But the pattern which she traces obviously applies *a contrario* to a supreme capacity for work, to artistic creativity. What if a subject has managed precisely 'to put the bits together in the right way and at the right time', 'to bring the object to life when it [had] been put together', to replace the state of 'disintegration' with the realisation of a 'beautiful and "perfect"' object? The hypothesis is possibly applicable, in a general sense, to all successful sublimation. But it seems to apply, in the most direct sense, to the creativity of Sir Walter Scott. Abbotsford is precisely the 'perfect' object, replacing the 'disintegrated' Melrose of his 'early associations'. And the process which has ensured the successful substitution is the removal of the partial object from the latter (the morsel from the Stilton cheese) and its incorporation into the former. The 'oral sadism' implied in this choice of imagery is thus transcended when the partial object recovers its wholeness in the new structure.

No doubt it is appropriate that such an exemplary figure of the Romantic period, and one so closely identified with the revival of historical studies, should provide us with the possibility of such a reading. Du Sommerard's constitution of the Musée de Cluny is obviously a minor achievement by comparison with those of Scott, and, even if we are tempted extrapolate the psychological basis of a collector's fetishism, we are not likely to be led to the discovery by hand as we are in the recorded conversations of Scott. In Scott's case, we might say, a quite exceptional case of overdetermination takes place. Childhood experience and environment powerfully conspire to make the stages of psychological development interlock with the poet's identification with the past. History is recognised as a mother, or rather as *the mother*, creatively recovered. Architecture, both that of his environment and that of his creation, provides the relay. In this respect, as in the others that we have considered, Byron provides not simply a counter-example, but the very example which might have been ideally conceived to show the contrary of Scott's situation. For Byron does not simply subsume Newstead Abbey in an ironic text, assailing its antiquity with the effects of satire and catachresis, emphasising its irreducible heterogeneity as 'Mix'd Gothic'. He also adopts a strategy in architectural description which is very precisely the fragmentation of the whole into partial objects. His description of St Peter's in *Childe Harold* takes this form, both sustainedly and deliberately:

> Thou seest not all; but piecemeal thou must break,
> To separate contemplation, the great whole;
> And as the ocean many bays will make
> That ask the eye – so here condense thy soul
> To more immediate objects, and control
> Thy thoughts until thy mind hath got by heart
> Its eloquent proportions, and unroll
> In mighty graduations, part by part,
> The glory which at once upon thee did not dart,
>
> Not by its fault – but thine: Our outward sense
> Is but of gradual grasp – and as it is
> That which we have of feeling most intense
> Outstrips our faint expression . . .[28]

Surely these lines demonstrate, in the displaced architectural setting, a most spectacular case of *resistance*? Byron's determination to defer the appreciation of the architectural interior in its wholeness not only runs counter to the prescriptions of such post-Romantic architectural theorists as Ruskin. It seeks to perpetuate, in its delaying strategy, a refusal of the 'perfect' object, and a relentless commitment to vision 'part by part'. Indeed Byron's initial reference to St Peter's as 'the vast and wondrous dome' must surely send us back, with these descriptive stanzas in mind, to the earlier qualification of Newstead Abbey:

> Monastic dome! condemn'd to uses vile!

It has been noted already that Byron uses the designation 'dome' for 'any large building',[29] and, in the case of St Peter's, the apparent synecdoche might appear more appropriate than in many other cases. But it is also obvious that this usage, applied to the ruined Gothic church of Newstead, is the very height of absurdity, unless we are willing to conclude that the term 'dome' is simply and exclusively a metonymy for 'any large building' – dissociated, indeed wrenched apart from any vestige of aesthetic perception or architectural knowledge. The point is further underlined, if there is any need for further corroboration, by the quite special significance which the architectural dome has come to have in the psycho-analytically based criticism which is anticipated in Ruskin and elaborated in Adrian Stokes. For Stokes, the dome is the paradigm of the good object, recovering in the most direct way the relationship to the mother's breast which is the prototype of all good subject/object relationships. Byron's architecturally absurd, sexually vilified 'dome' is doubtless a sure index of the powerful and unresolved sadism that lies latent in his attitude to Newstead.

Up to this point, we have been concerned with a programmatic contrast between Scott and Byron, which Washington Irving's travelogue incites us to make. The comparison is between a relation to a building which enacts the subject's relation to history as wholeness, and one which reflects the subject's resistance to whole-object identification of any kind. In Byron's view of Newstead, we might say, the question of history does not really arise. It is foreclosed by the strategy of fragmentation for which the most general description is irony. But it may be reasonably argued at this stage that Scott and Byron were not, in fact, antagonists. Quite the opposite, they had a healthy mutual respect. This point, though it does not in any way impugn the foregoing analysis, may lead us to examine more closely the actual situation of Scott in the period when Irving made his visit. For if he was not in any direct sense embroiled in conflict with the demons of Byronic irony, he was, in no uncertain terms, involved with another such ironic horde. Irving mentions in passing that the ruins of Dryburgh Abbey, a few miles along the Tweed from Melrose, had passed into the possession of the Earl of Buchan; and with them, the family vault, tombs and monuments of Scott's own ancestors, the Haliburtons. 'He appeared to feel much chagrin at their being in the possession, and subject to the intermeddlings, of the Earl, who was represented as a nobleman of an eccentric character.'[30] Irving certainly does not insist enough on the threat which the eccentric David Erskine, Earl of Buchan, posed to Scott's sense of historical place and propriety. Not only was Scott forced to feel himself disinherited from the site that would have been his own, were it not for his ancestor's financial imprudence. But he was crudely reminded by the egregious Earl that his final resting place among the Haliburtons was subject to another jurisdiction. One of Lockhart's most curious anecdotes concerns the occasion when Buchan forced himself into Scott's sick-room, and proved to have already in his possession a complete schedule for the celebrated poet's funeral at Dryburgh, 'in which, it may be supposed, the predominant feature was not Walter Scott, but David Earl of Buchan'.[31]

The Earl of Buchan's interference may have become a subject of much amusement when Scott began to mend. His absurd pseudo-medieval monuments, one of which survives still at Dryburgh,[32] may have irritated Scott rather than causing him any real distress. But the reference serves to remind us that Scott was committed to a struggle which was very much in earnest. The 'master-spell' of irony, as Byron expressed it in relation to Gibbon, was an antagonist whom Scott chose for his own, and fought with all the cunning that was at his disposal.

Washington Irving has recorded in a remarkable passage the manner in which Scott's public personality reflected the dualism between ironic dismissiveness and poetic enthusiasm, at the very point where he engaged with the historical material which he had made his own:

> Whenever Scott touched, in this way, upon local antiquities, and in all his familiar conversations about local traditions and superstitions, there was always a sly and quiet humour running at the bottom of his discourse, and playing about his countenance, as if he sported with the subject. It seemed to me as if he distrusted his own enthusiasm, and was disposed to dwell upon his own humours and peculiarities; yet at the same time, a poetic gleam in his eye would show that he really took a strong relish and interest in the theme.[33]

Such a characterisation of Scott seems pertinent not merely as a psychological study, but as an index of the careful balancing act which he has to undertake in the 'discourse' of the novels. A historian like Prosper de Barante, born a decade after Scott, could set himself the task of breaking radically with the ironic discourse of the eighteenth-century historian; he could model his narrative history directly upon the 'naive' style of Froissart, and thus aspire (as I have argued) to achieving a basic 'code' of historical discourse.[34] In Scott's case, engagement with the 'code' is deftly indicated in the Preface to *Quentin Durward*, where 'showing the code' is transcribed as a phonetic rendering of a French Marquis' pronunciation of 'chewing the cud'.[35] This Preface, which refers to the 'old family memorials' found in the Marquis' château as the basis of the narrative of *Quentin Durward*, is, in the most literal sense, about 'showing the code'. And yet, of course, it is itself purely fictional, a mere device for 'framing' the main narrative and establishing a notional authenticity. Doubtless the appearance of the term 'showing the code', which communicates to the attentive reader on quite a different level from the involved hypothesis of the mispronunciation, is a recognition of the historical novelist's unavoidable deviousness. He is concerned not with the signs of authenticity, not with the real but with Roland Barthes' 'reality effects'.[36] Yet, in Scott's case at any rate, he balances naiveté against irony; the 'poetic gleam' in the eye is proof against too exclusive a 'sporting with the subject'. Indeed one of the major dividends of concentrating, as this chapter has done, upon the relationship to architecture and the visible relics of the past is that it helps us to bring that 'poetic gleam' down to earth. It provides us with objective correlates to the 'lust of the eye'.

Beginning with Washington Irving's anecdotal account, we have thus reached a point where it is possible to formulate the different components of Scott's relationship to the past, mediated as it was by his relationship to the original Gothic architecture of the Tweed valley, and to his own neo-Gothic creation. Of course it is also mediated by the historical novels which, at the time of his visit at any rate, Washington Irving could not have associated with their still anonymous author. In order to assess more exactly the balance between irony and naiveté which I have suggested as distinctive to Scott, it is worth paying brief attention to the novel which had appeared a year before Irving's visit, and which was noted by Lockhart as the author's 'chief favourite among all his novels': *The Antiquary.*

Editors and biographers of Scott have drawn attention to the obvious possibility of identifying the author with the principal personage of this novel: Jonathan Oldbuck alias The Antiquary. Indeed this identification was cemented by Scott himself when he began the descriptive catalogue of his museum at Abbotsford with the allusive title *Reliquiae Trottcosianae – or the Gabions of the late Jonathan Oldbuck, Esq.* Yet so simplistic an identification is no less slighting to Scott than it is to the critical acumen of those who make it. What proves to be of interest in *The Antiquary* (and can indeed be effectively separated out from the other, more conventional aspects of the novel) is precisely the distance which the author takes in relation to Oldbuck, who represents a particular point, but certainly not Scott's point of equilibrium, on the scale between irony and naiveté. On the one hand, Oldbuck is suitably cutting about the sham historical reconstructions of 'this Gothic generation'.[37] Thoughts of Scott's vehemence against the Earl of Buchan arise when we read his expostulations against 'A monument of a knight-templar on each side of a Grecian porch'. Oldbuck is also right, in principle, about the inauthenticity of the poems of Ossian, and returns to convincing his Highlander nephew of the fact at several junctures. But if he is right in principle, we are made to feel that he is wrong in the tone of his vindications, particularly as regards his correspondence with his learned friends:

> ... I will show you the controversy upon Ossian's Poems between Mac-Cribb and me – I hold with the acute Orcadian – he with the defenders of the authenticity – the controversy began in smooth, oily, lady-like terms, but is now waxing more sour and eager as we get on – it already partakes somewhat of old Scaliger's style.[38]

It is interesting to compare this instance of antiquarian controversy with the previously cited introduction which Alexandre du Sommerard wrote to his publication, *Vues de Provins*, in 1822. Du Sommerard refers specifically to the controversies about the antiquity of the town of Provins which have raged for centuries, and recently become particularly bitter: 'The discussion thereafter lost the character which it ought to have kept; and polemics, borrowing the language of satire, envenomed discussion instead of clarifying it.'[39] Effectively Du Sommerard's *Vues de Provins* proposes to liquidate these ancient and tedious disputes, substituting 'a simple (visual) description of the monuments and ruins in their actual state'[40] for such unproductive sparring. One suspects that Scott would have been in agreement. This comparison with Du Sommerard gains added interest when we recall that in 1825 Du Sommerard had been painted in his 'Cabinet d'antiquités' under the title of 'L'Antiquaire' – The Antiquary. Any doubts that a direct reference to Scott's novel is intended must surely be dispelled if we compare the scene of Du Sommerard's Cabinet with the uproarious description of the Antiquary's den which Scott has provided.[41] But, of course, the interest of Du Sommerard's career lies precisely in the fact that he went beyond the simple accumulation of historical objects – that he organised his collection into a museum which represented an orderly vision of the historical past. By the same token Oldbuck remains decidedly on the eighteenth-century side of the barrier between the old history and the new history. Scott is affectionately celebrating a type whose relationship to his own creative work is that of the *amateur* to the artist: Oldbuck is to Scott as Swann is to the hero of *A La Recherche*.

It is for this reason that Oldbuck is set off, in *The Antiquary*, against the figure of the king's Bedesman, Edie Ochiltree, who is at one point described as the 'historian of the district'.[42] Ochiltree is able to disprove, by simple knowledge of the local terrain, Oldbuck's elaborate theory about the 'Ancient Fortifications at the Kaim of Kinprunes'. Ochiltree represents experience against hypothesis and, more precisely, the tradition of oral history in the locality against the classicising, polemicising historical style. Indeed Oldbuck's deficiencies in this respect can be related directly to the terms which we have been using to establish Scott's distinctive relationship to his architectural surroundings. Oldbuck discovers 'hewn stones' in his vegetable garden and sends them 'as specimens to [his] learned friends, and to the various antiquarian societies of which [he is] an unworthy member'.[43] Scott takes the 'morsels' (Irving's term) from the ruins of Melrose and rehabilitates them into the 'kind of Gothic shrine' which is the precursor and, in a sense, microcosm of the future Abbotsford. The antithesis is just the one which I have indicated between Lenoir's Musée des Petits-Augustins and Du Sommerard's Musée de Cluny: on the one hand, 'specimens', that is to say part-objects which are disjoined from each other and from any transcendent whole; on the other hand, part-objects which are linked synecdochically both to an architectural whole and to the mythic system of 'History'.

The architectural activities of Scott, like the collecting and museum-founding of Du Sommerard, thus turn out to have a direct and incontrovertible relationship to the establishment of the new notion of 'History'. Where Du Sommerard works merely (as it were) in the register of objects, Scott perfects a technique of transference and assemblage which will finally transcend the heterogeneity of its origins. The anonymous Waverley Novels, like the neo-Gothic surrogate of Abbotsford, are seamless creations. And it is pure chance, and good luck, that Washington Irving's timely visit has enabled us to lift the veil on a uniquely revealing stage of Scott's creative life. But, in both cases, there remains the common feature that a kind of conjunction has taken place between history and psychology: the prefiguration of the past has been (so to speak), overdetermined by psychic patterns which it is hard to ignore. At an earlier state, I quoted a passage from the writings of Melanie Klein about the need to achieve integration with the complete, good object. Mrs Klein diagnoses the anxiety of wanting 'to put the bits together in the right way . . . to bring the object to life when it has been put together', and 'the effort to undo the state of disintegration' to which the 'perfect' object has been reduced. Is it not striking that, when Michel Foucault attempts to characterise the myth of history as continuity, he should do so in terms which directly echo this analytic interpretation?

L'histoire continue, c'est le corrélat indispensable à la fonction fondatrice du sujet : la garantie que tout ce qui lui a echappé pourra lui être rendu ; la certitude que le temps ne dispersera rien sans le lui restituer dans une unité recomposée ; la promesse que toutes ces choses maintenues au loin par la différence, le sujet pourra un jour – sous la forme de la conscience historique – se les approprier derechef, y restaurer sa maîtrise et v trouver ce qu'on peut bien appeler sa demeure.[44]

[Continuous history, that is the indispensable correlate for the subject's founding function: the guarantee that all that has escaped from the subject can be restored to it; the certainty that time will not dissipate anything without restoring it to the subject in a recomposed unity; the promise that all these things which are kept at a distance by difference will be available for the appropriation of the subject once again – in the form of historical awareness, that it will be able to reinstate its mastery there and find there what can well be called its dwelling.]

'What can well be called its dwelling' – Foucault's formulation helps us to appreciate why, in the historical movement of the early nineteenth century, Scott exerted so unique and powerful an effect. Indeed Foucault's hygienic project of an 'archaeology of knowledge' encounters in Scott its primary source of contamination. The poet who did in fact establish his dwelling in a historical milieu to which mastery had been cunningly transferred, is in a genuine sense the anti-Foucault, whose web we glimpse in the processes of Foucault's unravelling.

And yet, of course, Scott was not alone in creating the potent myth of history which Foucault identifies. He was not alone in underpinning this myth with a psycho-sexual identification that gives it exceptional cogency. In his brief introductory comments to Lionel Gossman's study of 'Augustin Thierry and liberal historiography', Hayden White remarks: 'Like many of his generation, and especially Benjamin Constant (whom Gossman explicitly likens to Thierry), the dream of unity, continuity, and peace seems to be a projection of a more basic fascination with androgyny.'[45] In the case of Augustin Thierry, as Gossman makes clear, this fascination is borne out by a concern with myths of origin which displace on to the past the state of conflict which modern Utopianism seeks to transcend:

History, in Thierry's narrative, begins, therefore, not with the defeat and humiliation of the woman at the hands of the man but with the defeat and humiliation of the patriarch at the hands of the rebellious sons who covet his possessions. Thereafter, throughout all history – for every historical father is inevitably revealed as a parricide, just as every people turns out to have conquered another – authority has no foundation and law commands no respect, since they rest on an initial act of violence, or breaking of the law. The history of England, as Thierry writes it, and as Michelet was to see it after him, is a history of sons rising up against their fathers.[46]

If it is this mythic structure which underlies the 'progressive' historiography of Thierry and Michelet, then how are the terms shifted in the very different historical physiognomy of Sir Walter Scott? Since we began with a comparison between Scott and Byron, let us conclude with another – however conscious we may be of the tenuous and hypothetical nature of such claims as are being advanced. Newstead was Byron's paternal inheritance. But it was inherited across generations, from a patriarchal figure whose archaic quality must have been accentuated by his name, 'The Wicked Lord', as well as by his deliberate attempts to squander the inheritance of his son and grandson, both of whom predeceased him. Byron's succession, as a child, to this inheritance, seems to have brought about a passionate desire for identification, and a corresponding inability to dwell harmoniously in the 'Monastic dome'. Washington Irving quotes from a letter in which Byron states: 'Newstead and I stand or fall together. I have now lived on the spot. I have fixed my heart upon it; and no pressure, present or future, shall induce me to barter the last vestige of our inheritance.'[47] Yet, as Irving continues, Byron's 'residence at the Abbey . . . was fitful and uncertain'. His desire had been drawn, and rejected, by his kins-woman Mary Chaworth of Annesley Hall, herself the descendant of a victim of the 'Wicked Lord's' hot temper and swordsmanship. It was to seduce him into a perpetual 'pilgrimage', without fixed destination but always eccentric to his inherited home.

In Scott's case, the disinheritance was not threatened, but actual – and felt as such. He writes in his brief *Autobiography*:

The ancient patrimony was sold for a trifle (about £3000), and my father, who might have purchased it with ease, was dissuaded by my grandfather, who at that time believed a more advantageous purchase might have been made of some lands which Raeburn thought of selling. And thus we have nothing left of Dryburgh, although my father's maternal inheritance, but the right of stretching our bones where mine may perhaps be laid ere any eye but my own glances over these pages.[48]

Scott's childhood, therefore, took place not at Dryburgh, but adjacent to it, in the 'old Smailholm grange' where he was 'under the care of his grandmother and aunts'.[49] This 'grandame's child', having been cheated of his 'father's maternal inheritance', was to recreate it at Abbotsford. That he was able to do so is perhaps connected with the particular circumstances of his inheritance, or rather disinheritance. It was not a question of 'sons rising up against fathers', but of circumventing, or leaping over, the paternal bar to reach the 'maternal inheritance'. And this maternal inheritance, concretised in the new Abbotsford, was also the inheritance of history, reestablished in its continuity through the massive effort of reconstruction which was to be Scott's whole creative life.

Those who consider this hypothesis fanciful might at least ask themselves the following question, which relates to Scott's well-known division of labour (in the first stages of the Waverley Novels) between the eighteenth century and the medieval period. At the stage when Abbotsford is still an 'air castle', Scott lays claim, in *Waverley, or 'Tis Sixty Years Since*, to the very period in which his ancestors 'enjoyed the part of Dryburgh, now the property of the Earl of Buchan, comprehending the ruins of the Abbey.'[50] As Abbotsford nears completion, he gradually extends his historical realm, with *Ivanhoe* (1820) entering the Middle Ages, and with *Quentin Durward* (1823) transplanting the action into a European setting. It is as if the construction of Abbotsford, serving as direct compensation for the loss of the maternal inheritance, at the same time opens up the wider historical field for his appropriation. From remedying the improvidence of father and grandfather, Scott is enabled, through Abbotsford as relay, to explore the whole domain of history as a beneficent mother.

6   Defences against irony: Barham, Ruskin, Fox Talbot

In 1856 the child Henry James was 'thrilled' by the French painter Delaroche's 'reconstitution of far-off history', which his elder brother William regarded as being of little interest. The anecdote reminds us that by this stage (and for a decade or so before that date), the freshness and evocative power of the historical recreations of the 1820s and 1830s were tempered by familiarity. As the novel and popular works of the earlier period progressively lost favour with the sophisticated, they were in the same process reclassified as appropriate material for the entertainment of the immature, the young and the simple. Even in the case of Scott, this process is undeniable, though it takes place over a long period, perhaps culminating at the stage when Scott is omitted from Dr Leavis's 'Great Tradition', well over a century after the first appearance of the Waverley Novels. In the case of a historian like Barante, the transformation takes place with bewildering rapidity. During the late 1820s the *Ducs de Bourgogne* had gained the respect and enthusiasm of such high authorities as Stendhal, Guizot and Villemain. When Barante finally died in 1866, the anonymous obituarist in the *Journal de Bruxelles* thought it most apt to celebrate his galvanising effect on an audience of adolescents:

> When I was pursuing my studies in a provincial college which had kept the old traditions, I recollect having heard the twelve volumes of this work being read from beginning to end, at mealtimes. A pupil ascended, at the beginning of dinner, to a raised platform at the end of the refectory, and from there, in a loud and slow voice, he tried to dominate the terrible noise of clattering dishes which arose from all the tables. At the end of the a month, when we were used to it, we ended up by not losing a word, while carrying on with munching and swallowing our food.[1]

The meals so graphically described in this passage probably took place in the 1830s or early 1840s. From the same period (recollected towards the end of the century) comes Anatole France's account of the avidity with which he and his school-fellows devoured Barante's text. He adds, however, an important rider: 'As for the *History of the Dukes of Burgundy*, I have not re-read it. But I have read Froissart.'[2] Barante had evidently succeeded in creating, for his contemporaries, a 'chronicle effect'. But such an effect was radically undercut when readers acquired the opportunity of comparing the text with the authentic material which it was designed to simulate. Once that comparison could be made, the ersatz authenticity of the *Ducs de Bourgogne* became, in Michelet's cutting phrase, 'nothingness'. When the real Froissart beckoned, only the immature would continue to enjoy the substitute.

But it would be foolish to imply that mid-nineteenth-century adult readers were all qualified to make the leap, with Anatole France, from Barante to Froissart. For the more popular taste, an intermediate stage existed. This is well demonstrated by the appearance in 1843 of a collection like Barry St Leger's *Stories from Froissart*. No less than Barante, St Leger is obliged to rely for much of his material on the *Memoirs* of Commines. But whereas Barante contrasted the qualities of the two chroniclers very much to the advantage of Froissart's 'naiveté', St Leger rather surprisingly gives the benefit of his arbitration to Commines. Froissart is termed 'the butterfly only of the court . . . contented with its externals'; Commines, by comparison, is credited with having 'with the industry of a bee, studied the main-spring of diplomatic machinery', and with being 'contented only with the treasures of truth'.[3] Such a preference, which squares oddly with the title of the collection, involves St Leger in precisely that discrediting of his main source which Barante had hoped to eliminate from the historical narrative. Froissart, for all his vivid presentation, is arraigned in footnotes for treating 'the insurgent people as mere swine'. The reader is treated to sudden spasms of protest like: 'Thank heaven! this, among other opinions of the 14th century, is obsolete.'[4] St Leger's reformist conscience keeps him constantly on guard against the seductions of Froissart's prose.

Of course St Leger knows perfectly well that there is some ambivalence in his attitude to his main source. He takes advantage of a 'Prefatory Essay' to develop the whole issue of the relation between credulity and scepticism in the study of the past. Here his chief explanatory tool is an extended analogy with the cycle of the individual life, from youth to age, which fits well with the argument that we have begun to develop in this chapter:

It has been observed that the latter part, or, rather, the more advanced periods of life, are spent in unlearning a great deal of that which has been acquired at its commencement. Sentiments and thoughts are engendered by early reading, which are destined to be changed by experience; the ardours of boyhood are quenched by the coldness of that maturity by which they are considered follies; and the dreams of youth are dispelled by the dull realities of manhood. Romance is succeeded by reason, and the illusions of our early sentiments and opinions vanish before the touchstone of our maturer judgment. The destruction of these early illusions is painful, but it is unfortunately in the natural course of events in the history of the human mind. In youth we *read* for entertainment, and without analysing what we read; but at a more advanced age we *think* for instruction, and look with very different eyes upon what had formerly conferred pleasure and excited admiration. As one prominent illustration of this change of feeling, who is there, that in his early readings and conversation, has not learned to boast of what are called the 'golden days of good queen Bess', and looked back at that monarch as the honour of our country, and considered her as a model fit for the imitation of any future sovereign? And who is there that, on a cool and dispassionate perusal of the times of Elizabeth, in the days of his maturer judgment, has not pronounced her to

have been little else than a capricious tyrant – her reign characterised by her own favour-
itism and cruelty, and by the cupidity and exactions of her ministers?[5]

It is interesting that St Leger does not acknowledge the fatal flaw in this
analogy. If 'reason' follows 'romance' as maturity follows youth, then how
can he explain the cultural morphology of his own period? The fact that an age
of Romance, or Romanticism, succeeded an Age of Reason squares oddly with
such a naively developmental attitude to history. But if St Leger's analogy fails
to explain an earlier generation's fascination with Froissart, it compels attention
as a rhetorical figure. And it can be used to suggest, not only that we abandon
naive credulity as we (and the human race) grow up, but that 'illusions' and
maturer 'judgment' are inextricably bound up with one another. Just as we
preserve within our own past the youth who '*read* for entertainment', so we
cannot entirely blot out our vision of the 'golden days of good queen Bess' and
replace it with 'a cool and dispassionate perusal'. De Quincey, writing on
Michelet's 'Joan of Arc' in 1847, uses a similar, though less ambiguous figure
when he frankly confesses that credulity and scepticism follow one another as
day follows night: the gloomier the night, the less the temptation to remain
sceptical:

I believe Charlemagne knighted the stag . . . Observe, I don't absolutely vouch for all
these things: my own opinion varies. On a fine breezy forenoon I am audaciously
sceptical; but as twilight sets in, my credulity grows steadily, till it becomes equal to
anything that could be desired. And I have heard candid sportsmen declare that,
outside of these very forests, they laughed loudly at all the dim tales connected with
their haunted solitudes; but, on reaching the spot notoriously eighteen miles deep
within them, they agreed with Sir Roger de Coverly, that a good deal might be said on
both sides.[6]

With De Quincey's remarks, we are of course in the province of irony. His
statement about the relativity of credulity and scepticism itself invites a somewhat sceptical reading. But if De Quincey suggests an ironic attitude to history,
this is not to be confused with the more integral irony of an eighteenth-century
historian like Gibbon. As Lionel Gossman has persuasively demonstrated,
irony in Gibbon is a means of vindicating, through particular linguistic forms,
'the value of urbanity, of cool and imperturbable detachment, and of deliberate,
controlled, timeless elegance of form, against the ugly formlessness of uncon-
trolled passion and disorderly content'.[7] For De Quincey, irony consists in
retaining and exploiting a kind of existential ambiguity. Its purpose is not to
affirm values, but to insist upon the absolute relativity of the positions alter-
nately adopted.

Irony should be seen in this context as much more than a stylistic effect.
It is a method of vindicating, through style, a cultural stance – of responding in
the appropriate way to a cultural predicament. For Gibbon, in the eighteenth
century, it had been a question of establishing urbane values, and sharing them
with the elite which was alone qualified to appreciate them. For the men of the
1840s, it was a matter of counteracting the unprecedented and perhaps excessive

faith in historical recreation which had characterised the immediately previous ✓ period. Such a reaction might take the form of Barry St Leger's editorial petulance. The naive source was hedged about with intrusive annotations, which held up to ridicule the hollowness of so-called chivalric values. But it is clear that such sniping from the side-lines risked creating incoherence and confusion, and contributed little to forming a revised and revitalised image of the past. Now that historical recreation had inevitably entered its Mannerist phase, a more vivid imagination and a more resourceful poetic talent were needed to mark the distance travelled from the earlier period. In England, these qualities combined triumphantly in the unique figure of the Rev. Richard Barham, author of the *Ingoldsby Legends*. Scott had been the commanding presence of the first phase of historical rediscovery. Barham was to be his epigone, mimicking but also subverting the poetic modes which Scott had developed and popularised.

It is neither possible, nor necessary for the purposes of this argument, to establish a direct and documented relationship between Scott and Barham. To Scott, at the end of his life, the name 'Barham' would have meant above all the English frigate in which he embarked for the Mediterranean in 1831 – an enterprise which was to be doomed to a sad ending, since he had hardly arrived at his destination when a premonition assailed him, and he hurried back overland to Scotland in unceremonious haste, reaching Abbotsford and dying there shortly afterwards in the early autumn of 1832. The future author of the *Ingoldsby Legends* had been born a generation after Scott, in 1788, and as a young man he was close to (though by no means familiar with) Scott's circle. An entry for his diary in 1827 records, if not a meeting, at least a near miss: 'Sir Walter Scott had been there the day before.'[8] Of more significance than these jottings, perhaps, is Barham's well-attested friendship with Mrs Hughes, the wife of a Canon of St Paul's, who was also a close friend and correspondent of Scott. Barham's biographer indeed cites Mrs Hughes as the origin of 'a large proportion of the legendary lore which forms the groundwork of the "Ingoldsby" effusions' and quotes the dedication to the lady in her presentation copy of the *Legends*:

> To Mrs. Hughes who *made* me do 'em,
> Quod placeo est – si placeo – tuum.[9]

Yet this connection weighs little beside the very striking symbolic parallels which can be drawn between the careers of Scott and Barham. If they imply the existence in the younger poet of some considerable 'anxiety of influence', then it is hardly surprising that Barham should have made so little explicit reference to his interest in, or knowledge of, the work of Scott.

The symbolic parallels can be demonstrated best if we refer to the previous chapter, and particularly to Maynard Mack's suggestive use of the notion of 'composition of place'. In the earlier argument, I contrasted the ironic, fragmentary treatment of Newstead Abbey in Byron's poetry with the constructive procedures (both poetic and real) which Scott employed to build Abbotsford. I also suggested that the profound psychological effect of Scott's 'loss' of Dryburgh was a contributory factor in his zeal for the building of Abbotsford. Deprived of Dryburgh (the authentic medieval building which would, but for a senseless economic transaction, have devolved upon his father and then upon himself), Scott used the substantial resources of his purse and his imagination to construct a surrogate.

Richard Barham's construction of place, by comparison, arose from an even more pressing menace of disinheritance. Succeeding to his father's property in the vicinity of Canterbury in 1795 (when he was still a child), Barham was almost killed as a result of a carriage accident in 1802. Indeed his over-hasty executors had already taken steps to send their surveyor to look over the Manor of Tappington Everard, with a view to establishing its value and selling it. Barham recovered, and the property was not sold. He therefore escaped Scott's compulsion of having to create a new, substitute inheritance in another place. But the very possibility of loss seems to have stimulated his poetic capacities in a similar direction. If Scott palliated a *real* loss with a *real* construction, Barham was to offset the threatened loss with a new, but totally fictional, construction. His poetic strategy was to build, upon the very modest foundations of the Kentish manor-house which he hardly ever occupied, the legendary house of Ingoldsby with its ancestral crusading connections, its comic spectres and its skeletons in the cupboard. To quote Barham's son and biographer once again: 'the description of the mansion therein given is rather of what it might, could, would, or should be, than of what it actually and truly is...'.[10]

A strange logic, or morphology, seems to be at work in the cycle which leads from Byron and Scott to Barham. With Byron, first of all, the ironic text is used to register the anomalies of the 'Mix'd Gothic' building, and to stigmatise Newstead as:

> Monastic dome! condemn'd to uses vile!

But Newstead remains what it was: to its many other vestiges and associations, it simply adds the mythic presence of the Romantic poet. In the case of Scott, by contrast, the building which was created in an attempt to realise a personal vision of the medieval past becomes above all a monument to the creative genius of the author of Waverley. By the time of Scott's death (it would appear), Abbotsford had become known throughout Europe through the medium of cheap prints – the master himself had to decline an example offered to him in June 1832 by a Frankfurt bookseller with the testy remark: 'I know that already, Sir.'[11]

In both these cases, the 'place' exists independently of the poet, despite the mythic connections between the two. In Barham's case, however, the real Tappington Everard is hardly an adequate reference point for the very much more splendid and richly historical 'place' which is built upon its name. This is

Barham = baroque of immersion

not to say that the point of reference is entirely unnecessary. For Barham's *Ingoldsby Legends* engage in a systematic exploration of the areas of Kent which form the geographical context of the paternal manor. But it does mean that the relationship between text and 'place' has been significantly changed. The gap between the modest farm of Tappington and the proliferating poetic construction is as wide as the gap between fact and fantasy. The Manor which we discover exists, and can only exist, in the form of a book.

A parallel could be drawn with the strategy of a much greater Romantic figure, who nevertheless shared Barham's experience of coming slightly too late, as a young man, to the banquet of European Romanticism. Victor Hugo puts into the mouth of one of the characters in *Notre Dame de Paris* (the priest Claude Frollo) the suggestive prediction: 'Le livre tuera l'édifice.' 'The book will kill the building.'[12] This remark could be explained, in its primary sense, as a comment on the development of European history from the Middle Ages to the Renaissance, at which time the construction of cathedrals did indeed decline whilst the first printed books were being published and disseminated. But Hugo's dictum also (as has been pointed out by Jeffrey Mehlman) applies to his own fictional achievements. *Notre Dame de Paris*, the novel which takes for its title the name of a great cathedral, can be regarded as an attempt to measure up to the highly diversified symbolic achievement of the medieval architect, through the imaginative potentiality of the fictional text. But at the same time it is the index of a kind of struggle between medieval and modern creativity; in a sense, Hugo seeks to cover the pre-existent building with his text, to make the proliferating channels of his fiction a substitute for the manifold passages and stairways of Notre Dame. An extended comparison between Hugo and Barham would rapidly fall into incongruity. But it is worth retaining at least this notion of the building – the historical building – as, one might say, the *pretext*. The secret stairway which Barham discloses as his solution to the enigma of 'The Spectre of Tappington' is no more than a fictional device, which permits an unexpected resolution to a carefully developed plot. To this extent it has blatantly left behind, or passed beyond, its supposed location in the actual manor-house of Tappington.

The mention of Victor Hugo prompts one further comment, if only to underline once again the crucial difference between the epitome of French Romanticism and Richard Barham. The relatively late flowering of Romanticism in France, which was due in part to the artificial effects of Napoleonic censorship but also to the persistence of the classicising Academy, gave Hugo his opportunity to become the most comprehensive of all French Romantic authors – both a poet and a novelist, as Scott had been. For Barham, on the other hand, the sense of late-coming must have been an omnipresent one. Signs abound throughout the *Ingoldsby Legends* of the awareness that we are no longer in the infancy of the Romantic movement. If Ossian is referred to, his name is glossed with the ironic comment '(or Macpherson for him)'.[13] Where Scott is invoked, it is in order to bring out the utter incongruity of the reference, as in 'The

Witches' Frolic', which quotes without acknowledgment the well-known line from 'Young Lochinvar' – applied to a rather different type of ceremony:

> Now tread we a measure, said she.[14]

As if the incongruity of the reference were not absolutely patent, we are obliged to suffer it again, at a later stage in the poem, when Barham makes a mock acknowledgment to his source in the manner of Belloc's *Cautionary Tales*:

> One touch to his hand, and one word to his ear, –
> (That's a line that I've stolen from Sir Walter, I fear,)[15]

Of course, it is not only Scott, but the whole range of contemporary historical representation that Barham includes within his repertoire of reference. In 'A Lay of St Dunstan', he cites a well-known historical painting in the following terms:

> You must not be plagued with the same story twice,
> And perhaps have seen this one, by W. DYCE,
> At the Royal Academy, very well done,
> And marked in the catalogue Four, seven, one.[16]

As this quotation makes clear, the problem of belatedness aquires a particularly acute form where the representation of history is concerned. For the historical poet, novelist or painter is – whether actually or notionally – telling a story for the second time: he works on the basis of the real or supposed text which is the primary source. Barham, in making ironic references of this kind, proclaims himself to be even later in the field. He tells his own 'Lay' or story with acknowledgment to his immediate predecessor – who has himself made use of an original story, or history, of the period in question. Clearly, at this remove from the supposed events, the audience's credulity is bound to be tested severely. But the question of credulity can also be seen from the other side. This is how we might interpret the apparently casual anecdote which Barham records in his diary for 8 December 1828.

The subject, indeed the hero, of this uproarious anecdote is Barham's great friend, Theodore Hook, who was said to rival the Rev. Sidney Smith as one of the most noted wits of his period. As Hook relates (in Barham's account), the scene is the trial of Lord Melville in the House of Lords. Hook is asked for information on the processions, as they enter the House, by 'a country-looking lady' from Rye, and succeeds in fobbing her off with solemnly delivered, but cumulatively outrageous, falsehoods. First of all, he maintains that the Bishops, in their elaborate state dress, are 'not gentlemen', but 'ladies, elderly ladies – the Dowager Peeresses in their own right'. The information is accepted and conveyed to the country-looking lady's offspring. But more is to come:

All went smoothly, till the Speaker of the House of Commons attracted her attention by the rich embroidery of his robes.

'Pray, Sir,' said she, 'and who is that fine-looking person opposite?'

'That, Madam,' was the answer, 'is Cardinal Wolsey!'

'No, sir!' cried the lady, drawing herself up, and casting her informant a look of angry disdain, 'we knows a little better than that; Cardinal Wolsey has been dead many a good year!'

'No such thing, my dear Madam, I assure you,' replied Hook, with a gravity that must have been almost preternatural, 'it has been I know so reported in the country, but without the least foundation in fact; those rascally newspapers will say anything.'[17]

The little scene is instructive, as well as being extremely funny. For it cannot have escaped Barham's biographer that his own subject behaves with the same scant regard for historical fact as his friend, Theodore Hook. After all, Hook is playing a game with his interlocutor's credulity. He initially gives correct information, and then is tempted into the minor falsehood of proclaiming the Bishops to be Peeresses – a statement that is apparently not contradicted by the evidence of the 'country-looking lady's' eyes. But his master stroke is a projection into the past, when he asserts the presence of a celebrated historical figure, and maintains his ground, with 'preternatural' gravity and against all reason. Obviously Hook's harmless joke takes for granted the context of a decade in which even the 'country' public were witnessing the imaginative recreation of Richard Coeur de Lion, Louis XI of France, James I, and a host of other historical figures, in the pages of Scott and his successors. His ploy is a *reductio ad absurdum* of the notion of historical resurrection. But if this must be conceded, then Barham must be acknowledged to be closer to Hook than to Scott, in the way in which he cites and introduces his historical characters. When Barham gives us a 'Lay of St Dunstan', it is not simply that we disbelieve the events attributed to the Saint's agency. The text systematically subverts every expectation that we might have of a standard of fidelity to the past. Where the achievement of Scott was to stimulate credulity and so to provide a new wealth of iconic references for the imaginative recreation of the past, that of Barham is to manipulate incredulity. We are continually made aware of the artificial, and indeed grotesquely contrived, devices through which past events are purportedly evoked.

The 'Lay of St Dunstan' illustrates this distinction effectively as the following extract will show:

> The monks repair
>   To their frugal fare,
> A snug little supper of something light
> And digestible, ere they retire for the night.
> For, in Saxon times, in respect to their cheer,
> St. Austin's rule was by no means severe,
> But allow'd, from the Beverley Roll 'twould appear,
> Bread and cheese, and spring onions, and sound table-beer,
> And even green peas, when they were not too dear;
> Not like the rule of La Trappe, whose chief merit is
> Said to consist in its greater austerities;
> And whose monks, if I rightly remember their laws,
>   Ne'er are suffer'd to speak
>   Think only in Greek,
> And subsist as the Bears do, by sucking their paws.[18]

Up to a point, and especially in the first few lines, Barham's verse mimes the process of offering correct historical information. There are indeed such institutions as the rules of St Austin and La Trappe, and the latter is certainly more austere than the former. The phrase 'in Saxon times', and the shift in tenses from present to past historic, prepare us for the itemisation of the monks' diet: 'bread and cheese, and spring onions'. Since there is a fair degree of plausibility in the catalogue, we are inclined to accept its minute detail as a 'reality effect'. But (as with Theodore Hook) our credulity is then tested, step by step, until it reaches breaking point. The 'green peas' (with their suspicious qualifications) are already questionable. The statement about the rule of La Trappe, though veracious, is partly undercut by the whimsical rhyming of 'merit is' and 'austerities'. By the end of the extract, the information strikes us, of course, as completely worthless, and our attention is transferred to the outrageous vagaries of the rhyming scheme – which, capitalising on the presence of 'Bears', produces a delightful anomaly only a few lines later by rhyming Reginald Heber (the eminent divine) with 'She-bear'.

This extract puts us in mind of the fact that Barham's 'historical' evocations are mostly in verse. This fact alone would not, of course, suffice to account for their distinctiveness. Sir Walter himself was universally known as a writer of historically evocative ballads before he was unveiled as the author of Waverley. But there is a blatant difference between a poem like the 'Lay of St Dunstan' and one like the 'Lay of the Last Minstrel'. Where Scott maintains an equilibrium between narrative function and metric pattern, never inhibiting the former for the sake of the latter, Barham continually interrupts the narrative, digresses and dilates, while at the same time drawing our attention to metre and rhyming scheme. In Jakobson's terms, he foregrounds the 'poetic' at the expense of the 'referential' function.

The infallible sign of this practice is, of course, his cult of the pun. An illuminating comparison might be made with Daumier's contemporary series of satirical prints, the *Histoire ancienne*, whose irreverent portrayal of classical subjects was much appreciated by Baudelaire.[19] When Daumier gives us his 'Oedipus and the Sphinx', he treats the famous riddle as a ridiculous pun: 'Why can't you count on the pyramids?' – 'C'est qu'ils sont près Caire ('by Cairo' being in French the homophone of 'precarious'). In any form of realist or would-be realist discourse, the pun is bound to be anathema, since it violates the distinction between *signifier* and *signified*. Through combining two distinct *signifieds* (Heber/She-bear; 'Près Caire'/précaire) in one *signifier*, it implicitly raises the problem of the transparency of discourse to reality. Both for Barham and for Daumier, therefore, the insistence upon the pun is an anti-realist tactic, which successfully subverts the conventions of historical discourse.

One could in fact go further in Barham's case, and conclude that his verse forms are selected deliberately for their disjunctive and mechanistic effects; not only the obtrusive rhyming scheme and the urge to digress, but almost every aspect of Barham's prosody works against the principle of narrative 'flow', challenging the natural assumption that we have to do with a representation of past events. And this effect is accentuated by the design, or rather lack of design, in the *Ingoldsby Legends* as a whole. Barham's biographer recorded after his death: 'He intended, had he been spared, to have thrown together the *disjecta membra* of his design into a more systematic form, and to have rendered it more perfect and compact.'[20] But, despite the pious claim, it is unthinkable that so ragged a bunch of yarns could have been, to any noticeable extent, systematised.

In fact, we can single out the significant phrase 'disjecta membra' (disjointed limbs) not only as an apt characterisation of the structure of the *Ingoldsby Legends* as they now appear, but also as further index of the opposition between Barham's discursive procedures and those of Scott. I suggested in the earlier chapter on 'Abbotsford and Newstead Abbey' that Scott's originality can be detected in his shift from a strategy of metonymic reduction (whole to part) to one of synecdochic integration (part to whole); the case of the 'antique little lion' from Melrose aptly summed up this shift, which was also epitomised in the theme of the 'Talisman'. By comparison Barham certainly tries to mimic – at innumerable stages in his work – the process of integration by synecdoche. But because he treats the process ironically, he actually succeeds in inverting the effect: a reductive process of metonymy is uncovered beneath synecdoche, and his apparently organicist strategy revealed as mere mechanism. The opposition may seem unduly schematic. But a few verses from the 'Lay of St Gengulphus' will demonstrate the point. The saint has, by this stage, been dismembered. But he does not stay so for long:

> Kicking open the casement, to each one's amazement,
>   Straight a right leg steps in, all impediment scorns,
> And near the head stopping, a left follows hopping
>   Behind, – for the left leg was troubled with corns.
>
> Next, before the beholders, two great brawny shoulders,
>   And arms on their bent elbows dance through the throng,
> While two hands assist, though nipp'd off at the wrist,
>   The said shoulders in bearing a body along.
>
> They march up to the head, not one syllable said,
>   For the thirty guests all stare in wonder and doubt,
> As the limbs in their sight arrange and unite,
>   Till Gengulphus, though dead, looks as sound as a trout.[21]

It is difficult to miss the pathological element in this description, as in so many others by Barham which re-enact the fantasy of dismemberment and rehabilitation. Probably a psychoanalytic interpretation of his work would make much of the details of his accident as a child, which involved the mutilation of his right arm. But such an explanation (if it can be classed as an explanation) in no way accounts for (or diminishes the relevance of Barham's work to) the 'ironic' stage of historical discourse which is being described here. If, in the 1820s, historiography was able to draw sustenance from and contribute to the new ideal of 'life-like' representation, this was because it was one aspect of a widespread cultural reorientation which was organicist in character, and synecdochic in its poetic procedures. Barham signals the belated stage at which those procedures have themselves become a vehicle for ironic play: St Gengulphus is rehabilitated, limb by limb, before the assembled audience. But even after he has been restored to wholeness – 'sound as a trout' – there is a troublesome remainder, his beard, which determines to adhere to the wicked wife who chopped him up in the first place. As Barham's verse records, she is punished for her own reductive activities by becoming a walking *catachresis*:

> She shriek'd with the pain, but all efforts were vain;
>   In vain did they strain every sinew and muscle, –
> The cushion stuck fast! – From that hour to her last
>   She could never get rid of that comfortless 'Bustle'![22]

There is no need to multiply the examples from 'A Legend of Sheppey', 'The Jackdaw of Reims' and many more *disjecta membra* of the *Legends* – to show that Barham's ironic discourse, however light-weight we may find it, is organised with a purpose in mind. Instead of following Barry St Leger's system of juxtaposing the 'naive' source with an 'ironic' modern commentary, Barham invents a distinctive form of doggerel which very frequently (though not exclusively) uses historical material, but subverts its own claim to authenticity through the pervasive use of ironic devices. If Scott's achievement was that of a historical discourse more comprehensively *integrative* than that of his predecessors, Barham responded to the challenge of a *dispersive* historical discourse, which took for granted the antecedent coding and contrived to rearrange some of its central elements in an original and subversive way. In a sense, Barham had simply inherited Scott's public at a later stage in the cycle of taste; the *Ingoldsby Legends* were to have a popularity in the 1840s which could reasonably be compared with that of the Waverley Novels in the 1810s and 1820s. But where Scott's achievement was orderly and coherent – an almost unique example of a creative *persona* imposing its new rhetoric upon the European mind – Barham's offered the timely relief of disorder and incoherence. His first preface uses the authority of Shakespeare to proclaim:

> The Devil take all order!! – I'll to the throng!

No doubt the best way of characterising, in two images, the difference between Scott and Barham is to compare the sedulous medieval recreation of the entrance hall at Abbotsford (still garnished today with its suits of armour, niches, weapons and coats of arms) with the title-page of the *Ingoldsby Legends* – furnished in a very similar manner, but in such a style as to turn the references to ridicule. With Scott, the decor of the entrance hall partakes of the utter seriousness of his engagement with the past, an engagement which characterised not only his literary production but also his building of Abbotsford. In the case of Barham, Gwilt's lively design – with its supporting comic bears punning upon the origin of the author's name – is a farrago of false medievalism. The Jackdaw of Reims stands perched upon the highest pinnacle of the uncertain structure, as if to say: 'Abandon credulity, all ye who enter here!'

I have spent some time on the *Ingoldsby Legends* because of their amusing and intriguing historical flavour. But it must be admitted that Barham only accentuates (and carries to an excessive degree) the ironic features which are already becoming perceptible in more traditional forms of historical representation. The publishing of the *Legends* took place between 1840 (the date of the preface to the first edition of the First Series) and 1847, when Barham's son provided the preface for the Third and last series. Barry St Leger's *Stories from Froissart*, with their ineffectual mixture of credulity and criticism, appeared in 1843. I have already mentioned, in connection with Barham, Daumier's splendid series of lithographs, *Histoire ancienne*, which Baudelaire saw as a response to the ironic question: 'Qui nous délivrera des Grecs et des Romains?' – 'Who will deliver us from the Greeks and Romans?'[23] This series of fifty plates appeared in *Le Charivari* between December 1841 and January 1843, to be followed in 1851–52 by an English equivalent in Leech's uproarious *Comic History of the Romans*. Nor should the diagnosis of the onset of irony be confined simply to these parodic forms, in which historical representation is undisguisedly satirical or ironic.

I argued earlier, when discussing the histories of Barante and Thierry, that there is a crucial shift when illustrative material ceases to be metonymic (a simple adjunct to historical recreation), and becomes metaphoric, capable of substituting for an action related in the text. This change takes place (in the case of Thierry's *Histoire de la Conquête*) in the edition of 1838, and (for the *Ducs de Bourgogne*) in 1842. Though there is no particular reason to suppose that these new full-page illustrations to such well-known historical works were taken as anomalous or absurd, there can be little doubt that they established an alternative system to the pure order of narrative. The texts of Barante and Thierry were juxtaposed with the vivid and dramatic evocations of contemporary French painters like Deveria and Ary Schefer, who had learned from the evolution of Salon art over the previous twenty years. Even if there is no necessary anomaly, there is certainly the 'double vision' of irony which threatens to be involved here. Historical representation registers the effects of a prodigious extension and development from the 1820s onwards, which has marked a great variety of different fields. But when such diverse models are placed in confrontation with one another, the conventional nature of the strategies of representation threatens to come into view. It is difficult to imagine what Thierry's readers made of the illustration which was unmasked in an adjacent note as being 'not historical' but 'taken inadvertently by the draughtsman from a legend that is cited as being a mere fable'.[24] But such a lapse must surely have raised doubts about the degree of credence that could be accorded to the other plates, or indeed to the work as a whole.

12. *Sedulous medieval recreation:* The entrance hall at Abbotsford (from a water-colour by William Smith Jnr, reproduced in Lockhart, *Life of Sir Walter Scott,* 1912 edition)

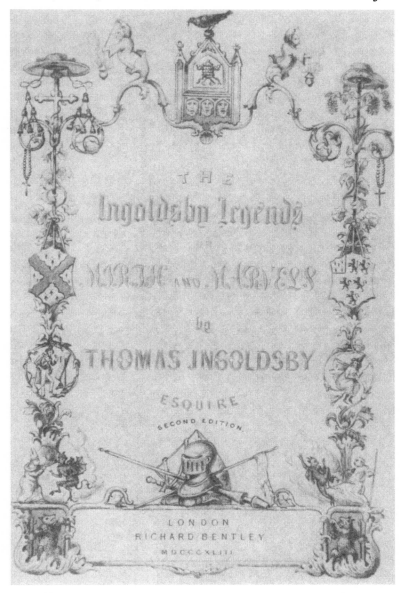

13. *A farrago of false medievalism:* frontispiece by I. S. Gwilt for Barham, *Ingoldsby Legends* (1843)

However I do not propose to investigate at greater length the ironic and fractured historical discourse of the 1840s. What is more fruitful is to consider two completely different, though parallel, defences against the onset of irony in historical representation. It will perhaps appear curious that aspects of the work of John Ruskin and William Henry Fox Talbot are being shown in this light. But such an interpretation can surely be justified. Ruskin clearly was pre-occupied, from an early stage in his career, with the extent to which a building could retain, for all to see, the evidence of its origin in history. He seeks an aesthetic standard which will not conflict with this visible attestation of histori-city. In this way he anticipates (although he does not in fact resolve) the problems of restoration and authenticity which remain paramount in any consideration of the way in which 'History' manifests itself in the lived environment. Fox Talbot of course was a pioneer in the development of photography; in particular he was the first person to perfect the negative process. Analysis of the implica-tions of this contribution will allow us to develop some of the points about representation initially raised with reference to Daguerre.

Over the spring, summer and autumn of 1845, the young Ruskin made an extended journey through France, Switzerland and Italy, in the course of which he was to have the opportunity of seeing far more than on the earlier visits which he had made in the company of his parents. The great towns of Tuscany – Lucca, Pisa and Florence – detained him for most of the summer. A strenuous programme of artistic visits, followed by long hours spent in detailed sketching of the monuments, helped him to take stock of Italy, and his dutifully regular letters to his parents show how absorbing was his engagement with the intellectual and aesthetic problems posed by the new environment. Two years earlier, Ruskin had published the brilliant first volume of *Modern Painters*, with its dedication to 'The Landscape Painters of England'. But he had written this startling text on the basis of a very selective knowledge of the history of art; what Italian paintings he knew were for the most part studied through prints or formed part of the relatively small number that had found their way by this stage into British collections. In 1845, Ruskin was able for the first time to envisage the entire urban setting – architecture as well as paintings and sculpture – as an integrated phenomenon. His initial reaction, however (as the following early letter from Lucca demonstrates) was frank bewilderment and sorrow at the degeneracy of the modern city, compared with what it might have been:

Such sorrow as I have had this morning in examining the marble work on the fronts of the churches. Eaten away by the salt winds from the sea, splintered by frost getting under the mosaics, rent open by the roots of weeds ... fallen down from the rusting of the iron bolts that hold them, cut open to make room for brick vaultings and modern chapels, plastered over in restorations, fired at by the French, nothing but wrecks remaining – and those wrecks – *so* beautiful. The Roman amphitheatre built over into a circular fishmarket. The palace of Paul Guinigi turned into shops and warehouses.[25]

Ruskin's initial perception is of ruinous beauty, which he epitomises with a vivid figure of anomaly. Gibbon heard 'the bare-footed friars' singing Vespers in the

'Temple of Jupiter'.[26] Ruskin notes the collocation of the Roman amphitheatre and the modern fishmarket. Two months later, in Florence, this ironic vision of the historical setting as a medley of disjunctive elements (not excluding the most absurd) is updated to incorporate an explicit reference to the *Ingoldsby Legends* – that manual of disrespect for the past:

You would like to see the sacristy of Sta Maria in the morning at five to eight – with its beautiful *cistern* for washing carved or cast rather by Luca della Robbia – all over lovely angels – and its press doors open where are the relics and the Fra Angelicos – and its ivory carvings above the altar – and its painted window – and azure roof – and me drawing and all the monks playing with a Kitten, that goes like the Jackdaw of Rheims, into the very Cardinal's chair and nobody says it nay.[27]

Through the jocularity of the filial letter, it can be seen how carefully Ruskin seeks to organise his perceptions and evaluations of the Italian environment. One method – the method followed in this extract and in the last two sentences of the previous one – is through catachresis and metonymy. The relationship of past glory to present utility is a mismatch, which makes any apprehension of history necessarily ironic. The elements of the present environment are listed, one after another, with no attempt to convey any overall vision or spatial effect. But it is important to bear in mind that Ruskin was not only providing this animated commentary for his absent parents. He was also (as the last extract makes clear) recording through drawings the very scenes which he described in his letters. The type of draughtsmanship which corresponds to this style of description is, of course, the detail. And, for the most part, Ruskin's record of this Italian tour consists of exquisitely detailed drawings of small sections of buildings: columns, colonnades, archways and the occasional façade.

A full and fascinating letter from Lucca, dated 6 May, gives a comprehensive account of Ruskin's daily round of duty, while at the same time touching upon several of the themes already mentioned in this analysis of historical representation. The draughtsman begins his day in the 'old Lombard church' of San Frediano, sketching after the mosaics and frescoes displayed there. Then, after one or two other church visits, he goes to the Duomo 'where there is a most delicious old sacristan, with the enthusiasm of Jonathan Oldbuck, and his knowledge to boot, and perfectly enraptured to get anybody who will listen to him while he reads or repeats (for he knows them all by heart) the quaint inscriptions graven everywhere in Latin ... and interprets the emblems on the carved walls'.[28] With the mention of Walter Scott's 'Antiquary', we are back in the realm of antiquarian scholarship, characterised precisely by an attachment to the curious, 'quaint' detail, and a corresponding neglect of the wider framework within which that detail has its fuller meaning. Adapting to that selective viewpoint, Ruskin then spends his afternoons drawing the façade of San Michele, in the most painstaking way imaginable. 'I have been up all over it and on the roof to examine it in detail. Such marvellous variety and invention in the ornaments, and strange character. Hunting is the principal subject – little

Nimrods with short legs and long lances – blowing tremendous trumpets – and with dogs which appear running up and down the round arches like flies, heads uppermost – and game of all descriptions . . .'[29]

Naturally, Ruskin's drawings convey in particular this precision of detail. But he continues the description of his afternoon in a rather different register. While he is recording the fine detail of San Michele, he is also becoming uncomfortably aware of the seriously dilapidated state of the marble cladding, which is breaking up and 'uncoating' the façade in a most disconcerting way. 'Fragments of the carved porphyry are lying about everywhere. I have brought away three or four, and restored *all* I could to their places.'[30] To remove the detached fragment, or to rehabilitate it? Up to a point Ruskin's decision had to be based on practical considerations – whether the original 'place' could be found or not. But the very formulation of such an alternative remains significant, in the light of the discussion which has already taken place. The 'fragment', removed from its original site, is a metonymy – like the 'specimen' in Lenoir's museum or Oldbuck's vegetable garden. The restored fragment, by contrast, is part of a mythic wholeness, the rehabilitation of an original unity through synecdochic integration.

To insert this comment in the intervals of Ruskin's industrious sketching may seem to be special pleading. But the evidence of Ruskin's letters to his parents suggests that the Italian journey of 1845 was a momentous episode in his early life, in which a good deal more was involved than the superficial recording of what he saw and valued. It is clear that this unprecedented period of separation from his parents and his country caused him to take stock of his earlier life, and to recognise that the spontaneous creativity – the naiveté – of childhood was no longer a resource to be drawn on without reserve. Ruskin was being assailed for the first time, in these circumstances, by the demons of irony. He was experiencing the disconcerting onslaught of 'double vision', as he explained in a letter of 10 May:

I don't know how it is, but I almost always see two sides of a thing at once, now – in matters poetical – and I never get strongly excited without perceiving drawbacks and imperfections which somehow one lost sight of when one was younger. When I see an olive tree, for instance hereabouts, though I may perchance think of the scriptural expressions concerning it, or the triumphal (use) of it, I am just as likely to remember the outside of a shop in St. Giles's – 'Fine Lucca Oil'!! and an orange tree, instead of carrying me to the south, is just as likely to take me in spirit to the gallery at Astley's – 'China or Harrange?'!! I cannot make up my mind whether the poetry or prose of life be its humbug, whether, seeing truly, there be most to feel, or most to laugh at. Yesterday as I was drawing at St. Romano, a finely faced beggar came in with a dog on a string. He went to the holy water font, and crossed himself with an expression of devotion almost sublime, while at the *same instant*, the dog bestowed some water of a different kind on the *bottom* of the marble vessel so revered at the top. It was a perfect epitome of Italy as she *is*.[31]

It is interesting that Ruskin begins by speaking of 'matters poetical'; he has to apologise for not being able to send his father the verses which he began to compose at Conflans on the journey to Italy. This was the stage when Ruskin seemed to falter in his ability to produce a stream of precocious Wordsworthian verse, and perhaps resigned himself to the vocation of a belated Romantic.[32] But, from our point of view, the rhetorical form in which Ruskin's self-consciousness is expressed is hardly less important than his sense of estrangement from any 'Intimations of Immortality'. Ruskin as poet falls a prey to the reductive effects of metonymy: the olive tree is for him not simply an olive tree and 'nothing more', but a perverse connection to the slogans of Oxford commerce. The synecdochic function (the power of the orange tree 'carrying me to the south') is bizarrely inverted as the evocative fruit is pinned down within the English waitress's banal mispronunciation. Even Ruskin as draughtsman has to see his subject as demonstration of catachresis: the sacred font submits at the same time to the rituals of adoration and abuse. The experience of Italy concretises for Ruskin that ineradicable dualism – between the spiritual and the material, the high and the low – which will become a leitmotiv of his later writing and an obsession of his private life ('One hardly knows which hath the upper hand in her, saint ... or beast.')[33]

However we are not directly concerned here with the vicissitudes of Ruskin's later life. What is important is to trace Ruskin's tactics before the onset of irony. He had come to acknowledge regretfully, on this lengthy journey of 1845, the duties of adult judgement: 'I think much of the blessed imaginative power of childhood is gone from me', he wrote from Milan on 16 July, 'and nothing can pay for it.'[34] Yet throughout his intense communion with the spirits of past Italy, he was attempting to recover an image of historical wholeness from the disorder, fragmentation and sheer anomaly of the contemporary Italian environment. How was this image to be secured? Obviously it had to be through the strategy of synecdoche – through the precise description or the detailed drawing that gave imaginative access to a whole greater than its parts. In a moving passage which quotes *Praeterita*, Adrian Stokes draws attention to the way in which, on an earlier journey on the continent, Ruskin had helped to terminate a period of hypochondria and psychosomatic illness by the drawing of an aspen tree: 'in the forms of an exterior perception Ruskin regained the measure of a good incorporated object and of potency feeling, focused by the integrated body of the aspen tree'.[35] But on this later journey, the need for an image of cultural wholeness, and a conviction of the integrity of the past, was inextricably intertwined with the longing for the 'good incorporated object'. Ruskin tried to see his olive tree, and his orange tree, as touchstones for an unspoilt, uncontaminated Italy; instead, they became caricatural expressions of English vulgarity. He looked to the detailed drawing as an evocation of the sacred space of the Romanesque church. But the beggar and his dog cast their chequered shadows on the idyll.

It could not be claimed that Ruskin ever escaped the anxieties and ironies which appear in this sequence of letters. His defence against them, however, was to create a unique type of critical writing, which registered the strains and stresses of his situation. For Ruskin, synecdoche was a perilous but necessary wager against the ironic predicament. Proust was able to detect and analyse the results of his strategy when he explained that 'the object to which a type of thought like Ruskin's applies ... is not immaterial, it is distributed here and there over the surface of the earth. One must go and look for it where it is found, at Pisa, Florence, Venice, in the National Gallery, at Rouen, Amiens and in the mountains of Switzerland.'[36] For Proust, therefore, the achievement of Ruskin's critical writing is that it draws the reader into that quest for detail, for the precious object, which was also the ideal of Ruskin's draughtsmanship. The justification for this quest lay in the fact that:

> ... it greatly embellished the universe for us, or at least some individual parts of it, some named parts, because it has touched them, and initiated us into them by obliging us, if we wish to understand them, to love them.

But in Proust's equivocation between 'the universe' and 'some individual parts of it', we can see once more the problematic of the part and the whole. For Proust, the inevitable danger of Ruskin's approach is that a concentration on the detail can lead to a kind of 'idolatry' or 'fetishism': the virgin in her niche isolated from the immediate environment of the cathedral and detached from the humdrum but living market-place, offers a wholly factitious image of integrity. When the young Marcel visits the famous Virgin of Balbec for the first time, he is horrified to observe how inseparably the venerated object merges with the work-a-day environment of the French village. As Proust implies, Marcel's proclivity to set the Virgin in the ideal world of the past, rather than in the real world of the French village, is a natural consequence of his enthusiasm for Ruskin.[37]

Yet Ruskin does not stake everything upon the energising power of the object, or detail. One of his later solutions to the problem of the integrity of the past is to reimpose, definitively, a mythic division between wholeness and fragmentation which the young traveller on his Italian journey would never have anticipated. To Ruskin in 1845, Italy abounds in evidence of the abusive treatment of the treasures of the past. To the writer of the last two volumes of *Modern Painters*, over a decade later, Italy and indeed the entire continent of Europe has become the mythic repository of history as wholeness. Not only is Giorgione's Venice used in 'The Two Boyhoods' as an ideal, Jerusalemic city to contrast with the squalid state of Victorian London, but the 'old tower of Calais church' (first rendezvous for Ruskin on any journey to the mainland) has become the symbolic shifter to a Europe which is irradiated with history:

> I cannot tell the half of the strange pleasures and thoughts that come about me at the sight of that old tower; for, in some sort, it is the epitome of all that makes the Continent of Europe interesting, as opposed to new countries; and, above all, it completely expresses that agedness in the midst of active life which binds the old and the new into harmony. We, in England, have our new street, our new inn, our green shaven lawn, and our piece of ruin emergent from it, – a mere *specimen* of the middle ages put on a bit of velvet carpet to be shown, which, but for its size, might as well be on a

museum shelf at once, under cover. But, on the Continent, the links are unbroken between the past and the present, and, in such use as they can serve for, the grey-headed wrecks are suffered to stay with men; while, in unbroken line, the generations of spared buildings are seen succeeding each in its place. And thus in its largeness, in its permitted evidence of slow decline, in its poverty, in its absence of all pretence, of all show and care for outside aspect, that Calais tower has an infinite of symbolism in it, all the more striking because usually seen in contrast with English scenes expressive of feelings the exact reverse of these.[38]

This entire passage is, of course, a demonstration of the rhetorical usages which we have traced in earlier chapters. England is portrayed as the realm of metonymy, in which the ruin is no more than a 'specimen', detached from its context like Oldbuck's 'hewn stones' or Lenoir's sepulchral fragments. At the threshold of Europe, by contrast, the Calais tower offers that imaginative access to wholeness which the olive tree and the orange tree (in 1845 at any rate) refused to provide. In England, there is fragmentation: past and present, old and new, are irremediably divided, and their conjunction can therefore only be experienced as an anomaly – the catachresis of the 'green shaven lawn' with a 'piece of ruin emergent from it'. In Europe there is continuity: 'the links are unbroken between the past and the present'. An organicist metaphor comes to the foreground as Ruskin describes the 'grey-headed wrecks ... suffered to stay with men', and traces the 'generations of spared buildings' as if the different stages of human history could be made simultaneously present in the syntagm of the built environment. There would be obvious clues for interpreting this passage in psychological terms: as an attempt to overcome the alienation of adulthood, to which the letters of 1845 repeatedly testified. We might also point out the oddity of Ruskin's sharp dualism, in so far as it implies a cultural division between nineteenth-century England and the continent. Certainly an author like Washington Irving, fresh from the genuinely 'new' country of America, tries to locate in Britain itself the very same 'links' between past and present which Ruskin declares to have been cut.[39] But the very precariousness of Ruskin's thesis, its psychological overdetermination and its hazardousness as a cultural diagnosis, all testify to the vigour with which he took up the task of reassessing the Romantic heritage. Where Barham had ironically retraced the process of synecdoche, Ruskin seeks, by a prodigious effort of creativity, to evacuate irony and reinstate synecdoche as the integrative bonding of the cultural and historical world. That he does not really succeed in doing so is hardly surprising. Yet the splendour of his effort not infrequently redeems the failure.

Barham vs Ruskin [handwritten margin note]

For Ruskin, therefore, 'History' – as a seamless web – begins at Calais, with the 'old tower'. In England, her mythic presence cannot be apprehended. Echoes of Ruskin's powerful conception can be picked up a century later, in the autobiographical *Inside Out* of Adrian Stokes, which makes a similar distinction between the fragmented, repellent London scenery of his childhood and the 'counter-landscape' of Italy. Yet in Stokes, the aesthetic dualism has been divested of its specifically historical character; the psychological import is moreover quite freely admitted, since Stokes's Italian 'counter-landscape' is also 'the rested mother . . . love and life'.[40] The significance of Ruskin's position, developing as it did in the ironic aftermath of Romanticism, lies in the way it harnesses latent psychological drives to reaffirm the otherness and the wholeness of history: a history that was to be perceived throughout the environment of everyday life, but from a distance (as it were) since Ruskin is the foreigner disembarking on the continent, who carries within himself the secret of his insular origins. It is easy enough to see how Ruskin's historical perception could be transformed, in the writings of his successors, into a purely aesthetic vision. Such is the case if we put 'The Two Boyhoods' beside Walter Pater's famous essay on the 'School of Giorgione'. For Ruskin, the ideal Venice of Giorgione is still anchored, in concrete historical terms, by the precision of its documentation and by the programmatic contrast with modern London; Pater, however, negates any such historical distance by postulating a trans-subjective ideal of style – 'the Giorgionesque . . . an influence, a spirit or type in art, active in men so different as those to whom many of his supposed works are really assignable'.[41] How could the notion of history survive, not indeed as an intellectual construction, but as an aesthetic and cultural perception, when the sharp dualism of Ruskin's writings was superseded by such an exquisitely flexible, trans-historical vision of the past?

Such a question is saved from being merely rhetorical by a detail in Ruskin's biography which deserves a place in this study. During his 'last days at Oxford' (that is to say around January 1840), Ruskin learned from a member of his college of 'the original experiments of Daguerre'.[42] A rapid message to friends in Paris helped him to procure a few examples of Daguerre's plates, which he held to have been 'the first examples of the sun's drawing that were ever seen in Oxford, and, I believe, the first sent to England'. Yet the precious daguerreotypes remained a mere curiosity for Ruskin until the Italian journey of 1845, when his reiterated attempts at detailed sketching made him welcome with unguarded enthusiasm such infallible aid to draughtsmanship:

I have been lucky enough to get from a poor Frenchm[an] here, said to be in distress, some most beautiful, though small, Daguerreotypes of the palaces I have been trying to draw – and certainly Daguerreotypes taken by this vivid sunlight are glorious things. It is very nearly the same thing as carrying off the palace itself – every chip of stone and stain is there – and of course, there is no mistake about *proportions*. I am very much delighted with these and am going to have some more made of pet bits. It is a noble invention, say what they will of it, and anyone who has worked and blundered and stammered as I have for four days, and then sees the thing he has been trying to do so long in vain, *done* perfectly and faultlessly in half a minute, won't abuse it afterwards.[43]

It is quite clear, from this passage, why Ruskin was so struck with the new 'invention'. The daguerreotype was not simply an aid to correct drawing; it was, in a real sense, a detail of the actual world – 'very nearly the same thing as carrying off the palace itself'. But it also offered immediate access to a new, remade world in miniature: looking back on this period in *Praeterita*, Ruskin comments on these plates 'about four inches square' which contained 'the Grand Canal or St. Mark's Place as if a magician had reduced the reality to be carried away into an enchanted land'.[44]

We should remember, while noting these reactions to some of the initial experiments in photography, that Ruskin's responses (both in 1845 and in the later source of *Praeterita*) fell into a pattern which pre-dated the work of Daguerre and his competitors. Reference has been made several times in this study to the technical effects and popular success of Daguerre's earlier invention, the diorama. But, even in the later eighteenth century, it is possible to find equivalents for the reactions registered by Ruskin, elicited on this occasion by William Storer's 'Accurate Delineator'. Storer's contraption, which was bought and ecstatically received by Horace Walpole, was also both an aid to correct perspectival drawing, and an instrument of miniaturised reproduction, 'a new discovery that . . . will bring all paradise before your eyes'.[45] A recent critic has stressed the telling similarity between the language which Walpole uses to describe the effects of his 'Delineator', and the reactions of an American journalist to his first daguerreotype in September 1839: 'It looks like fairy work, and changes its color like a camelion.'[46]

The evidence goes to show, therefore, that photographic reproduction aroused no absolutely new types of response. On the epistemological level, photographs appeared to present no distinctive and unprecedented vision of the external world. Or rather, whatever was novel about them could be contained within the existing framework of responses to non-mediated forms of representation, which were already becoming established by the later eighteenth and early nineteenth centuries. Even the English pioneer of photography, William Henry Fox Talbot, strikes us initially as minimising the transgressive effects of his new technique in the field of representation, however farsightedly he envisages its scientific application. We can picture him, in 1833, on the shores of Lake Como, viewing the 'fairy images' of the 'camera lucida' and frustrated at the same time by his lack of drawing ability. His 'flash of inspiration' consists in the idea that Herschel's experiments in the fixing of light-produced images with the aid of platinum salts might be employed in the fixing of the images of the 'camera obscura'.[47] But he still remains wedded to the notion that photographic reproduction will be the handmaid of the traditional arts. When he writes to Herschel about Daguerre's experiments, it is evident that he sees the countervailing strengths of his own 'photogenic' process exclusively in these terms:

Although Daguerre is said to succeed so admirably with the camera, it does not follow that he can copy an engraving, a flower, or anything else that requires *close contact*. I say this, on the supposition that he uses a metal plate covered with a *liquid* from which light precipitates something previously held in solution.[48]

Yet, despite the assumptions which Fox Talbot made in justifying his invention, it is possible to discern even at this early stage in the history of photography the origin of the debates that have pursued it up to the present day.

Without drawing too schematic an opposition between Daguerre and Fox Talbot, we may conclude that Daguerre (the showman of the diorama) exemplifies the notion of the photograph as 'fairy work', in the sense of projection into an imaginary space – Ruskin's 'enchanted land'. Fox Talbot (at any rate with his initial, 'photogenic' process) emphasises the possibility of 'close contact', of an indexical link between the image and its referent. And this criterion of fidelity, whatever Fox Talbot may have conceived as its utilitarian dividends, brings with it a cognitive by-product that is, in the long term, impossible to disregard. A photograph of a picture or engraving is, after all, not simply an automatic, and to that extent a more efficient, means of reproduction. It is (at least in so far as it can be perceived as a photograph) *that* picture, or engraving, as it was at a precise historical juncture. It is a reproduction with a signature in time.

Here we touch upon the lively issue which has been raised, among others, by John Berger, as to whether photography is more essentially concerned with time than with space.[49] Berger argues that photography's primary effect is to convey an instant of time, abstracted from a narrative process which the spectator constructs for himself, though he is sometimes aided by a caption or other relevant verbal information. Whatever conclusions we might reach about the primary function of photography, there is no doubt that, in the context of this study, the relation of photography to time is of paramount importance. To be more precise, the crucial relevance of photography to historical representation lies in the fact that it gradually converts the otherness of *space* – Ruskin's 'enchanted land' – into an otherness of *time*, which is guaranteed by the indexical nature – the 'close contact' – of the photographic process. The fact that Daguerre and Fox Talbot did not, initially, view their technical innovations in these terms is of course perfectly understandable. For it was only in the measure that their daguerreotypes and calotypes, which remained novelties to them, became progressively older that they began to take on photography's unique function of representing the past, of making manifest to the spectator what Roland Barthes has called the 'having-been-there . . . the always stupefying evidence of *this is how it was*'.[50]

Barthes finely assesses the difference between film and the photograph in a way which recalls the antithesis sketched here between Daguerre and Fox Talbot. In the photograph, he suggests, the '*this was so* easily defeats the *it's me* . . . the photograph must be related to a pure spectatorial consciousness and not to the more projective, more "magical" fictional consciousness on which film by and large depends'.[51] His distinction will perhaps enable us to disentangle some of the threads which have been closely woven together in this study of historical representation in the nineteenth century. It is possible that we could identify Ranke's 'wie es eigentlich gewesen' with the 'pure spectatorial consciousness' of the 'having-been-there' which Barthes equates with perception of the photograph. The difference between Daguerre and Fox Talbot might therefore correspond, at least on one level, to the distinction between the 'projective

do not lose yourself in photos in same manner as film.

possibilities of the historical novel and the authenticity of narrative history which relies not on 'fictional consciousness' but on the intermittent 'reality effects'.

Yet this analogy need not blind us to the fundamental difference between historical discourse, on the one hand, and the photograph. Throughout this chapter, we have been concerned with the effects of irony on the apprehension of the historical past. In their different ways, St Leger, Barham and Ruskin all testify to the irreducible gap between the 'naive' historical recreation of the 1820s and the 'ironic' predicament of the 1840s, when the strategies of the earlier period had to be subverted (Barham), accentuated to the point of crisis (Ruskin), or simply placed in suspension (St Leger). Now it is the curious property of the photograph that its 'naive' character is not obliterated, but actually confirmed by the passage of time. Since it forms (in Barthes' phrase) a 'message without a code', it simply persists, gathering historicity as the distance in time between the moment of photographing and the moment of the spectator's perception grows greater. Walter Benjamin has succinctly pointed out how, while the portrait becomes after a few generations no more than a 'testimony to the art of the person who painted' it, the photograph affords a 'new and strange phenomenon': 'in that fish-wife from Newhaven, who casts her eyes down with such casual, seductive shame, there remains something that does not merely testify to the art of Hill the photographer, but something that cannot be silenced, that impudently demands the name of the person who lived at the time and who, remaining real even now, will never yield herself up entirely into art'.[52]

Where art abandons its claims therefore, the photograph is emancipated both from its author and from the treadmill of morphology. It persists as a kind of ephemeral monument. Susan Sontag is surely right to associate the relatively recent boom in the popularity of nineteenth-century photographs with the Romantic cult of ruins, bearing in mind the crucial difference that the photograph does not emulate the giantism of the ruined monument, but instead monumentalises a fragment of everyday life.[53] Du Sommerard, who first gave the everyday objects of the past a place within the ordered historical series of the museum, can be seen as a kindred spirit to his contemporaries, Daguerre and Fox Talbot. Yet at the same time, the relative security of the institutional framework which Du Sommerard created stands in sharp contrast to the precariousness of the photograph as 'monument'. Roland Barthes expressed with memorable force, in *La Chambre claire*, the consequences of photography's vulnerability for the human apprehension of time:

Earlier societies made arrangements for memory, as a substitute for life, to be eternal and for at least the thing which told of Death to be itself immortal: that was the Monument. But in making Photography, which is mortal, the general and – as it were – natural witness of 'what has been', modern society has renounced the Monument. A paradox: the same century invented History and Photography. But History is a form of memory fabricated from positive recipes, a purely intellectual discourse which abolishes mythic Time; and Photography is a sure testimony, but a fleeting one; to such an extent that, today, everything tends to prepare our species for an incapacity, which will soon be with us: an incapacity to conceive, either affectively or symbolically, of *duration*: the era of Photography is also that of revolution, contestation, assault and explosion – in short of different forms of impatience, of all that is opposed to the notion of maturing. – And no doubt, the astonishment of saying 'That has been' will vanish, that as well. It has already vanished. I remain, I don't know why, one of its last witnesses . . . and this book is its archaic trace.[54]

Barthes' plangent passage, made more solemn by his death a few days after the publication of *La Chambre claire*, sharpens to the finest point the division between photography and every other form of representing of the past, and thus it leaves the fragile photograph perilously exposed. A less drastic polarity could however be suggested, in which the unique 'testimony' of the photograph remained as the extreme boundary of a continuum of forms of historical representation. The present-day visitor to Lacock Abbey, once the home of Fox Talbot and the scene of many of his finest photographs, will find a country-house constructed (like Newstead Abbey) on the foundations of a medieval abbey. Yet Sir William Sharington's Tudor mansion scarcely stresses the anomaly of this convenient

14. *A country-house constructed on the foundations of a medieval abbey:* Sharington's Tower at Lacock Abbey (photographed by Fox Talbot)

superimposition of cloister and corridor, chapter house and long gallery; even Sanderson Miller's imposing neo-Gothic entrance hall (added in 1753) seems not to detract from the general effect of harmony. At the gateway to the Abbey, the visitor will come upon a sixteenth-century tithe barn which contains the Fox Talbot Photographic Museum. He will find the village of Lacock itself hardly very different from the image conveyed in Fox Talbot's photographs, since it has been preserved from modern development by the National Trust, after a bequest by Fox Talbot's descendant in 1944. It is hardly fanciful to associate, as they are in practice associated at Lacock, the photographic technique which resurrects past appearances and the national institution which preserves the structures of the past for the entertainment and profit of the present. As Pierre de Lagarde effectively shows in the case of France, the various associations and institutions which concern themselves with the preservation and restoration of ancient buildings have their roots in the pioneering achievement of the early nineteenth century: in Lenoir's salvaging of the monuments at the time of the Revolution, in Arcisse de Caumont's founding of the first conservation society, in Guizot's ministerial inventory of historic buildings, in Mérimée's tours of regional inspection, and in Viollet-le-Duc's elaborate practice of restoration.[55]

A quite separate list could of course be provided for the other side of the Channel. Both would show how the historical preoccupations of the early nineteenth century acquired organisational form, and developed gradually in both France and England to a point where, today, their practical functions may appear to be detached from any overall concept of history. In other words, the mythic values attached to history – those values which underlie and support such universally accepted practices as the preservation and restoration of historic buildings – survive the onset of irony in the 1840s. The myth of history remains underground, as it were, while historical discourse in its written form (Barthes' 'purely intellectual discourse') begins its own purposeful assault on myth. It is indeed interesting to speculate on whether this antagonism between the mythic idea of history and the intellectual practice of historiography remains absolute, and whether it is still possible to infer a continuum of forms of historical representation, from the photograph to the ruin, from the historical treatise to the historic home.

Anti-history and the ante-hero:
     Thackeray, Reade, Browning, James

In the different modes of historical representation which have been covered
here, it has been possible to trace a number of separate, but parallel, modes of
development. In the sphere of historiography proper, we have looked at the
'cyclical' evolution from Barante through Thierry to Michelet. For the historical
museum, we have considered the formation of two distinctive collections, and
their fusion in the novel achievement of Du Sommerard's Musée de Cluny. Sir
Walter Scott has come to our attention in several different connections, notably
in relation to the building of Abbotsford but also as the pretext for Barham's
mannered manipulation of historical credulity in the *Ingoldsby Legends*. Although
different approaches and different analytic concepts have been used to investigate these widely differing themes, the central assumption has remained the
same: that analysis of the internal and external constraints upon these different
modes of discourse would reveal a morphology, or a pattern of formal development. The 'historical-mindedness' of early nineteenth-century France and
Britain would be revealed as being dependent on certain specific and recurrent
rhetorical techniques: in the earlier period, at any rate, these would merit the
title of a 'historical poetics'.

Yet we were also obliged to take account at several junctures of the epistemological dimension of historical recreation. The urge to make the past live
again could not be viewed in isolation from other Romantic fantasies of human
omnipotence, most of which could be related (in Foucault's terms) to the wide-
ranging reinterpretation of the map of knowledge that took place during the last
years of the eighteenth century. Particularly important from our point of view
was the succession of technical developments, beyond the sphere of language,
which offered a temporary or more long-lasting effect of illusory recreation: from
lithography and the diorama to the photograph. These were seen to be integrally
bound up with the new historical sensibility, striving to annihilate the gap between
the model and the copy, and offering the Utopian possibility of a restoration of
the past in the context of the present. The fact that only the photograph, with
its capacity to record and perpetuate light rays on a chemically-prepared
surface, was able to achieve this effect with complete success, does not mean that
the other aspirations must be treated as negligible. More significant than the
achievement of photography, from our point of view, is the more general evidence of a concern with non-mimetic equivalences, and with the chronological

and metaphysical transgressions that consequently ensued. This was, on the one hand, a powerful stimulus to historical reconstruction, since an interval of time provided the most striking example of a gap that defied closure. But, on the other hand, it was also an incitement to more and more far-fetched and abstruse historical investigation; the quest for historical realism risked becoming a vicious circle in which the period details could never be sufficiently copious, and the effect of resurrection never overwhelming enough.

One significant manifestation of this tendency can be found in the development, towards the end of the century, of the technique of the facsimile edition. When Barante wrote his substitute chronicle in the early 1820s, it would never have occurred to him to make the published version similar, in some way, to the original manuscript of Froissart's *Chronicles* which he had seen as a young man in Breslau. Even the painters of the 'Style Troubadour', though they strove for effects which were to be generally reminiscent of the Middle Ages, did not aspire to resurrect in any detailed way the forms of late medieval art. The notion of the facsimile edition was, of course, a much less ambiguous one. It required simply the reconstitution, from one historically authentic object, of a particular number of exact copies. To set a precise date on the initiation of this practice is difficult, and in any event not central to the argument of this study. By the 1870s, at any rate, such authenticity seems to have been in demand. A sumptuous edition of the *Poems and Letters of Thomas Gray*, produced privately by the Chiswick Press in 1874, not only reproduces the inhabitual quarto format and large type of an original eighteenth-century model, but includes photographic vignettes of such relevant scenes as Stoke Poges Church and Eton College which offer their own immediate index of fidelity.[1] Ten years later, an entire series of smaller, but much more painstakingly accurate, facsimiles is being produced by Elliot Stock editions: their *Compleat Angler* claims to be an 'absolute facsimile' making use of a 'photographic process which is simply infallible', while their edition of George Herbert's *The Temple* (dated 1885) dilates upon the care which has been taken with 'type, paper, binding'.[2] It should be emphasised that the 'photographic process' mentioned in connection with the *Compleat Angler* only applies to some of the visual effects reproduced; the seventeenth-century print has been re-set and re-utilised, where possible, and only the types and 'cuts' which are 'altogether obsolete' have been resurrected by photography.

However significant the emergence of the facsimile edition may be, it is obviously not a great imaginative feat. Like the photograph – though not to the same compelling extent – it has a formal correspondence with its model: it is a direct *analogon*. But the very fact that facsimile editions flourished at this time (no doubt as a by-product of photographic technology) leads us to some general hypotheses about the conditions of historical recreation in the second half of the century. We can speculate that the concern with the rediscovery of the past (inseparably yoked in the earlier period to the imaginative enterprises of historians, painters and novelists) had by this stage migrated to a more restricted, if more secure, field of investigation. If it was no longer possible to overwhelm the public with a brilliant historical fiction, or a narrative representation of a period which was barely known before, then at least it was possible to tempt them with a technically impeccable reproduction of a seventeenth-century book. But what had happened, in the mean time, to historical narrative and the historical novel?

This chapter is an attempt to answer the question. It takes as its subject matter a sequence of notable achievements of historical fiction, from Thackeray to James. My argument is that in all these examples, though with very different results, the text is produced in response to a crisis in the notion of historical reconstruction and period authenticity. The writer does not exactly fail at his task: with the single exception of James's incomplete novel *The Sense of the Past*, all of these books were highly acclaimed by contemporaries and have been classed by competent judges among their authors' finest works. But the price of their avoidance of failure is an unprecedented complication of plot, structure and sometimes characterisation. Scott's *sancta simplicitas* lies a long way behind them.

To begin this survey with the work of Thackeray is to be reminded straight away of the close link between historical fiction in the mid-century, and the complicated issues of authenticity which have been debated throughout this study. In the 1840s, as has been noted, Thackeray's astringent reviews of the Royal Academy exhibitions made pointed references to the authenticity of historical costume, reproaching Landseer because the dress of his 'gentlemen and ladies' appeared to have been 'put on for the first time', and acclaiming John Herbert's 'Trial of the Seven Bishops' because 'the men are quite at home in their quaint coats and periwigs of James the Second's time'.[3] Perhaps the more generous tone of the second review, which appeared in 1844, is bound up with the fact that Thackeray himself was offering to the public in the same year his own first full-scale historical reconstruction, in the form of the novel *Barry Lyndon*. Adopting the persona of a charming profligate who has compiled the memoirs of his eventful life during a final stay in the Fleet prison, Thackeray insists on the differences between late eighteenth-century and mid-nineteenth-century European society. Significantly enough, these differences are symbolised above all by the change in fashions of dress:

Why, when I danced with Coralie de Langeac at the fêtes on the birth of the first dauphin at Versailles, her hoop was eighteen feet in circumference, and the heels of her lovely *mules* were three inches from the ground; the lace of my *jabot* was worth a thousand crowns, and the buttons of my amaranth velvet coat alone cost eighty thousand livres. Look at the difference now! The gentlemen are dressed like boxers, quakers, or hackney-coachmen; and the ladies are not dressed at all. There is no elegance, no refinement; none of the chivalry of the old world, of which I form a portion.[4]

But Thackeray does not merely aim for authenticity of costume. *Barry Lyndon* is conceived as a novelist's riposte to the all too simple patterns of plot development found in the works of Scott. In one of a series of ironic annotations which punctuate the first-person narrative, the authorial persona shows a dissatisfaction with 'those heroic youths' who figure in the novels of Scott. 'There is something *naive* and simple in that time-honoured style of novel-writing by which Prince Prettyman, at the end of his adventures, is put in possession of every worldly prosperity, as he has been endowed with every mental and bodily excellence previously.' The indictment is all too telling when we think of the blatant and uncomplicated careerism of the Scott hero, ably aided and abetted by his generous creator. 'The novelist thinks that he can do no more for his darling hero than make him a lord.'[5]

Yet Thackeray's challenge to the Scott prototype, in *Barry Lyndon*, does not go far enough. Despite the evidence of research into the dress and manners of the eighteenth century, and despite the peripheral introduction of a figure like Dr Johnson, we gain hardly any sense of a concrete historical milieu. In inverting the success story of the Scott hero, Thackeray has in fact done little more than return to the well-established pattern of the eighteenth-century anti-hero, for whom Fielding's Jonathan Wild can serve as a good example. Certainly the irony is more subtle and more pervasive in Thackeray's case, creating a field of systematic distortion within the narrator's point of view. But this very instability undercuts the claim to historical authenticity which might have been made for *Barry Lyndon*. The cumulative effect is not so much that of a historical novel as that of a comedy of manners.

Eight years after the publication of *Barry Lyndon*, Thackeray returned to the attack with another novel which pressed its claims ostentatiously on the very title-page: *The History of Henry Esmond*. Indeed its pretence to be regarded as an authentic historical record might have struck the reader even in advance of the title-page, through the very apparel in which the text appeared. An early impression, published in 1853 in three volumes, comes in quarter calf binding, with a tooled leather spine and marbled end-papers.[6] Although the first title-page announces 'ESMOND, A STORY OF QUEEN ANNE'S REIGN BY W. M. THACKERAY, Author of "Vanity Fair", "Pendennis" etc.', there is a second title-page more in keeping with the archaistic appearance of the binding: 'THE HISTORY OF HENRY ESMOND, ESQ. A COLONEL IN THE SERVICE OF HER MAJESTY Q. ANNE WRITTEN BY HIMSELF'. It is worth pointing out that the latter title, or at least its abbreviated form, is the one that has stuck! Thackeray was not, however, content to give his novel a mock-authentic title-page and an eighteenth-century binding. Even the typography of this original edition was modelled on an earlier style of printing, with the characteristic 'f' for 's' (when it appears in the middle of a word) and a joined-up version of 'ct'. Not only at the outset, but on every page, the mid-nineteenth-century reader was offered all the outward signs of a text from the earlier period.

Of course, such a degree of historical mimetism was bound to be, in the last resort, self-defeating. The external appearance of Esmond, just like the carefully studied clothing of contemporary historical paintings, must have simply

THE HISTORY

OF

HENRY ESMOND, Esq.

A COLONEL IN THE SERVICE OF HER MAJESTY
Q. ANNE.

WRITTEN BY HIMSELF.

Servetur ad imum
Qualis ab incepto procefferit, et fibi conftet.

IN THREE VOLUMES.

VOLUME THE SECOND.

LONDON:

PRINTED FOR SMITH, ELDER, & COMPANY,
OVER AGAINST ST. PETER'S CHURCH IN CORNHILL.

1852.

underlined the fact that literary and stylistic devices were no longer enough for a public which had outgrown the naive enthusiasms of the Waverley period. Either because he recognised this difficulty or more probably for reasons of cost, Thackeray modernised typography and binding for the edition of 1858. But this was not the only respect in which *Esmond* caused its author quite unprecedented problems. Thackeray was well aware that a text which made such excessive claims for its authenticity offered at the same time an uncertain reward for all the labours of research. He had already confessed in a letter written during the composition of *Esmond*:

It has taken me as much trouble as 10 volumes, and for no particular good for most of my care and antiquarianism is labor thrown away, and there must be a blunder or two or perhaps 20 which the critics will spy out.[7]

The critics of *Esmond* later fulfilled this gloomy prediction. As Samuel Phillips wrote in *The Times*: 'One discrepancy in such a work is sufficient to take the veil from the reader's eyes and to put an end to the whole illusion.'[8] Given this carping attitude, it was not even necessary for the critic, or the informed reader, to identify a particular 'discrepancy'. The very fact of being on the look-out for one must have wrought havoc with the delicate veil of illusion. Why then – we may ask – did Thackeray embark upon the ridiculously time-consuming and self-defeating project of writing so ambitious a historical novel? The answer seems to lie not so much in his stated intentions, as in the objective fact of his relation to literary tradition. It is not simply that Thackeray was anxious to write a 'historical novel' and willing to incur the accompanying risks, but that he was drawn irresistibly to a form of fiction which entailed an equivocal relationship to the reality of his characters, and an exploitation of the credence accorded to them by his public. If he could not repeat the triumphs of Scott, he could use to the full the opportunity of not being Scott. Much more effectively than *Barry Lyndon*, his *History of Henry Esmond* would be, under the most consummate of disguises, an Anti-History.

This claim needs to be examined in detail, since it is the initial presupposition of my argument in this chapter. My hypothesis is that Scott's historical novels make use of a distinctive set of devices, which in combination help to explain the remarkable strength and (as it were) solidity of the Romantic genre. Thackeray, and the subsequent authors who will be mentioned here, inherit these devices and, to a certain extent, make use of them. But they employ them to create abrupt reversals and fascinating contradictions within the genre. The Waverley prototype is undermined from within, and the structure which seemed to enclose a capacious edifice is discovered to be barely self-supporting. This transition is one aspect (but perhaps a major aspect in the British context) of what Roland Barthes has called the end of the classic text. From being an art of 'plenitude', resembling 'a household cupboard in which meanings are arranged, piled up and stored away',[9] the novel has to come to terms with an evacuation of sense, a disarrangement of meanings and a dissipation of symbolic richness. The text as *plenum* gives way to the text as *vacuum*.

To plot this course in the particular evolution of British historical fiction, we need to be able to label, at least provisionally, the stock-in-trade of Waverley. A series of terms which relate broadly to the Formalist analysis of literary genres will help us to locate the distinctive features of the 'historicity' of the Waverley Novels, and to trace their future development. These are *framing*, or establishing the authenticity of the text with respect to an external model or document; *singularisation*, or establishing the 'empty scene' of the narrative and peopling it with individual 'heroes' and other characters; *objectification*, or endowing particular objects with a providential or talismanic role in the fulfilment of the plot; and finally, *action*, or the constitution of a central person-age or 'hero' as transitive in historical time. Each of these devices performs a specific function in advancing the narrative. Equally, each device holds a special stake in the historicity of the historical novel, contributing to its effect of overall authenticity.

It would be a long task to illustrate these categories from the full range of Scott's historical fiction. At the risk of over-simplifying Scott's complexity, we shall take *Quentin Durward* (1823) as the exemplary case, in the knowledge that Lukács also chose this novel for an extended comparison with *Esmond*, in his wholly different analysis of the genre.[10] Scott begins *Quentin Durward* with a highly sophisticated piece of framing, when he recounts the origin of the novel in some old 'family memorials' which have been supposedly discovered in the Château de Hautlieu.[11] The story which follows is not 'based on' these sources, as a historical work is based upon documents. Notionally, it 'is' the source which has been brought to light. Or rather, since the gap between the two cannot in the fictional world be made perceptible, Scott's narrative simply does duty for the original source. Scott even seems willing to admit, through a verbal conundrum, the transparency of this device, when he has the Marquis of the Preface mispronouncing an English phrase as 'chewing the cud'.[12] The Marquis is trying to say 'showing the code' – which is exactly what Scott himself is doing at this juncture.

After this preliminary framing, Scott launches into a classic demonstration of his technique of *singularisation*. It is 'a delicious summer morning': two men 'who appeared in deep conversation' watch the arrival of the traveller 'at a considerable distance'.[13] We eavesdrop upon the empty scene, and gradually our attention is rewarded by details of the stranger's dress which seem to betoken his origins: his 'short grey cloak' in the Flemish fashion, and 'smart blue bonnet, with a single sprig of holly and an eagle's feather',[14] by which Scott's compatriots would not be wrong in recognising one of their fellow countrymen. So much for the future hero of the novel. But Scott has a trick to play with respect to some of the more important accompanying characters. The senior of the two men in the foreground who initially await the arrival of Quentin announces himself as Maître Pierre, a rich bourgeois. Quentin is in some doubt about the identity of this character, and later compares his behaviour to that of a 'cunning vassal'. It is only after a period of deliberate deception that the bourgeois or vassal is revealed as King Louis XI of France. A more carefully managed effect is achieved with the young Countess de Croye, whom Quentin first remarks in the guise of a serving girl, then hears (but does not see) singing a doleful song from a turret, and finally identifies as a fugitive lady of high rank. 'The reader will easily imagine', writes Scott, 'that the young soldier should build a fine romance on such a foundation as the supposed, or rather the assumed, identification of the Maiden of the Turret, to whose lay he had listened with so much interest, and the fair cup-bearer of Maître Pierre, with a fugitive Countess, of rank and wealth, flying from the pursuit of a hated lover.'[15]

Scott's singularisation therefore involves a dual process: we move from the strange (and the fictional) to the familiar (and the historical), and we exchange richness and plurality of signs (Bourgeois/vassal/King, serving maid/damsel of the lute/fugitive Countess) for precise inscription within the historical milieu. This is also the pattern of the romance as a whole, since the young and penniless stranger who has been placed before us at the outset will end up by owning a substantial tract of the fair land of France. Scott often provides his hero, and his readers, with an interim guarantee that this happy ending will not be denied to us. He *objectifies* a property that will, at a crucial juncture, provide the key to the dénouement. The most obvious example, in the range of Scott's fiction, is the Talisman (in the novel of the same name) which performs its healing work and then passes into the keeping of a historic Scottish family. In *Quentin Durward*, there is no such assurance of a successful outcome. But it could be argued that Quentin's own name serves as a talisman. When he has won his fair lady, his love match is at last made socially acceptable by the genealogical explanations of the Earl of Crawford: 'He is of the House of Durward, descended from that Allan Durward who was High Steward of Scotland.'[16]

It must be clear already what a high premium is set by Scott on the transitive *action* of his hero. We are conducted from an intimate and private scene to an ever broadening canvas of historical events, a process which culminates in the (authentic) episode of the assassination of the Bishop of Liège, and the battle before the city which ensues. Quentin participates in this development becoming himself an ever more effective instrument of the action, until the moment of his final recognition and acceptance. The contrast with *Esmond* is immediately apparent on this general level. Where *Quentin Durward* begins with a king incognito, *Esmond* terminates with a prince incognito. Where Scott leads us up to a climax in a genuine historical event, Thackeray produces the sorry anti-climax of the Young Pretender's visit to Castlewood – planned as an exercise in high politics but resulting in little more than a moment of princely dalliance with Beatrix Esmond. The critic George Brimley complained in his review in the *Spectator* that such an ill-starred and inauthentic episode was indeed hard to swallow: that 'these violations of received tradition with respect to such well-known historical personages, force upon the reader unnecessarily the fictitious character of the narrative, and are therefore better avoided'.[17]

Brimley thus castigates Thackeray for not having the same circumspection as Scott. And his reactions seem to imply that *Esmond* was no more than a sorry parody of Scott, or a ham-fisted attempt to play upon the established chords of response to the historical novel. *Quentin Durward* acquires its sense of momentum and sure resolution from the fact that the penniless adventurer is finally recognised and rewarded by the sovereign power. *Esmond*, by contrast, takes on a kind of dubiety and irresolution as a result of the fact that the hero eventually throws up his allegiance to the House of Stuart, and abandons the family estate for a substitute Castlewood in the New World. The predominant movement is not centripetal, but centrifugal. What had promised, initially, to be a consoling account of a rightful heir barred from his inheritance, and recovering his birth-right from a sovereign power after numerous vicissitudes, turns out to be both more and less than that. For the Young Pretender is, in effect, the *Deus ex machina* who speeds the plot to its conclusion. But this is not because he confirms Esmond in his inheritance, and grants him his long-desired bride. It is precisely because Prince Charles has compromised Beatrix that Esmond is cured of his passion for her; happiness in the New World is to consist in marriage with Beatrix's mother, Rachel, Lady Castlewood, who is no longer merely a mother-substitute for Esmond, nor a pale reflection of her daughter, but a desirable wife.

Even on this schematic level, comparison between Scott and Thackeray illuminates the extreme subtlety, even to the point of perversity, of the latter author, who has effectively turned the prototype inside out. At the detailed textual level, Thackeray displays an even more remarkable ingenuity in maintaining ambiguities and suspending apparent differences. In *Quentin Durward*, the paradigm of serving maid/damsel of the lute/fugitive Countess is developed in the plot, but it is finally superseded by the revelation that all three images are manifestations of the same character. In *Esmond*, there are three important female characters: the old Viscountess, past mistress of Charles II; Rachel, Lady Castlewood; and her daughter Beatrix. The plot depends on the assumption that Esmond is blinded by his love for Beatrix, and does not recognise the real merit of Rachel; it also depends on the notion that Beatrix emancipates herself from the beneficent influence of her mother, and is transferred to the baleful sign of the old Viscountess, thereby anticipating Esmond's disillusionment. But this process takes place not so much on the thematic and psychological levels, as on the level of textual imagery. Metonymic chains extend throughout the work, bringing together the related images of sun, moon and stars and other closely associated terms. Although the full range of this imagistic patterning cannot be demonstrated here, it is worth citing a particular and central example, especially as it leads us directly to the question of the status of historical characters within the novel.[18]

We start with the motif of the priceless diamond necklace, symbol of the old Viscountess's liaison with Charles II. This passes at her death to Henry Esmond, who makes a present of it to Beatrix. Up to this stage in the narrative, Thackeray has been careful to associate the beneficent image of the sun (and gold) first of all with Rachel, and then with Rachel and Beatrix seen in harmony:

Esmond long remembered how she [Rachel] looked and spoke, kneeling reverently before the sacred book, the sun shining upon her golden hair until it made a halo round about her.[19]

He sees them now [Rachel and Beatrix] ... as they used to sit together of the summer evenings – the two golden heads over the page – the child's little hand and the mother's beating the time, with their voices rising and falling in unison.[20]

These two visions – of morning and evening, of mother and of mother and daughter identified – are overtaken by a marked change in astronomical imagery, when Esmond begins to transfer his attentions from the mother to the daughter. Rachel is now associated with the moon, while Beatrix blazes out in her full glory:

The moon was up by this time, glittering keen in the frosty sky. He could see, for the first time now clearly, her [Rachel's] sweet careworn face.[21]

Esmond thought he had never seen anything like the sunny lustre of her [Beatrix's] eyes. My Lady Viscountess looked fatigued, as if with watching, and her face was pale.[22]

It is precisely at this stage, when Esmond has provisionally transferred the solar metonymy from Rachel to Beatrix, that the ominous motif of the diamonds (and stars) is introduced. Having celebrated the 'sunny lustre' of Beatrix's eyes, he proceeds to identifying them next with diamonds: 'little shining toys' which, with 'other glittering baubles (of rare water too)' men have quarrelled over 'since mankind began'.[23] From this juncture, no doubt, Beatrix is no longer moving under the sign of her mother and instead becomes progressively associated with the sterile legacy of the old Viscountess. The completed process is signalled by the Young Pretender's exclamation on first seeing Beatrix in her diamonds, which picks up both the astral imagery and the earlier identification of the old Viscountess with a portrait of Diana by Lely:

... qui est cette nymphe, cet astre qui brille, cette Diane qui descend sur nous?[24]

It is relevant that, in addition to the Esmond diamonds, Beatrix attracts another, less precious gift of brilliants at this crucial juncture of the narrative. At a ceremony where the three ladies of the Esmond family in concert present Henry with a fine sword, Beatrix is described as 'wearing on her beautiful breast the French officer's star which Frank [her brother] had sent home after Ramillies'.[25] The association is made doubly significant by the fact that when Frank captured this 'star with a striped ribbon, that was made of small brilliants', his original idea was to destine it as 'a pretty present for mother',[26] i.e. Rachel.

Just as Rachel is denied the French star, so she never succeeds in wearing the Esmond diamonds, even when she becomes Henry's wife. Yet in a most ingenious way, Thackeray keeps the sun/gold motif in reserve throughout the period of Esmond's infatuation with Beatrix by identifying it with the golden sleeve-button which Rachel takes from Henry during his imprisonment and continues to preserve in a safe place. At the conclusion of the novel, the ascendancy of the gold button is triumphantly affirmed, in explicit contrast to the depreciation of the diamonds:

Our diamonds are turned into ploughs and axes for our plantations . . . and the only jewel by which my wife sets any store, and from which she hath never parted, is that gold button she took from my arm on the day when she visited me in prison, and which she wore ever after, as she told me, on the tenderest heart in the world.[27]

This shifting sequence of related metonymies extends, therefore, over the entire course of the novel. In fact, it is hardly too far-fetched to see in the very name 'Esmond' a covert allusion to the prevailing astronomical images of the text, since 'S-mond' (*Mond* being the German word for moon) might plausibly represent the eclipse of the sun by the moon (Diana), which is the central complication of the plot. If this notion is bound to be conjectural, there is certainly a similar *jeu de mots* involved in the introduction of the authentic historical character Lord Mohun at various critical stages of the narrative. The correct pronunciation of 'Mohun' makes it a homophone of 'Moon'. The point is specifically underlined in a letter from the old Viscountess (Lely's Diana) who refers in her antique spelling to 'M. de Moon'.[28]

Lord Mohun's role in *Esmond* is in many respects a determining one. By successively murdering Henry's guardian, Lord Castlewood, and Beatrix's fiancé, the Duke of Hamilton, he causes a radical transformation in the position of the narrator. Indeed the power which he exercises over the development of the plot establishes him as a rival to the narrator – an implication which is borne out by his having the same Christian name and thus being mistaken for Esmond at one crucial moment. It is worth paying some attention to the way in which Thackeray deploys this sinister character, who is no less historically authentic than the unfortunate Duke of Hamilton who died at his hands. Through reviewing the devices which Thackeray uses to domesticate the brute material of history, we can appreciate the fine oscillation between fiction and fact which is his unsettling achievement.

In his study of the Balzac novella, *Sarrasine*, Barthes notes the extreme discretion with which Balzac handles the historically authentic name or detail. He suggests that it is through not bringing them into the foreground – through citing them almost *en passant* – that Balzac safeguards the impression that the action is taking place against a genuine historical background. 'It is precisely the lesser importance which confers upon the historical personage his *exact* weight of reality . . . for if the historical personage were to assume his *real* importance, the discourse would be obliged to endow him with a contingency which, paradoxically, would make him less real . . . it would only be necessary to make them speak and, like impostors, they would expose themselves.'[29] By this test, Lord Mohun appears at first sight to pass muster. His entry on to the scene is extremely discreet. The chapter in which he makes his appearance is entitled 'My Lord Mohun comes among us for no good', but his initial role is simply that of a Rosencrantz to Lord Firebrace's Guildenstern (Lord Firebrace being programmatically devoid of all the qualities that Lord Mohun possesses, including the prime one of historical authenticity). In this establishing chapter, Lord Mohun is never so close to the front of the stage as to be allowed direct speech. The household at Castlewood discusses him, and has its daily routine interrupted by him. But the power which he exerts remains curiously impersonal.

Yet Mohun's discretion is merely the calm before the storm. He is destined to kill two of the main male characters, the first (Lord Castlewood) being fictional and the second (Hamilton) historical. In so far as his second murder is 'historically' given, he holds a kind of dual sway over the fictional world of *Esmond*. He is bound, by a necessity which overrides the contingency of the narrative, to come victorious out of the duel with Castlewood, since that is the condition of his surviving to challenge Hamilton. Indeed it could be said that he is bound to come victorious out of the conflict with Castlewood by virtue of the simple fact that he is historical while Castlewood is fictional. Or, to put the matter in a less provocative way, it is inconceivable for a character whom the reader knows (and the author proclaims) to be historical to suffer death at the hands of a character whom the reader knows to be fictional.

These considerations go some way to explaining the equivocal role of Lord Mohun in the central sections of *Esmond*. Like Beatrix (the moon, Diana), he exercises a delaying influence over the plot, which is at the same time the deflection of the course of Esmond's life and a pre-condition of the fulfilment of the action. It is impossible to view him as a 'character', as if he were credited with psychological density. The *signified* for which he acts as *signifier* is simply the irreducible challenge represented by the incorporation of the real into the fictional. This becomes obvious when Thackeray brings Esmond and Mohun into direct contact. Both are out riding on the Downs, when the rein breaks in Mohun's hands and the two gentlemen are forced to jump from the carriage. Henry soon recovers, but Mohun remains on the ground 'dead to all appearance': 'he was bleeding profusely from a wound on the forehead, and looking, and being, indeed, a corpse'.[30] But Henry saves the situation:

Harry, with a penknife, opened a vein in his arm, and was greatly relieved, after a moment, to see the blood flow. He was near half an hour before he came to himself, by which time Doctor Tusher and little Frank arrived, and found my lord not a corpse indeed, but pale as one.[31]

In this little episode, Thackeray narrows to a very fine point the tension between the historical and fictional levels. The phrase 'being, indeed, a corpse' is a stark contradiction. Mohun not only happens not to be dead (since, in the fictional world, appearances can turn out to be misleading), but is *necessarily* not dead, since his historical role is still to be played. Furthermore, the fact that Henry revives Mohun by bleeding him underlines the absurdity of the supposition that the 'blood' which is let with the pen-knife (the blood of fiction) can either diminish or strengthen the 'life' which Mohun holds by a non-fictional guarantee.

Yet this association of Mohun with blood has a further part to play in the intrigue. When Mohun finally kills Lord Castlewood, Esmond is involuntarily caught up as 'an actor in that ghastly midnight scene of blood and homicide'.[32] Thrown into prison, he has to suffer Rachel's imputation that he was to blame for the death of her husband and his benefactor. 'Take back your hand – do not touch me with it,' she cries, 'Look! there's blood on it!'[33] There follows a long speech of reproach in which the unhappy widow finally refers to her husband as lying 'in his blood . . . and you let him die, Henry!'[34] Of course there is a latent ambiguity in this repeated use of the motif of blood at this point. Henry is very far from having been responsible for the death of his patron. At the same time, Castlewood's death-bed confession has in effect given him a new identity by confirming the purity of his own blood and lineage. The blood motif thus plays a role somewhat like that of the gold button, as a residual guarantee of the eventual rectification of Esmond's position, after the intervening period of disequilibrium has passed.

In writing of the disequilibrating effect of Mohun in the central sections of the novel, one should not neglect to mention that there are other historically authentic figures – Addison, Dick Steele, etc. – who come to the forefront and yet do not generate the atmosphere of crisis associated with Mohun. It is as if Thackeray wished to make use of both *beneficent* and *maleficent* historical figures, the latter being intimately involved with the *peripeteia*, while the former provide a kind of redundancy within the historical milieu. It is significant that both Steele and Addison are literary figures, identifiable by their language, and that is also the aspect of them which Thackeray chooses to emphasise (in Addison's case, there are extensive quotations from his poem, 'The Campaign'). Neither of them has any significant influence on the plot. Indeed one of Addison's most prominent interventions is to urge Esmond to refrain from the drastic political action which he is planning on behalf of the deposed House of Stuart:

Esmond marched homewards to his lodgings, and met Mr. Addison on the road that night, walking to a cottage he had in Fulham, the moon shining on his handsome, serene face. 'What cheer, brother?' says Addison, laughing. 'I thought it was a footpad advancing in the dark, and behold 'tis better than fighting by daylight. Why should we quarrel because I am a Whig and thou art a Tory?'[35]

Addison's moonlight advice, if taken by Esmond, would have led to the cessation of quarrels, and the liquidation of the political rivalry which is the mainspring of the plot. But before Esmond can abjure his divisive loyalty to the Stuarts, the maleficent Mohun has an appointment to keep: he must fight the historical duel with the Duke of Hamilton which is to be (and was) the cause of both their deaths. Esmond's fictional destiny must pass by way of this fated appointment.

The previous analysis touches on only a few of the features which make *Esmond* a uniquely disquieting historical novel. But the contrast with Scott is already clear. Thackeray's *framing* – the exceptionally audacious device of a bibliographic replica – sets up the pattern for an authenticity that continually tries too hard, and rebounds upon itself. The poetic richness of *Quentin Durward* always aids, and does not merely complicate the action. But whereas Quentin's name remains as a talisman, capable of revealing his high birth at an opportune moment, the name of Henry Esmond is caught up in a pattern of word-play and subjected to the shifting patterns of imagery. For Thackeray to select as one of his historically authentic characters the notorious Mohun, and then to make the imagery of sun/moon/stars an integral element in the metonymic patterning of the work, is in itself a sufficient demonstration of the problematic character of *Esmond*. To insist upon the name as *signifier* (and in particular the historical name), is to violate the prescriptive realism of the genre and to call in question the relation of words to things in the historical milieu. Even Esmond's talisman, his gold button, is part of the chain of signifiers which signals the shifting relationships of the main characters and their relative positions from the hero's point of view. In other words, the processes of *singularisation* and *objectification* (to which I drew attention in the case of Scott) are systematically subverted. Where Scott connects and earths every stray wire, Thackeray leaves the circuit without insulation and seems to be trying to provoke the spark of live electricity.

It is hardly surprising that Thackeray himself should have had mixed feelings about this achievement, which he declared to be 'clever . . . and also stupid'.[36] Charlotte Brontë showed a similar indecision when she called it 'admirable and odious'. But such reactions were in fact appropriate for a novel which was both History and Anti-History – which both admitted and subverted the canons of the genre. That this was by no means an easy achievement can be demonstrated if we look briefly at another unsettling historical novel which was published in the next decade, George Eliot's *Romola* (1863). In *Romola*, the perspective is far from ironic, and the names are not drawn into a texture of significant word-play. But George Eliot's moral concerns have led to the establishment of a fissure down the very centre of the work, which separates the impressive and authoritative persona of Romola from the more light-weight and ultimately condemned character of Tito Melema. Poor Tito seems to play the role of a Scott hero in the dog-house, who must learn by harsh experience that the blithe careerism of his predecessors is no longer a passport to fame and fortune.

Indeed George Eliot plays a particularly nasty trick on Tito, since all the ingredients for success are at first apparently present. He is singularised impeccably, raised from sleep before our eyes in the centre of Florence after a providential escape from shipwreck. Almost immediately his interlocutor notices a ring on his finger. Is this Tito's talisman, which will at some future stage ensure his recognition and be his passport to consequence within the city of Florence? The truth turns out to be the reverse. This is the onyx ring by which his guardian wished to identify himself, when he sent Tito a despairing message to redeem him out of slavery; it is the ring which Tito subsequently sells to a shopkeeper, thereby hastening his unmasking as an ungrateful son, and leading to a gruesome dénouement by the Arno, while the feeble old man strives to press the last breath out of Tito's lungs. If the Scott hero can therefore count upon reconciliation, however tardy, with the all-powerful father-figure of the monarch, Tito is the unlucky victim of his adoptive father's acute sense of justice. His death is, designedly, not the end of the novel, for Romola survives and is reconciled to his fate. But the moral growth of Romola scarcely cancels out the unsettling demise of the abbreviated hero: it is as if George Eliot were deliberately trying to mutilate the historical novel because of its simple-minded and amoral assumptions about human behaviour.

It would be wrong to omit from this brief account of *Romola* the fact that George Eliot undertook painstaking research into the sources of the Renaissance period. So unremitting was her labour that she described herself as emerging from it 'an old woman'. But her failure to transmute this primary material into the stuff of historical fiction was generally acknowledged. Swinburne called her studied portrait of the friar Savonarola 'a laborious, conscientious, absolute failure – as complete as the failure of his own attempt to purge and renovate the epoch of the Borgias by what Carlyle would have called the "Morison's Pill" of Catholic Puritanism'.[37] With his usual acuteness, Swinburne also identified the strengths and weaknesses of the portrayal of Tito: on the one hand, a triumphant 'exposition of spiritual decay', but on the other hand, a character presented 'as a warning or fearful example, rather than simply represented', which made him 'for some readers an insurmountable impediment to the fullness of their pleasure and admiration'.[38] Finally Swinburne was harsh, but surely just, in his diagnosis of the lamentable failure of plot contrivance in *Romola*:

There is an almost infantine audacity of awkwardness in the device of handing your heroine at a pinch into a casually empty boat which drifts her away to a casually plague-stricken village, there to play the part of a casual sister of mercy dropped down from the sky by providential caprice, at the very nick of time when the novelist was helplessly at a loss for some more plausible contrivance, among a set of people equally strange to the reader and herself. Such an episode as this – an outrage at once on common credulity and on that natural logic of art which no school of romance can with impunity permit its disciples to ignore or to deny – neither Scott nor Dumas nor Reade would have allowed himself...[39]

In the brief essay from which this passage is taken, Swinburne uses *Romola* to make a retrospective comparison with the masterpiece of the last named and least well-known of these disciples of the 'school of romance': Charles Reade's *The Cloister and the Hearth*. First published two years before *Romola*, in 1861, it provoked (as Swinburne tells us) frequent comparison and contrast with the later work. But apart from the common focus in the Renaissance period, the two novels are about as appropriate for comparison as chalk and cheese. Swinburne indeed emphasises this fact, and takes it as a measure of Reade's significance that he must be placed in the company of the two acknowledged masters of the historical romance, Scott and Dumas. Reade is 'by far the greatest master of narrative whom our country has produced since the death of Scott'. His skill in narrative is inferior to that of Dumas only because of 'the inability to keep his hand close, to abstain from proclamation and ostentation'. His creation of pathos falls below Scott only because of 'the lack of seeming unconsciousness and inevitable spontaneity'.[40] Both blemishes, we might say, are those of a late-comer!

Swinburne's high estimate of Reade's importance helps to establish his relevance to our theme, although Swinburne does not, of course, judge him by the criteria that we have been using. Born in 1814, Reade made his initial reputation as a dramatist and a writer of novels on contemporary social themes. But he was at the same time an indefatigable collector, filling his house in Albert Terrace (opposite Sloane Street in Chelsea) with historical and documentary materials. His patronage extended to the Pre-Raphaelites, and his surviving correspondence with Millais demonstrates the high excitement with which he viewed the purchase of Millais' Arthurian 'Sir Isumbras' for his collection.[41] Emerging from this rich and promising background, *The Cloister and the Hearth* is a singular and fascinating product. It is no less different, in its conception, from *Henry Esmond* than it is from the novels of Scott. Inheriting the ironic vision of the mid-century, Reade radically revises and revitalises the conditions of historical fiction.

A comparison from outside the field of fiction helps to set the scene for this distinctive achievement. One year before the final publication of *The Cloister and the Hearth* (but one year after the appearance of an early draft in the periodical *Once a Week*), the Swiss historian Jakob Burckhardt published his great essay on *The Civilisation of the Renaissance in Italy*. Hayden White gives detailed consideration to Burckhardt's work in his study *Metahistory*, emphasising in particular the distinctive relationship of the Swiss historian to Ranke and the German school. As White notes, Burckhardt has often been reproached for his 'inadequate vision of history as *developmental process* and *causal analysis*'.[42] But these supposed defects are not simply the result of a failure to achieve the confident narrative construction of a Ranke or a Michelet. Burckhardt's effects of syntactic disruption and causal discontinuity are carefully designed. They are the precise equivalents, in terms of style and narrative structure, to his ironic vision of history, and represent at the same time a critique of the conception of history as chronological process which had been current earlier in the century.

Without wishing to stretch the comparison between historiography and historical fiction to an implausible degree, I would suggest that Reade's *The Cloister and the Hearth* is a parallel achievement. It is not to be thought of (as even Swinburne implies) as an unsuccessful attempt at a classic model, but as a successful realisation of a new pattern whose intricacies deserve special study and appreciation. Two salient characteristics should be mentioned first of all. Hayden White contrasts Burckhardt's ironic vision with the tragic or comic 'emplotment' which is a feature of the work of most of his predecessors. In *The Cloister and the Hearth*, there is an extraordinarily scrupulous avoidance of either of these two types of emplotment. As we learn in Ch. xxviii: 'Things good and evil balance themselves in a remarkable manner, and almost universally.'[43] In the light of this principle, we can be almost infallibly certain that, throughout our reading, a period of celebration will be followed by a period of disaster, and *vice versa*. Besides this indifferentist tendency of the plot, we can see straight away that a bizarre (and possibly unprecedented) range of mannerist devices has been used to stress the discontinuity of the narrative on the structural and syntactic levels: chapters of varying lengths, ranging from a few paragraphs to an immense tract; variations of size of type and type-face; incorporation of bars of music and even an interpolated sketch which is definitely not an 'illustration' but an integral part of the narrative discourse. The first, rather disconcerting, impression is of a cross between Scott and Sterne. Although all the finer details of this presentation have not been slavishly retained in later and cheaper editions of the novel, they should not be regarded as mere inessential trimmings. No less than with Thackeray's counterfeit eighteenth-century edition, they are the signs of the author's coherent attitude to historical representation.

If we return to the four procedures originally defined in relation to Scott, we can see at once the novelty and astuteness of Reade's approach. *The Cloister and the Hearth* begins with what appears to be a classic framing device: a reference to 'a musty chronicle, written in intolerable Latin, and in it a chapter where every sentence holds a fact'.[44] Reade repeats the resurrectionist claim of his predecessors:

For if I can but show you what lies below that dry chronicler's words, methinks you will correct the indifference of centuries, and give those two sore-tried souls a place in your heart – for a day.[45]

The assurance is, however, deceptive. The two sore-tried souls, Elias and Catherine, are not only curious subject matter for a Latin chronicle, but also far from being protagonists of the story. This role is reserved for their youngest son, Gerard. Soon the plot shifts from the family background and becomes essentially the story of Gerard's fortunes and misfortunes. He is singularised, in an unexpected and dramatic way, by being stifled in a chest and then virtually raised from the dead. ('"THERE IS LIFE IN HIM!" said Jorian Ketel to himself.')[46] He has something which appears to be destined for his talisman: an amethyst ring which he is given as an earnest of devotion by a lady innkeeper. But even here the divergence from the pattern of Scott (and Thackeray) is already apparent. Gerard is not rescued from desperate straits (as we confidently expect on several occasions) by the help of the amethyst ring. It is mentioned, and admired, after the parting from the lady innkeeper. But its role in the plot turns out to be quite gratuitous. It has no power of eventual resolution, no promise of reconciliation. That would be to endorse the providential structure which Reade has abandoned.

However the most decisive transformation effected by Reade concerns the transitive action of the hero, his role in history. If Quentin accomplishes his destiny through feats of arms, and Esmond through the attempt, and the failure, to figure as a man of action, Gerard is unequivocally an artist. Poor Tito is a mere dilettante, whose engagement to teach Greek lies to the side of more worldly ambitions. But Gerard, despite his picaresque travels, progresses through a scale of artistic accomplishments; he is copyist, illuminator, musician, storyteller and incomparable preacher. Reade therefore displaces to a great degree the problem of narrative action and surface texture which Thackeray so pronouncedly heightens. In *Esmond*, the play of image, allegory and name seems to call into question the authenticity of the narrative. In *The Cloister and the Hearth*, rhetorical and illustrative techniques are (as it were) borrowed from the developing consciousness and the increasingly expert craftsmanship of Gerard himself. Illumination – that heightening of the pages of the 'dry chronicler' with sumptuous colour and attendant imagery – is for Reade a potent metaphor of the novelist's art; it is also the very skill which Gerard learns, at the outset, from Margaret Van Eyck.

Reade thus achieves a highly sophisticated type of authenticity, which applies to the manner rather than the matter of the story. Where Thackeray, in the original edition of *Esmond*, makes a consistent but implausible use of antique typography, Reade uses the occasional resource of Gothic script for a purely indexical function. Gerard, masquerading under the name of Clement during his conscience-stricken return to medieval asceticism, carves out religious texts unremittingly on the walls of his solitary cave. The elaborate typography, contrasting visibly with conventional script, indicates the manner of Gerard's carving and enables us to picture it, without the aid of an illustration. In an even more curious way, Reade's vignette of clasped hands breaks into the discursive sequence between two parts of an undivided sentence. Gerard has included the drawing in a letter to his illiterate family, meaning it as a sign of farewell. Reade takes the opportunity to praise the language of images. 'It is at the mercy of no translator: for it writes an universal language.'⁴⁷ But, of course, the presence of this image only makes sense to us (as it did to Gerard's family) within a highly determinate context. Its narrative function apart, it seems to suggest that implicit contract which binds an audience to its narrator.

There is a final and (for our purposes) conclusive demonstration of Reade's perspicacity in the closing pages of the novel. Gerard's passage through mid-fifteenth–century Europe has been, to a great extent, an artist's education. But in spite of his contact, in Italy, with the first stirrings of the Renaissance, he is sent back again to Northern Europe, where he is exposed to self-mortification and eventually to death. The admonitory note of George Eliot is absent. Equally, the read, they could all tell it was Gerard's hand-writing.

'And your father must be away,' cried Cathe-rine. 'Are ye not ashamed of yourselves? not one that can read your brother's letter?'

But although the words were to them what hieroglyphics are to us, there was something in the letter they could read. There is an art can speak without words: unfettered by the penman's limits, it can steal through the eye into the heart and brain, alike of the learned and unlearned: and it can cross a frontier or a sea, yet lose nothing. It is at the mercy of no translator: for it writes an universal language.

When, therefore, they saw this,

which Gerard had drawn with his pencil between the two short paragraphs, of which his letter con-sisted, they read it, and it went straight to their hearts.

---

16. *The implicit contract which binds the audience to the narrator:* vignette of clasped hands, a page from Reade, *The Cloister and the Hearth* (first edition, 1861)

sense of resolution appropriate to Scott is foreclosed. Gerard does not inherit, and neither is he disinherited, at the end of the novel. But his young son is destined to inherit as a unity the strains of cultural experience which have failed to come together in Gerard's own life:

The yellow-haired laddie, Gerard Gerardson, belongs not to Fiction but to History. She has recorded his birth in other terms than mine. Over the tailor's house in the Brede Kirk Straet she has inscribed:—

'HAEC EST PARVA DOMUS NATUS QUO MAGNUS ERASMUS;'

and she has written half-a-dozen lives of him. But there is something left for her yet to do. She has no more comprehended magnum Erasmum, than any other pigmy comprehends a giant, or partisan a judge.[48]

Such sleight of hand achieves, at this final stage of the novel, an overwhelming effect. Reade has improved on the discretion which Barthes attributes to Balzac, by making the most renowned historical figure of the book not simply distant from, but posterior to, the action. *The Cloister and the Hearth* is not an Anti-History, but Gerard is indeed an Ante-Hero, the progenitor of the historical hero whose genius we all recognise. Reade's antithetical play with the notions of History and Fiction is nowhere more evident than in this closing section. Erasmus 'belongs not to Fiction but to History', and for that reason the novel stops short at the very threshold of his career. But, on the other hand, the 'half-a-dozen lives' which History has so far provided are woefully inadequate. Erasmus – who belongs to History – stands vis-à-vis the historical accounts that have been written as a giant to pigmies. Perhaps the oblique shaft of historical fiction can in fact do more than has been overtly suggested, if it sets up the circumstances in which this inscription – HAEC EST PARVA DOMUS NATUS QUO MAGNUS ERASMUS – will offer us a sense of authentic resolution.

Reade played for high stakes in *The Cloister and the Hearth*, and his audacity was acclaimed by his critics. Swinburne rated his achievement as only just inferior to the two acknowledged masters of nineteenth-century historical fiction. Walter Besant praised the novel as 'the greatest historical novel in the language ... more faithful than anything in the works of Scott'.[49] Acknowledging the chasm of irony which separated his own period from the age of High Romanticism, Reade had contrived to write a Janus-like book, which faced the past but also foreshadowed the future. If one side of Gerard harked back to the rumbustious adventures of Quentin Durward, another side pointed forward to that distinctive product of the Aesthetic Movement, Walter Pater's 'imaginary portrait'. For Pater's young heroes – Sebastian van Storck, Duke Carl of Rosenmold and Denys l'Auxerrois, not to mention Marius the Epicurean and Gaston de La Tour – are never wholly artists; almost always they are burdened with the responsibility of playing some practical role in life. But having reserved for the benefit of the narrative the minimum of incident which it requires, Pater casts the major emphasis on artistic creativity – though not so much upon the production of work, as upon the refinement of sensibility which will prepare the way for the new work to be conceived. Duke Carl of Rosenmold is a clear example. Sovereign of a small German state in the eighteenth century, he senses the incipience of the German Renaissance of letters, but does not survive to see it. As if in recollection of the closing pages of *The Cloister and the Hearth*, Pater ends his imaginary portrait with an evocation of the youthful Goethe's brilliant skating display, drawn from his mother's correspondence.[50] Like Gerard, Duke Carl is an ante-hero. The historical achievement to which his premonitory intuition testifies belongs to the authentic artist – to Goethe, who requires no fictional dress.

The Cloister and the Hearth, which was published during Pater's student days at Oxford, may or may not have been a significant influence on his work. That is not our concern. What needs to be emphasised here, however, is the fact that Pater's 'imaginary portraits' so far tip the balance from transitive action to aesthetic consciousness that the result is no longer historical fiction in any but a notional sense of the term. The collection bearing the title *Imaginary Portraits* was published in 1887. The unfinished novel, *Gaston de La Tour*, appeared posthumously in 1896. Even in the transition between the two publications, the ever more fastidious rejection of the husk of historical incident becomes increasingly noticeable. Gaston comes close to being a transparent lens through which the fresh vision of the early French Renaissance is filtered. Yet in so far as he shows this infinitely receptive consciousness, he is forced to abandon his historical specificity. The fictional character becomes, with virtually no concealment, the fantasised projection of Pater's own premonitory consciousness. In the chapter on 'Modernity', particularly, we can sense the urgency of Pater's own concern to 'father the future'.[51]

Writing towards the close of the nineteenth century, Pater is therefore at the exact antipodes from Scott. Instead of the man of action, he gives us the dreamer; in place of the scrupulously reconstituted historical milieu, a delicately woven atmosphere which is traversed – as if by a sunbeam – by the epiphany of an artistic renaissance. With Scott, there is an extraordinary confidence in the appropriation of the past: Abbotsford can serve as the symbol (no less than the Waverley Novels) of the urge towards concrete realisation which brushes out of its way any niggling questions of authenticity. With Pater, there is a hard-won, but ultimately secure, confidence in the future: the idea of renaissance is culturally and historically given, but the predicament of the aesthete is that he must survive the uncertainty of not knowing right up to the end his place in the new age. Yet if these two figures strike us by their incongruity, it remains the case that our chief concern in this chapter has been with the interim stages between Scott and Pater: with writers whose attitude to past and future has been less clear-cut, but whose devices for responding to the progressively more stringent requirements of historical fiction have been for that reason all the more ingenious. Compared to Scott and Pater, both Thackeray and Reade appear to have a relatively small psychological investment in history. But that very fact

Pater Imaginary Portraits

makes their precarious achievements all the more enlightening from our point of view.

One final issue emerges as a logical sequel to this investigation. We have been looking at the stage when the writing of the historical novel becomes exceptionally difficult, because of the ironic reaction against earlier modes and the ever more stringent claims of historical authenticity. What of the stage at which it becomes impossible? I do not, of course, intend to expatiate upon the great unwritten historical novels, but simply to mention two limit cases of historical fiction: a poetic metamorphosis of a novel that might have been, and a failed novel that raises the stakes of authenticity to an impossibly high pitch. The two works are Robert Browning's *The Ring and the Book* and Henry James's *The Sense of the Past*.

Browning came by chance upon his copy of what he was to call the 'old yellow Book', while idly searching a market barrow in the Piazza San Lorenzo, Florence, in June 1860. We know this to be so because he recounts the circumstances in the opening section of *The Ring and the Book*.[52] Immediately this information is conveyed, however, the problems which mark the statement in this particular context come to the fore. This is not simply a framing device, like Scott's 'family memorials' or Reade's 'musty chronicle'. The 'old yellow Book' existed (and presumably still exists). We are told by his editors that Browning first considered writing a historical novel on the basis of the materials gathered there, and that he even offered the plot to one of his literary friends.[53] This information is merely apocryphal. But the fact remains that the original discovery of the book does form part of the opening section of the poem. When Browning speaks, *in propria persona*, he is telling us about the *real* finding of a *real* book which is a *real* historical document. How can there be any legitimate comparison with the procedure of the historical novelist, who uses a fictional persona and a fictional 'real source' for his framing section?

Passing from 'the Book' to 'the Ring', we have another striking anomaly to pursue. The Ring is, as Browning's son has noted, 'a ring of Etruscan shape made by Gastellani (the famous Roman jeweller)'[54] for Elizabeth Barrett Browning; after her death, the poet wore it on his watch-chain in memory of her. But it is also the image chosen by the Italian poet Tommasei to symbolise the art of poetry, which was used in an inscription placed on the Casa Guidi by the municipality of Florence, to honour Elizabeth Barrett Browning after her death. These two data are historical, and the second is obliquely mentioned in the poem. But the literary function of the Ring is to serve Browning in an extended simile for the creative enhancement of brute fact by the poet. Just as fine gold can only be wrought into certain patterns through the admixture of an alloy – which acid subsequently burns away – so the poet brings his own creative imagination to the historical data:

> This was it from, my fancy with those facts,
> I used to tell the tale, turned gay to grave,

But lacked a listener seldom; such alloy,
Such substance of me interfused the gold
Which, wrought into a shapely ring therewith,
Hammered and filed, fingered and favoured, last
Lay ready for the renovating wash
O' the water. 'How much of the tale was true?'
I disappeared; the book grew all in all . . .
Lovers of dead truth, did ye fare the worse?
Lovers of live truth, found ye false my tale?[55]

As Browning continues his introductory section, it is the subordination of literal fact to the poetic level of discourse that is stressed. The Ring is, initially, a particular ring, which commemorates a particular person; but it also serves as the privileged simile for the operations of the poetic imagination, and then as a metaphor of the poetic achievement: *The Ring and the Book* as we have it. The Book is, initially, the historical source. But soon it has become the very book which we are reading: *The Ring and the Book*. This occurs because of Browning's absolute polarisation between the Book as source and the Book as poem: the first is 'dead truth', while the second is 'live truth'.

Browning's 'poetic' option therefore completely overrides the effects of *framing* and the *objectification* which recall the historical novel. The two seemingly objective references in the title both have their exact correlates in the real world. But this strategy of correlation only serves to enhance the sovereign power of the poetic imagination, which is the sole guarantee of resurrection. It is also worth making the point that Browning has definitively suspended the *action* of the story. The historical materials included in the 'old yellow Book' recount the trial of Count Guido Franceschini and his accomplices for the murder of Pompilia, his wife, in 1698. In the verse already quoted, Browning writes of telling the 'tale' of these events – which must presumably mean narrating the lives of Guido and Pompilia up to and including Pompilia's death and Guido's trial.

Yet (as is well known) Browning's poem is not a 'tale', but a sum of monologues on the events, spoken by the dying Pompilia and the evil Guido, by the unselfish Canon Giuseppe Caponsacchi, by the alternate voices of public opinion and the opposing lawyers, and by the final arbiter of Guido's guilt, the Pope. The 'action', though repeatedly recalled, is over and done with, although we still have a lingering element of uncertainty at the Pope's final verdict. All of Browning's psychological insight and dramatic talent is in fact put into the service of *singularisation*; the individual characters are singularised, however, not so that they may take their respective parts in a historical narrative, but so that their individual truth of expression may combine to make integral artistic whole:

So, British Public, who may like me yet,
(Marry and amen!) learn one lesson hence
Of many which whatever lives should teach:
This lesson, that our human speech is naught,

- again the use of literary structure to analyze but does not discuss the "why"

Our human testimony false, our fame
And human estimation words and wind.
Why take the artistic way to prove so much?
Because, it is the glory and good of Art,
That Art remains the one way possible
Of speaking truth, to mouths like mine, at least.[56]

In *The Ring and the Book*, Browning succeeds in uniting a Romantic view of the sovereign power of the poet's imagination with a perspectivist approach to historical and psychological reality. But his achievement is a highly personal and idiosyncratic one, and brought no new resources to the writers of historical fiction. First published in 1868, the poem closed the decade which had begun with *The Cloister and the Hearth* and *Romola*. Well aware as he must have been of the problems which these novels had created for their authors, Browning had not so much confronted as brilliantly side-stepped the issue of historical reconstruction.

To end this chapter with a brief reference to Henry James may at first sight appear arbitrary. But it is no part of our concern to trace the detailed evolution of the historical novel in this period. Our examples have been selected to demonstrate the successive reactions of some important British novelists to the ironic historical vision of the mid-nineteenth century and the new tests of authenticity which had developed contemporaneously. With *Esmond* and *The Cloister and the Hearth*, the historical novel was still close to the centre of imaginative writing – a position which it had occupied since the first fictional publications of Scott half a century before. By the 1870s, however, it had begun to slip into the *demi-monde* of literary production. Pater's historical fictions were (as has already been argued) explorations of the shades of aesthetic consciousness rather than of a concrete milieu. True historical novels of quality which continued to be written – like Stevenson's unfinished *Weir of Hermiston* (1896) and Conrad and Ford's collaborative *Romance* (1903) – used to the full the resources of Romantic melodrama without reviving in any noticeable way the techniques of representing history. Why then did Henry James, with the greater part of his career as a novelist of modern minds and manners behind him, decide to attempt *The Sense of the Past*? Why did he abandon it, then return to it again, eventually leaving it unfinished, though with a remarkable set of supplementary notes which indicate his unusual conception of the problem? The answer appears to be that James not only wanted to write a historical novel; he wanted to write a historical novel of a type which had never before existed, in which the main character actually stepped out of the present into the past, while keeping the self-awareness and many of the social marks of the contemporary period. J. C. Squire defined the ambition in the following terms:

Henry James, sending Ralph Pendrel back into 1820, could be satisfied with nothing less than a plausible transition and the most intimate research into the way in which he – with his modern mind and his consciousness of the huge imposture of his impersonation – would affect Regency people, and the way in which they and his situation would affect him. The branching avenues of speculation would have been numerous enough had Ralph actually conformed in all particulars with the behaviour of the 1820 relative whose place in 1820 he was taking; though, anyhow, the question (which he never quite faced, but must ultimately have faced) as to whether the 'past' had 'happened' or was metaphysically contemporaneous would have remained. But he made his theme far more intricate when he decided that the 1910 Ralph, going back, should 'go off the rails'.[57]

The comment is perfectly fair. James did not content himself with one momentous innovation in historical fiction, but multiplied the 'avenues of speculation' to the point where their ramifications threatened to spiral out of control. And yet it is possible to retrace – step by step – the intermediate stages which led him to this position. In 1856, the young Henry James had visited the retrospective exhibition of the work of Delaroche in Paris and (so James the autobiographer tells us) he had been overwhelmed by the painter's 'reconstitution of far-off history'. Ralph Pendrel, the hero of *The Sense of the Past*, is older and more sophisticated, with a well-bred American's fine nose for period; when he lets himself in to the empty but still furnished house in a London square which had belonged to his English ancestors, he is able to place the furnishings and pictures in their appropriate epoch. But across the divide which separates the connoisseur from the milieu which he is inspecting – and the American from the home which his family has abandoned – there intervenes a sudden and welcoming bridge: the young man in Regency costume who had been painted with his back to the artist turns round – and the face is Ralph Pendrel's own.

In the crucial Book Third of the novel (which James broke off in his first draft) Ralph Pendrel tries to explain this remarkable encounter to the American Ambassador. His explanation touches first of all on his desire for 'some better sense of the past':

'I've been ridden all my life, I think I should tell you' – for our young man thought it but fair to develop this – 'by the desire to cultivate some better sense of the past than has mostly seemed sufficient even for those people who have gone in most for cultivating it, and who with most complacency,' Ralph permitted himself to add, 'have put forth their results.'[58]

Against these complacent investigators of the past – connoisseurs, painters, historians, novelists perhaps – Ralph can pit his own direct and irreducible experience – but of whom or what?

'So you can fancy what a charm it was,' he wound up, 'to catch a person, and a beautifully intelligent one, in the very act of cultivating – '
    The Ambassador was on his feet at this, with an effect of interruption, as by the very quickness of his apprehension. 'His sense of the present!' he triumphantly smiled.
    But his visitor's smile reduced that felicity. 'His sense of the future, don't you see? – which had at last declined to let him rest, just as my corresponding expression had declined to let me.'[59]

What Ralph envisages is a perfect chiasmus. His wish to enter the past is intense, but it is exactly balanced by the wish to enter the future which he discerns in the young man in the picture. Once this mechanism of exchange has been set up, the force of its attraction on Ralph becomes irresistible. Yet he still needs to take the actual plunge into the past: a process which James masterfully accentuates with a series of accumulating metaphors as his hero passes through the door that divides the epochs:

Our young man was after that aware of a position of such eminence on the upper doorstep as made him, his fine tat-tat-tat-ah of the knocker achieved, see the whole world, the waiting, the wondering, the shrunkenly staring representative of his country included, far, far, in fact at last quite abysmally below him. Whether these had been rapid or retarded stages he was really never to make out. Everything had come to him through an increasingly thick *other* medium; the medium to which the opening door of the house gave at once an extension that was like an extraordinarily strong odour inhaled – an inward and inward warm reach that his bewildered judge would literally have seen swallow him up; though perhaps with the supreme pause of the determined diver about to plunge just marked in him before the closing of the door again placed him on the right side and the whole world as he had known it on the wrong.[60]

After this extraordinary passage, the remainder of the narrative (even Ralph's 'going off the rails') inevitably falls rather flat, and the absence of an ending does not appear an intolerable loss. James has achieved a kind of *mise en abîme* of the process of framing; the authenticity of the vision of the past is not displaced on to a supposed document or source, but wrung out of the psychological credibility of Ralph Pendrel. Equally, the process of singularisation of the historical hero has developed a psychological, rather than a purely rhetorical dimension. It is not enough that the Regency version of Ralph Pendrel should be brought to life in the empty house. We must be given, at the same time, Ralph's intensifying sense of the process as it takes place. Yet, after this climax, how could the newly perceived historical milieu and the tedious intrigue of the plot possibly retain our interest? How could we react as if the conventions of the historical novel were still in place, when those conventions have just been dissected metaphysically, and bound together again only by the compelling bravura of James's writing?

The Sense of the Past is therefore an appropriate valediction to this survey of historical novels and fictional forms in the nineteenth century. James directs his scrutiny towards England in the 1820s. He calls attention, from his vantage point in the next century, to the period of the most lively and resourceful interest in the recreation of the past – the period of Barante, Thierry, Scott, Daguerre, Du Sommerard and Delaroche. But he also draws attention to the declining capacity of the historical novel to sustain its own special mode of authenticity – a capacity which Thackeray and Reade had both, in their very different ways, tried to reaffirm. That 'sense of the past' which James evoked as 'an increasingly thick *other* medium' required new stimuli, and new techniques of recreation, if it was to flourish once again. Clio had finally taken off her Regency dress.

Postscript

'Who will deliver us from the Greeks and Romans?' asked Baudelaire in his laudatory review of Daumier's *Histoire ancienne*.[1] For the British public, relief from the solemnities of the Classics was to come nearly a decade after Daumier published his uproarious series, when Leech illustrated the *Comic History of the Romans* (1851–52). Yet already in its direct predecessor, Gilbert Abbott A'Beckett's *Comic History of England* (1847), Leech had created the caricatural type that was to stand him in good stead for the later publication. The frontispiece to the *Comic History of England*, which depicts the 'Landing of Julius Caesar', identifies the invading troops by an infallible test – that of their noses. Immense, aquiline, indeed 'Roman' noses, evidently red with cold, protrude over the tops of the legionaries' shields. By the time that he comes to illustrate the later work, Leech is repeating this formula *ad nauseam*. Admittedly a few of the more unimportant participants in the action of 'Marius discovered in the Marshes at Minturna' have quite modest probosces. But those who are directly involved in the discovery of the fugitive are endowed with magnificent specimens. And Marius's own enormous white head, emerging incongruously from the water, possesses the most splendid nose of all.

Over a century later, this caricatural type still seems to be inflexible. When Astérix accidentally witnesses the invasion of Britain by the Romans, Julius Caesar is instantly recognisable in the turmoil – by his nose.[2] Yet this specific code of 'Roman-ness' is not confined to the strict domain of caricature. Writing about 'The Romans in Films' in his *Mythologies*, Roland Barthes drew attention to a similar visual code which operates in historical films. How do we know that the characters in Mankiewicz's *Julius Caesar* are Romans? The noses of film actors can scarcely be made to fit the same formal rules as Leech's caricatural figures. But the hairdresser comes to the rescue. He has worked overtime to produce the sign of Roman-ness on even the most unpromising head of hair. Even the actors whose pates are almost bald have somehow been induced to show a raked forelock of straggling strands – just like Leech's Marius, shivering away in the marshes of Minturna. These wretched forelocks are the badges of historical authenticity.

Barthes uses this example of the rudimentary visual code in *Julius Caesar* to support a bitter attack on the corruption of the sign in western representation. He contrasts this 'degraded spectacle' of Roman-ness with the 'openly intellectual' sign language of the Chinese theatre, where a single flag is used to signify a regiment. By comparison, the code employed in *Julius Caesar* is an uneasy hybrid, 'equally afraid of simple reality and of total artifice'.[3] In our own argument, this kinship between Leech's code of caricature and the stereotypes of the Hollywood history film raises a no less radical question. This study has been concerned with the strategies of representation which reflected and determined the 'historical-mindedness' of the nineteenth century. Two crucial factors have recurred, in different guises, throughout the analysis. The first is the mythic aim of narrowing the gap between history as it happened, and history as it is written: Ranke's 'wie es eigentlich gewesen' is the totem of this tendency, but it has a technical correlative in the revision of systems of representation which was achieved in the various forms of spectacle leading up to the invention of photography. The second is the notion of a morphological cycle which passes from code to myth, from naive expression to irony; many instances were given of the constraints which operated on those who came late to the game: Michelet after Thierry and Barante, Barham after Scott. In the last chapter, account was taken of the predicament of historical novelists from the mid-century onwards. Assailed by irony, they secured their authenticity at an ever-escalating price.

The question which arises from these decorative examples of 'Roman-ness' turns therefore upon the relationship of historical representation to irony. No doubt it would be possible to investigate this particular issue in a number of different domains. The evolution of contemporary architecture in its 'Postmodern' phase would offer a unusually pure example of the ironic view of history: indeed one authority has recently affirmed that 'contemporary classicism can be measured by the extent to which the architect brings irony to the problem of relating the modern world to the values of the past'.[4] A parallel, but much more diverse, field of investigation would be the contemporary historical novel: here we have a strong indication that what J. W. Burrow calls 'modernist playfulness in the plotting of historical works'[5] is a fictional necessity, and not merely a luxury. Indeed the difference in quality between a popular historical novelist like Mary Stewart and a superior artist like Peter Vansittart can be gauged particularly in the latter's willingness to multiply the levels of irony, while the former remains attached to a naive model of historical narration.[6] But these are side issues in this study. Barthes' reference to 'The Romans in films' reminds us that it is in the contemporary cinema that we must look for the most telling evidence of the struggle between irony and authenticity which has been the emergent motif of the preceding chapters. The history film – a medium which was of course unavailable to the artists and writers of the nineteenth century – offers the clearest contemporary equivalent to our 'historical poetics'. Deriving from the invention of photography in the first instance, it has succeeded in integrating text and image, narrative sequence and archaeological accuracy. A short postscript on this historical *Gesamtkunstwerk* will bring to the fore the issues which relate this study of the nineteenth century to the abiding problems of historiography at the present day.

17. *Adventures of the Roman nose I:* Marius discovered in the Marshes at Minturna,
from J. Leech, *Comic History of the Romans* (1851–2)

To isolate the question of historical reconstruction in the cinema is in a sense
highly artificial. As with the nineteenth-century historical novel, a film which
attempts to represent a past period utilises the same machinery as a film which
purports to show contemporary life: the overriding motivation is one of 'Realism',
and to this extent a work like Von Stroheim's designedly 'realistic' but contemporary *Greed* (1924) is an advance on the extravagant costume melodramas
of the early commercial cinema – Pastrone's *Cabiria* (1913) and Griffith's
Intolerance (1916). It would be hazardous to try to fix a stage by which the
history film emerged fully fledged from these early developments. But there can
be no doubt that, by the time of Jean Renoir's *La Marseillaise* (1938), the complex issues of historical reconstruction have been integrated in a sophisticated
and provocative way. Renoir directs our attention to the problem of mass
consciousness in history: to the ways in which a mass movement like the
Revolution of 1789 can germinate from the minds of many individuals. But he
also exploits the uniquely inclusive nature of the cinema to pose the central
issue of representation as such: he retraces the process whereby historical
facts and images are constructed to represent particular values and ideologies.
The painter Javel, caught up in the revolutionary movement, adopts a neo-
classical pictorial mode like that of David and his school; he also pictures the
entry of the Marseilles contingent into Paris as a heroic fresco. Marie-
Antoinette talks of the particular historical juncture as ringing down the curtain

18. *Adventures of the Roman nose II:* Caesar faces the conspirators in Mankiewicz's
Julius Caesar (1953)

on a tragedy, while the newly arrived Marseillais are packed into the performance
of a shadow-play which represents the conflict between the King and 'La
Nation'.[7]

Renoir thus gives the history film a self-critical dimension. We not only see
the images of past events, but are made aware of the conventions upon which
such a representation depends. The King himself, neither cast in a heroic mould
nor conveyed as a caricature, is given the distance of a Brechtian protagonist as
he concerns himself with hunting, sleep and food (including the newly arrived
and exotic tomato). Although Renoir did not himself try to extend these possibilities of historical reconstruction in the post-war period, his example was
closely studied by the Italian post-war Neo-Realist school, and in particular by
Roberto Rossellini, whose career was increasingly dominated by the search of
appropriate technical and poetic means to represent historical events. Rossellini's
earliest post-war films (such as *Roma, città aperta* of 1945 and *Germania, anno
zero* of 1947) were addressed to contemporary historical circumstances. But in
1950 he completed *Francesco, giullare di Dio*, an episodic account of the life of

19. Non-actors and location shooting: St Francis and his companions in Rossellini's *Francesco, giullare di Dio* (1950)

Saint Francis of Assisi based on surviving medieval sources such as the *Fioretti*. In 1966, he directed the remarkable *Prise de pouvoir par Louis XIV*, in 1971 the biographical *Blaise Pascal*, and in 1972 *L'età dei Medici: Cosimo dei Medici e Leon Battista Alberti*. This brief list, which is far from exhaustive, shows the scope of some of Rossellini's films, ranging from the Italian Middle Ages to the Renaissance, and from the meditative life of Pascal to the *Realpolitik* of the young Louis XIV. But Rossellini also ventured much further afield, going back to Ancient Greece and the time of the Apostles, and forward to the nineteenth-century saga of Garibaldi's march.

One of the crucial components in Rossellini's historical 'Realism' was the type of effect which we labelled the 'technical surprise' in our discussion of history painting. Yet the fact that cinema is so much more complex an amalgam than painting necessarily implies that this effect, or combination of effects, extends over a number of different domains. In the case of *Francesco*, for example, we can single out the importance of the choice of non-professional actors for the majority of the roles, with the saint himself being played by a Franciscan friar. We can also draw attention to the consistent use of location shooting, with a consequent freedom of camera movement and an avoidance of the careful editing rhythms, 'shot-reverse shots', and other features of the well-made Hollywood film. As a direct result of Mussolini's insistence that non-Italian films should be dubbed, Rossellini was able to count on unusually good dubbing facilities while working in Italy, and his location shooting was thus free from the constraints of simultaneous sound shooting. Of course, this combination of factors did not remain constant throughout Rossellini's career as a director. When he made *Prise de pouvoir* in France – sixteen years after *Francesco* – he was able to profit from the French expertise in the recording of direct sound, improvising ingeniously when incongruous features like aeroplane noise found their way on to the sound track. By this stage, he was also able to utilise a newly developed moving lens which (in his view) worked 'more like an eye' and facilitated 'a system of constant direct participation' by the cinema audience.[8]

The French film critic André Bazin has defined the 'Realism' of films such as those of Renoir and Rossellini with the aid of the geological metaphor of the 'equilibrium profile'. Just as a river forces its way to the sea through rock that is at first resistant, then accommodates to the flow of water, so the impact of new techniques at first galvanises the audience, but then inevitably diminishes in intensity. The cinema director must constantly search for new technical devices to achieve the 'reality effect'. Obviously the issue of 'historical realism' is inscribed within this overall problematic of 'Realism'. To the basic questions of casting, location, camera movement and editing, it brings the additional problem of the reconstitution of a historical milieu. Yet in this particular respect, the challenge facing the cinema director is not very far removed from that which faced the historical painter in the nineteenth century. How to avoid what could be criticised as Delaroche's 'pretty and clean' scenography, or Storey's 'theatrical make-up of a scene dimly realised in the pages of some book', is still a lively issue. Thackeray offered a recipe which held good for the history film as well as for the history painting when he praised the figures in Herbert's 'Trial of the Seven Bishops' for being 'quite at home in their quaint coats and periwigs of James the Second's time'.[9] Both the 'quaintness' and the 'being at home' – complementary effects of strangeness and familiarity – are equally indispensable for a 'historically realistic' cinema.

It is certainly interesting to speculate on what the fastidious Thackeray would have made of one of the most ambitious of recent history films: Stanley Kubrick's *Barry Lyndon* (1975). From the point of view of fidelity to Thackeray's original novel, Kubrick's film is lamentably defective: characters are eliminated, conflated and misrepresented, while units of narrative are freely displaced in the commentary of the voice-over narrator. Location suffers from a bewildering inability to retain and develop one particular milieu: when Barry reaches the peak of his prosperity, he is shown almost interchangeably against the back-grounds of Castle Howard and Wilton House, occasionally taking his walks in a Stourhead smothered with nineteenth-century azaleas and rhododendrons. But these failings – if they are to be seen as failings – in no way detract from Kubrick's remarkable technical innovation, which is to make use of a number of special lenses for interior and exterior shots. He is able to record a candle-lit interior with a minimum of extra lighting, while his establishing shots of historic buildings and landscapes have a quality of finesse rarely, if ever, seen before. No doubt because this technical means enabled him to 'fix' a scene as if it were the product of the painter's brush, Kubrick has infiltrated a number of shots which appear like *tableaux-vivants* from eighteenth-century painting. Barry and his cousin, walking in the woods, seem to have stepped back into a Gainsborough portrait, while the drunken Barry, slumped into an armchair at his club, fits into a scene almost identical with a plate from Hogarth's 'Rake's Progress'.

Kubrick's approach in *Barry Lyndon* could almost be seen as an extended development of the technique of the 'establishing' shot. The camera moves into each scene, and finally moves out again: only very rarely do we have 'tracking' shots which follow lateral movement. This relatively unusual exploitation of technique enables us to see the whole film as an attempt to 'establish' a historical milieu, just as it follows the course of Barry's irrepressible attempts to 'establish' his own fame and fortune. But Thackeray's novel is not, as was pointed out before, an essay in the mode of the Waverley Novels, where 'Prince Prettyman' is endowed with all the benefits of a happy ending. If Thackeray allows his 'darling hero' to come within a hair's breadth of becoming a lord, he soon precipitates him from his high position to abject poverty and causes his life to end in a debtor's prison. Kubrick's film does not fully respond to the antithetical possibilities inherent in Thackeray's narrative. It offers us the irony of a story in time which is authenticated by a series of static 'establishments' of the eighteenth-century milieu. But it does not provide us with any effective equiva-lent for the process whereby Thackeray undercuts his anti-hero's progress in the very unfolding of the narrative. Once Barry has begun to slip from grace, Kubrick's film loses its credibility and interest. Our identification with the protagonist, which has been secured by fairly conventional means, cannot survive this unsettling reversal.

It may be asking a great deal of the cinema director that he should explore both the novel illusionistic techniques of film, and the issues of authenticity that depend upon the unfolding of a historical narrative. But this was certainly the aim of a recent and remarkable work: Daniel Vigne's *Le Retour de Martin Guerre* (1982). This unusual film, based on the account of a celebrated sixteenth-century trial for imposture which was compiled by a *conseiller* at the Parlement de Toulouse, tries to scale new heights of authenticity in its depiction of costume and milieu. It draws upon the collaboration of the American historian of early modern France, Natalie Zemon Davis, who had herself conceived the idea of writing a film scenario from this *cause célèbre* quite independently of the French director.[10]

It is interesting to note, on the most general level, the convergence of two paradigms of historical realism in the mise-en-scène and costume of *Martin Guerre*. On the one hand (as in *Barry Lyndon*), there is a specifically pictorial model. This seems to have been displaced from the following century, when pictorial modes in Italy and Northern Europe followed the precedent of a 'Caravaggiesque' chiaroscuro. The excellent colour photography, which is aided by strong side-lighting in the domestic interiors, suggests the model of the Lorraine painter, Georges de La Tour: artfully composed scenes reactivate the memory of particular paintings by La Tour, although the main female character bears a toque reminiscent of Vermeer's great 'Head of a Woman' in the Mauritshuis (The Hague). Paradoxically, this displaced pictorial model – which fits the conditions of cinematic reproduction exactly, even if it does not fit the sixteenth century – establishes an overall consistency of atmosphere which is conducive to authenticity. Combining with it, and yet necessarily conflicting in some respects, is the archaeological model of precise attention to period detail. At the peasant marriage close to the beginning of the film, the young bride and groom are dressed in striking red robes. Natalie Zemon Davis's knowledge of peasant life has afforded both a precious detail of authenticity and a powerful effect of de-familiarisation.

In fact, a *coup* like this resonates in the spectator's mind, preparing him to accept other attendant details as equally authentic. Shortly after the marriage scene, the young Martin goes to visit a village 'guérisseuse' to be cured of his sexual inhibitions. While this scene takes place, we have no difficulty in accepting that the curious language which the old woman uses is drawn from genuine folk-lore, and that the elaborate craft of basket-weaving, which is demonstrated simultaneously in the background, is a legitimate example of the traditional *vannerie*.

However, all these features are subordinate to the overall plot of *Martin Guerre*. It is here that the issues of falsehood and authenticity are most exhaustively played out. For the whole story turns around the question of the main character's right to the name which he has claimed. The young Martin, persecuted by his fellow villagers and disconcerted by a marriage forced upon him by his family, finally leaves home without leaving any explanation. A decade later, a man presents himself in the village and claims to be the Martin Guerre who took to his heels so many years before. Through his physical likeness, he succeeds in convincing a large number of the villagers, including the abandoned wife and several members of the Guerre family. Only an ensuing quarrel with his uncle over the profits which have been taken from Martin's lands during his absence can cloud the picture of renewed family harmony. But the uncle brands the new Martin as an impostor, and brings a legal suit against him, which is heard first of all in the village, and finally at the Parlement de Toulouse.

The film therefore consists in a kind of *mise en abîme* of the problem of authenticity. Just as the returning Martin must convince the village, so the actor, and the whole film, must convince us. The issue is complicated by the fact that the part of Martin is played, with great feeling and panache, by the most familiar young male actor of the present French cinema, Gérard Depardieu. If Rossellini used non-professionals to enhance the sense of authenticity, and thus avoided that interplay between the character and the 'star' playing the character which is powerfully exploited in the American cinema, Vigne does not discourage the 'interference effect' between character and star. This works in a curious, but perhaps positive, way in *Martin Guerre*. We become progressively uncertain about how far we should be convinced by Depardieu's strenuous defence of his identity as Martin. And when, in the final moments of the trial, a new character appears on the scene, we are quite willing to accept his credentials as the real Martin Guerre, who has up to that point been barred to us by Depardieu's forensic ability and the necessary *peripeteia* of the plot. The fact that the 'real' Martin is played by an actor less well known than Depardieu even seems to enhance his claim to historical authenticity.

This exploration of the issues of falsehood and authenticity, which is made inevitable by the plot, gives Vigne's film a dimension which is absent from those of Rossellini. Indeed it implies that the narrative structure of *Martin Guerre* will be in some respects closer to the pattern of the nineteenth-century novel than to the films of the Neo-Realist tendency. Guerre/Depardieu arrives upon the scene in a kind of second birth, like the hero of *The Cloister and the Hearth* being resuscitated from the laundry basket. The development of the narrative is by no means strictly chronological, but occurs through a series of 'flash-backs'. We start with the arrangements for the final trial being made, and it is with this hint of the problematic status of the new Martin that we scrutinise his return to the village and his behaviour to his reclaimed family. The script even incorporates small clues to the identity of the impostor Martin, letting us see that his encyclopedic knowledge of the life of the man whom he is impersonating is not complete in every respect. We note that he mistakes the cupboard in which the candles are traditionally kept. Is this merely a fault of memory, or something more significant? When we arrive at the dénouement, we realise that this lapse should have been enough to convince us of the impersonation.

All of this goes to show that *Martin Guerre* makes use of a specifically literary model in its narration. Contrasting it with the 'episodic' structure of (say) Rossellini's *Francesco*, we might recall the distinction which Barante draws between the historical novels of Scott and historiography proper: 'The beauty of history is to be the link in an uninterrupted chain. The literary composition closes its conclusion upon itself.' The fact that both Barante and Rossellini choose, within their respective domains, the narrative structure of the 'uninterrupted chain' is a measure of their wish to disavow the literary and fictional model. By contrast, *Martin Guerre* offers a characteristic fictional resolution. As Frederick A. Olafson has argued, the 'ending' of a fictional work is signalled by the *internal* recognition or *anagnorisis* of one of the characters, whilst the historical narrative cannot by definition incorporate such an element.[11] When the false Martin Guerre is unveiled in the film, it is crucial that he should be made to admit his impersonation. This dramatic moment – anticipated by Conseiller Coras's words: 'We await your confession, Arnaud du Tilh'[12] – is the climax which prepares the resolution of the film.

What then would be a more strictly 'historical' way of treating the story of the false and the true Martin Guerre? Natalie Zemon Davis has tried to answer the question in a supplementary account which was originally published together with the scenario of the film. She does not claim that the documentary evidence is decisive enough to leave us in no doubt about the imposture of Arnaud du Tilh, and she is candid enough to admit that her account is 'in part an invention'.[13] But this is an invention which has been conditioned by careful attention to the available evidence. Her view is that we can reconstruct a picture of Arnaud du Tilh which takes notice of the many elements involved in constructing a false identity, but relates them strictly to the individual and historical aspects of the case. The need for the securing of accomplices at an early stage in the plan, and obviously for suborning Martin's deserted wife, Bertrande, must have loomed large in Arnaud's preparation. But if we cannot be certain how or when this happened, we can at least learn about the network of communications which existed at that time between Pyrenean villages. We can retrace the probable path which the real Martin Guerre took on fleeing from his wife and family. We can follow the movements of Arnaud du Tilh as, presumably, he assembled his dossier on the absent husband.

In other words, Natalie Zemon Davis offers us the elements of a quite different scenario. It is one that takes its stand upon a fascinating probability: that Arnaud du Tilh had never even seen the real Martin Guerre, and would have been as much in doubt about the identity of the man with the wooden leg who turns up in the concluding stages of the trial as we are. In this scenario, we would be the accomplices of Arnaud du Tilh, sharing his own elation at the early success of his imposture and caught up in the suspense of not knowing how long his luck would last. A film produced on the basis of this scenario would be quite different from Daniel Vigne's film. But there is no reason to suppose that it would be any less fascinating for its abandonment of the major fictional resources.

This unusually cogent example helps me to re-state the position which has been implicit throughout this study. It is not difficult to think of cases where the historical and the fictional, the 'scientific' and the 'poetic', appear to exclude one another like oil and water. But this mutual exclusion is not as absolute as it is made to seem. As Louis Mink has argued, 'our understanding of fiction needs the contrast with history as much as our understanding of history needs the contrast with fiction. . . . If the distinction were to disappear, fiction and history would both collapse back into myth and be indistinguishable from it as from each other.'[14] This is a conclusion of great importance, since it lays stress on the cultural necessity of maintaining the distinction between history and fiction. But such a position does not in any way impugn the fact that to maintain the irrelevance to historiography of the fictional and 'poetic' procedures outlined here is itself a mythic attitude – a petrification before the Head of Medusa which (as I argued in my first chapter) Ranke's famous saying has unfortunately become. Natalie Zemon Davis's alternative scenario for *Martin Guerre* is a genuine alternative. The devil of fiction does not need to have all the best stories. What is required, however, is that the story-teller should be conscious of the particular options that are open to him, and should not disavow his poetics in a misguided regard for the signs of objectivity.

Here my earlier reference to the contemporary French *Annales* school becomes relevant once again. Hans Kellner concludes his well-judged estimate of Braudel's *Mediterranean World* with the assertion: 'no one can deny that Braudel has expanded a great deal of art and energy to create a linguistic solution for a linguistic problem'.[15] But such an assertion, which does not in any way conflict with our assessment of the historical value of Braudel's work, is not likely to pass without challenge. Relatively few historians or students of history can be persuaded, even by such accomplished advocacy, that there is a linguistic problem, let alone a linguistic solution. One sign of the paradoxes which ensue can be found in Adrian Wilson's critical consideration of Philippe Ariès' *Centuries of Childhood*. Admirably stringent though this article may be, and justified in much of its argument, it encounters at its limits a number of intractable difficulties. Ariès' ' "present-minded" point of view', writes Wilson, leads him to select categories which are 'personal and idiosyncratic as well as being time-bound and of contemporary origin'. The implications of this method would be that: 'No historians would write the same book; at the same time, the very success of *Centuries of Childhood* indicates that there is a fit between Ariès' categories and those of a wide public.'[16] What can be the basis of this 'fit', we might ask, if Ariès' categories are indeed personal and idiosyncratic? And what epistemological basis can there be for the hypothesis that, in the absence of such idiosyncrasies, two historians might indeed 'write the same book'? The answer to the first question lies perhaps in reassimilating Ariès 'categories' to Dan Sperber's definition of a rhetoric – something which is 'a function both of the text and of the shared knowledge'.[17] The answer to the second question was already given in Macaulay's reply to Dr Johnson: the truth of history is not 'one' and admitting of 'no degrees'; historiography is bound to observe 'the truth of imitation in the fine arts'.[18]

In putting forward these answers, we are not simply vindicating Macaulay's eighteenth-century stance against the new historiography of Ranke. Such a position would be unhistorical and absurd. The point is that the 'rhetorical' aspect of Ariès' style requires less negative treatment. Wilson tries to solve his problem by invoking the convenient distinction between the 'professional' and the 'amateur' historian. Ariès is an amateur. Yet, it must be conceded, *Centuries of Childhood* 'incarnates, with its own naive honesty . . . the very essence of the first stage of the historical investigation of a new field'.[19] No doubt we are returning to the idea (so aptly applied to Scott) that only the non-professional has a lever strong enough to jolt the world of historiography out of its orbit! But 'naive honesty' is not an adequate recipe for this achievement. Also at a premium is the specifically rhetorical ability which leads Ariès to state at the outset of his massive study, *L'Homme devant la mort*:

> Rediscovering from Homer to Tolstoy the constant expression of a same overall attitude before death does not mean that we recognise in it a structural permanence which is alien to specifically historical variation. A good many other elements have been superimposed on this elementary and immemorial background. But it has stood up to the pressures of evolution for about two thousand years. In a world subjected to change, the traditional attitude to death stands out like a mole of inertia and continuity.
>
> It is now so far effaced from our habits of living that we have difficulty in imagining it and understanding it. The ancient attitude whereby death is at once nearby, familiar, and of diminished importance, no longer impinging on our senses, is too much of a contrast to our own, whereby death causes such deep fear that we no longer dare to call it by its name.
>
> That is why, when we call this familiarity with death the taming of death, we do not mean by this that it was formerly savage and was later domesticated. We intend to say, on the contrary, that it has today become savage, where formerly this was not the case. Death at its most ancient was tamed death.[20]

Michelet tells us that the Joan of Arc whom we might have taken for a remote and mystical medieval figure is in fact close to ourselves as a result of her 'good sense'. Ariès argues that the 'taming of death', which we might have considered to be the achievement of modern rationalism and modern medicine, is in fact the achievement of any period but our own: we have given death a savagery which earlier cultural and social institutions were able to palliate. In both contrasted cases, the chiasmus serves to sharpen our awareness of difference: to make us aware of the truism that we can only recognise in the past what our 'present-mindedness' is capable of recognising – and to prepare us for the negation of that recognition. Adrian Wilson accuses Ariès, with some justice, of scrutinising his evidence for 'modern attitudes to the child',[21] discovering that these attitudes are absent, and merely recording this absence. But from *Centuries of Childhood* to *L'Homme devant la mort*, the strategy has been reversed. The 'absence' is in our modern incapacity to preserve the cultural and social mechanisms for the 'taming' of death. It is the infinite differentiation of those mechanisms, across the last millennium, that forms the fabric of Ariès' magisterial study.

Obviously there is no space in this postscript for a full-scale review of the strategies of the *Annales* school, but since we are concerned here with contemporary equivalents of the 'historical poetics' of the nineteenth century, it is worth looking at one further, preeminent example from historiography to balance our earlier concentration on the history film. Barthes wrote at the conclusion of his article on 'The Discourse of History' that 'the sign of History is no longer the real but the intelligible':[22] in his view historiography had previously relied on 'reality effects' to validate its claim to be transparent to reality, but this resource was no longer available in a period when the mythic purpose of such devices had been detected. No doubt this conclusion seemed appropriate to Barthes in 1967, just two years after the publication of Braudel's *Mediterranean World*. But would he have written the same thing ten years later, after the publication of Emmanuel Le Roy Ladurie's *Montaillou*?

Surely the enormous popular success of *Montaillou*, in the rest of the world as well as in France, was bound up with the fact that the whole book, and not merely a phrase here and there, formed a kind of 'reality effect'? The very purity of its conception – one medieval village, one privileged contemporary source, and very little more – was central to this effect. Even the italicisation of extracts from the testimony of the hapless inhabitants of Montaillou seemed to enhance the rhetorical point: that *this* was the real, and all the rest was commentary. It was as if Le Roy Ladurie had managed to detect and revive a particular psychological mechanism. He had shown that the past keeps coming back, given a good chance. But he had also demonstrated that this effect takes place not in spite of, but because of, its remoteness; not in spite of, but because of, the stylistic marks which identify the commentary as being produced by a writer of the present day; not because of our 'present-mindedness' but because of our ability to recognise the strangeness of what seemed the minimal unit of historical scrutiny.

In a different but hardly less cogent way, Le Roy Ladurie's later studies – *Carnival* and *Love, Death and Money in the Pays d'Oc* – re-enact this feat. It is the way in which the carnival events in the small town of Romans oscillate between extreme generality and exiguous particularity, that seems to confirm their historicity. Le Roy Ladurie epitomises the point in his conclusion: 'The Carnival at Romans makes me think of the Grand Canyon. It shows, preserved in cross section, the social and intellectual strata and structures which made up a "très ançien régime".'[23] In other words, the carnival is at the same time almost nothing and almost everything. It is an obscure series of events, smothered in symbolism, and it is 'a complete geology, with all its colours and contortions'. The historical effect resides, in its purity, in the gap between the two. With *Love, Death and Money in the Pays d'Oc*, we are back once again with the privileged single source, as in *Montaillou*. But Le Roy Ladurie has organised his study in a novel and provoking way. Instead of being split up into an infinite number of italicised quotations, the source is given in its entirety: the vivid tale of 'Jean-l'ont-pris' seems to serve as a magnet for the historian's massive and ingenious commentary, or (to adopt the publisher's phraseology) 'as a window through which the imaginative life of the peasant can be discerned'.[24]

Indeed the richness and the irony of Le Roy Ladurie's achievement are both brought out by the fact that his contemporaries – not only publishers, but distinguished historians and critics – have saluted his works in terms almost identical with those which were used to acclaim the historiography of the Romantic period. 'A classic adventure in eavesdropping across time' – 'a Chaucerian gallery of vivid medieval persons' – 'the widest-angled, deepest focused, most sharply detailed presentation of village life in the Middle Ages, which has ever

been or is ever likely to be proffered'[25] – such hyperbole, with its telling escala-
tion through fictional, pictorial and cinematic metaphors, is without any doubt a
tribute to Le Roy Ladurie's craftsmanship. But it is also evidence of the
extreme, perhaps excessive, value which our culture still places upon the myth
of recreating the real – on the image of the historian as taxidermist. Le Roy
Ladurie's historical poetics may have received its intellectual and cultural
validation. But it is exposed nonetheless to the exacting critique of Foucault's
'archaeology', which is concerned precisely with laying bare the mythic
response to history so effectively activated by *Montaillou* and *Carnival*.

   Perhaps it would be more exact to say that Foucault's diagnosis comes in at a
different, though logically related, level of analysis. Le Roy Ladurie contrives to
be both a Romantic and an Ironist. Not content with signifying the real, he is
also engaged in multiplying the signs of the historian's presence: he is a *metteur-
en-scène* who can arrange 'a pause in our narrative' or 'something akin to a
flashback', and he is also a man of the twentieth century, who can detect in
sixteenth-century Romans 'a protection-racket, mafia-style'.[26] No doubt he
offers a mode of historiography which is appropriate to his (and our) ambivalent
state. But it is Foucault's aim to make the institution of 'History' itself an
object of critical scrutiny. He aspires to provide an archaeological chart of the
territory which Le Roy Ladurie exploits so brilliantly.

   So we end this study where we began: with the ambivalent image of Clodion's
Clio. History as the Law, inscribed on tablets of stone, contrasts and combines
with history as a sustaining Otherness. History as science is interfused and
interwoven with history as myth. There is a real interest in exploring the
texture of this interrelation, which is so much more intricate when its threads
are not torn sharply apart.

Notes

INTRODUCTION

1. P. de Barante, *Souvenirs* (Paris, 1890–97), vol. III, p. 248.
2. Lord Acton, *Lectures on Modern History* (London, 1969), p. 32.
3. Cf. R. D. Townsend, 'Hagiography in England in the Nineteenth Century: A Study in Literary, Historiographical and Theological Developments', unpublished D. Phil. thesis, Oxford, 1981, p. 187: 'Raine concluded that the body of S. Cuthbert was decomposed during the first eleven years after his death, that the bones were taken out of the stone coffin, placed in juxta-position, and swathed so carefully as to make them appear coherent, and assume the form of a human body.'
4. Jonathan Culler, 'Making sense', in *20th Century Studies*, 12 (Dec. 1974), p. 31.
5. Dan Sperber, 'Rudiments de rhétorique cognitive', in *Poétique*, 23 (1975), p. 415.
6. Cf. Peter Gay, *Style in History* (London, 1975): Chapter 2 is on Ranke.
7. J. W. Burrow, *A Liberal Descent – Victorian historians and the English past* (Cambridge, 1981), p. 1.
8. Flaubert, *Correspondance* (Paris, 1927) vol. IV, p. 348 (letter to Ernest Feydeau, 29/30 Nov. 1859).
9. Quoted and translated in J. A. Giles (ed.), *Six English Chronicles* (London, 1878), p. xx. The original of the quotation is in Bertram's Latin preface to his edition of 'Richard of Cirencester', Gildas and Nennius: 'Longe melioris aevi multos pannos purpurae, & fragmenta egregia continet, quae singula frustra alibi quaesiveris' (C. J. Bertram, *Britannicarum Gentium Historiae Antiquae Scriptores Tres* (Copenhagen, 1757), opp. p. 4). Cf. W. Stukeley (ed.), *An account of Richard of Cirencester ... and of his works* (London, 1757).
10. P. de Barante, *Souvenirs*, p. 248.

1.   THE HISTORIAN AS TAXIDERMIST: RANKE, BARANTE, WATERTON

1. Leonard Krieger, *Ranke: The Meaning of History* (Chicago and London, 1977), p. 4.
2. Fritz Stern (ed.), *The Varieties of History from Voltaire to the Present*, second edition (London, 1970), p. 57.
3. Georg C. Iggers and Konrad von Moltke (eds.), *The Theory and Practice of History: Leopold von Ranke* (New York, 1973), p. xix.
4. *Ibid.*, p. 137.
5. David Hackett Fischer, *Historians' Fallacies* (London, 1971), p. xix.
6. Stephen Bann, 'Historical text and historical object: the poetics of the Musée de Cluny', *History and Theory*, 17, 3 (1978), 265. Chapter 4 is a revised version of this article.

7. Gareth Stedman Jones, 'History: the poverty of empiricism', in Robin Blackburn (ed.), *Ideology in Social Science*, (London, 1972), p. 97.
8. Iggers and von Moltke, *Theory and Practice*, pp. xix–xx.
9. Herbert Butterfield, *Man on his Past: The Study of the History of Historical Scholarship* (Cambridge, 1969 reprint), p. xv.
10. The 'supplement' consists of a 'Memorial Address' concerning Ranke, which was originally given on 23 January 1936 at the Preussische Akademie der Wissenschaften.
11. Friedrich Meinecke, *Historism: The Rise of a New Historical Outlook*, translated by J. E. Anderson (London, 1972), p. lx.
12. *Ibid.*, p. lviii.
13. Wilhelm von Humboldt, 'The Historian's Task', translated in *History and Theory*, 6, 1 (1967), 56–71.
14. Humboldt, *Werke*, 5 vols. (Darmstadt, 1960), vol. 1, p. 585.
15. Leopold von Ranke, *Geschichten der romanischen und germanischen Völker von 1494 bis 1514*, second edition (Leipzig, 1874), p. vii.
16. Cf. Peter Gay, *Style in History* (London, 1975): Chapter 2 is devoted to Ranke.
17. Humboldt, 'The Historian's Task', p. 56. I am aware that I may be accused, at this point, of creating an artificial distinction between the approaches of Humboldt and Ranke, and allowing my case to rest upon selective quotations and dubious linguistic distinctions. This hypothetical accusation requires a clear statement in response. On the one hand, I would not wish to minimise the indebtedness of Ranke to Humboldt, and the significance of their common adherence to the German tradition of historical thinking. It would not be difficult to select passages from Humboldt's address, for example those which relate to the poetic and creative vocation of the historian, which Ranke would have assented to with enthusiasm. My concern, however, is not to emphasise the common elements, but to identify what seem to me to be the significant, even if apparently minute, points of difference. This is where the difference between *darstellen* and *zeigen* comes in. Evidently these words could, in a particular circumstance, be used as synonyms. The dictionary however gives as meanings for *darstellen*: represent, depict, delineate, exhibit, limn, portray, and for *zeigen*: show, point out, indicate, exhibit, display. *Darstellen* is thus a term whose shades of meaning adhere, for the most part, to a traditional mimetic formula of representation. *Zeigen* is more appropriately used for direct *showing*, unmediated by a code or system of transcription. In terms of Peirce's semiotics, we could say that *darstellen* covers the 'iconic' and 'symbolic' sign, whereas *zeigen* involves also – and preeminently – the 'indexical' dimension.
   Nevertheless, I would not wish to lay too much emphasis on the assertion that Ranke *intended* to load his dictum with this new significance. What I am arguing is that, in 1824, the difference between *darstellen* and *zeigen makes sense* – provided that we relate it to the crisis in representation which is perceptible in other, related fields of expression. I am also arguing, moreover, that the 'mythic' status of Ranke's dictum is closely bound up with this *implication* of transgressive meaning.
18. Antoine Guilland, *L'Allemagne nouvelle et ses historiens* (Paris, 1899), p. 71. Guilland is described on the title-page as 'Professeur d'Histoire à l'Ecole Polytechnique Suisse'.
19. Cf. Jacques Derrida, *Éperons: les styles de Nietzsche* (Paris, 1978), pp. 43ff.
20. Rudyard Kipling, *Many Inventions* (London, 1898), p. 171.
21. Iggers and von Moltke, *Theory and Practice*, p. xx. I should emphasise that I am

not disputing the accuracy of this new translation. I have no doubt that 'essentially' is a more appropriate way of translating *eigentlich* than 'actually'. But I question the epistemological dividend that accrues from this change. After all, the distinctiveness of the 'dictum' does not reside in the fact that it implied an emphasis on 'factuality' rather than the 'essential'. What person could have been misled into thinking that Ranke aspired to a 'factuality' untouched by selection? The distinctiveness lies in what could be made of the claim that Ranke aspired to 'show how ... things happened'.

22. Fischer, *Historians' Fallacies*, p. 160.
23. Tzvetan Todorov, 'The fantastic in fiction', *20th Century Studies*, 3 (May 1970), 91–2.
24. Ranke, *History of the Latin and Teutonic Nations*, translated by P. A. Ashworth (London, 1887), p. vi.
25. Translated by E. Armstrong (London, 1909), p. x. Both translations omit the Preface.
26. Lord Acton, *Lectures on Modern History* (London, 1969), p. 32.
27. Michel Foucault, *Les Mots et les choses* (Paris, 1966), p. 379.
28. *Ibid.*, p. 380.
29. Quoted in Stephen Bann, 'Postscript: three translators, Silhouette, Barante, Rossetti', *20th Century Studies*, 11 (Sept. 1974), 89.
30. *Ibid.*, pp. 91–2.
31. Charles Waterton, *Wanderings in South America* (London, 1825), p. 122.
32. Charles Waterton, *Essays on Natural History chiefly Ornithology* (London, 1838), p. 300.
33 *Ibid.*, pp. 300–1.
34. *Ibid.*, p. 304.
35. Prosper de Barante, *Letters to Mme de Staël* (Clermont-Ferrand, 1929), p. 289.
36. *Ibid.*, p. 293.
37. Prosper de Barante, Letters to Mme Récamier, Bibliothèque Nationale, Paris, naf 14099, 24 Dec. 1808.
38. Letter from Mme de La Rochejaquelein to Barante, 10 March 1809, in *Andegaviana*, fifth series (Paris/Nantes, 1906), p. 357.
39. Alphonse de Beauchamp, *Histoire de la Guerre de la Vendée et des Chouans*, 3 vols. (Paris, 1806), vol. 1, p. 154.
40. Mme de La Rochejaquelein, *Mémoires* (Paris, 1889), p. 94. This edition, published by the author's family, reproduces the original text, before Barante's revisions.
41. Mme de La Rochejaquelein, *Mémoires* (Paris, 1817), p. 52.
42. Letter from Benjamin Constant to Barante, 25 Feb. 1808, in *Revue des deux mondes*, 34 (July 1906), 249–50.
43. Charles de Rémusat, *Mémoires de ma vie*, 4 vols. (Paris, 1958), vol. 1, p. 309, note 1.
44. Alfred Nettement, *Vie de Madame la Marquise de La Rochejaquelein* (Paris, 1858), p. 340.
45. Quoted in Guilland, *L'Allemagne nouvelle*, p. 71.
46. Stern, *Varieties of History*, p. 87.
47. Letters of François Guizot to Barante, Archives Nationales, Paris, 42 AP 200, 14 June 1823.
48. Letter of Guizot to Barante, Archives Nationales, 21 Nov. 1825.
49. *Journal des Débats*, 20 Feb. 1826.
50. Cf. Chapter 4.
51. Acton, *Lectures*, p. 32.

52. Ranke, *Latin and Teutonic Nations*, trans. Armstrong, p. xi.
53. Quoted in Douglas Crimp, 'Positive negative: a note on Degas' photographs', *October*, 5 (Photography special issue) (Summer 1978), 100. There can be little doubt that by 'black and white' Degas was referring to photography.
54. Quoted in Jean-Louis Schefer, 'Spilt Colour/Blur', translated by Paul Smith, *20th Century Studies*, 15/16 (Special issue on Visual Poetics) (Dec. 1976), 99. Cf. also Schefer, *Scénographie d'un tableau* (Paris, 1969).
55. Schefer, 'Spilt Colour/Blur', p. 90.
56. Cf. Marcelin Pleynet, 'La Lettre de l'incarnation', *Documents sur*, 2/3 (1978), 84–92.
57. Cf. Schefer, 'Spilt Colour/Blur', pp. 82ff.
58. Quoted in S. Lenel, *Marmontel* (Paris, 1902; reprinted 1970), p. 373.
59. *Ibid.*, p. 375.
60. Quoted in Arthur Gill, 'The London diorama', *History of Photography*, 1, 1 (Jan. 1977), 33: the source is Jeffreys Taylor, *A Month in London* (London, 1832).
61. Definition from the Dictionary of the Academy quoted in J. Hovenkamp, *P. Mérimée et la couleur locale* (Nijmegen, 1928), p. 4, note 3.
62. Marmontel, *Elémens de littérature*, vol. IV (*Oeuvres complètes*, vol. VIII) (Paris, 1787), p. 113.
63. *Ibid.*, p. 118.
64. *Ibid.*, p. 116.
65. Stern, *Varieties of History*, p. 75.
66. *Ibid.*, pp. 76–7.
67. Augustin Thierry, *History of the Conquest of England by the Normans*, translated by William Hazlitt (London, 1856), p. xxi.
68. *Ibid.*, p. xxx.
69. Stern, *Varieties of History*, p. 87.
70. Quoted by Ashworth in *Latin and Teutonic Nations*, p. vi.
71. It is worth quoting here, as a reminder of Ranke's relationship to *Historismus* and its Enlightenment origins, the following passage from Meinecke's *Idee der Staatsräson* which explicitly relates the perspectival view of history to the changes in thought consequent upon the Renaissance and the Reformation. 'This was perhaps the greatest revolution of thought the West had ever experienced ... All history now began to take on a different aspect. It no longer looked to be one simple flat level that could easily be surveyed; it was seen to be a matter of perspective, and to possess infinite depths of background.' (Quoted in Meinecke, *Historism*, p. xliii.)

2.   A CYCLE IN HISTORICAL DISCOURSE: BARANTE, THIERRY, MICHELET

1. Peter Geyl, *Debates with historians* (London, 1970), p. 111.
2. Roland Barthes, *Essais critiques* (Paris, 1964), p. 124.
3. Gustave Rudler, *Michelet historien de Jeanne d'Arc* (Paris, 1925), vol. 1, pp. 64, 67.
4. *Ibid.*, p. 3.
5. Cf. Paul Viallaneix (ed.), *Oeuvres complètes de Michelet* (Paris, 1978), vol. VI, p. 12: it is argued that Michelet's corrections with reference to the trial records were 'minor retouches ... nothing beside the innumerable corrections of style with which the manuscript text is covered'.
6. Sainte-Beuve, *Correspondance générale* (Paris, 1936), vol. II, p. 196, note 5.
7. Cf. Roman Jakobson, *Essais de linguistique générale* (Paris, 1963), pp. 214ff.

8. Claude Lévi-Strauss, *Le cru et le cuit* (Paris, 1964), p. 38.

9. Cf. Gérard Genette, *Palimpsestes* (Paris, 1982).

10. Cf. Paul Veyne, *Les Grecs ont-ils cru à leurs mythes?* (Paris, 1983), pp. 17–18.

11. Edward Gibbon, *Vindication* (Oxford, 1970), p. 10.

12. Ferdinand de Saussure, *Course in General Linguistics*, trans. Wade Baskin (London, 1978), p. 123.

13. Cf. Roland Barthes, *Elements of Semiology*, trans. Annette Lavers and Colin Smith (London, 1967), pp. 58–9, 64–5, 71.

14. *Ibid.*, p. 71.

15. Augustin Thierry, *Histoire de la Conquête de l'Angleterre par les Normands, de ses causes, et de ses suites jusqu'à nos jours, en Angleterre, en Ecosse, en Irlande et sur le continent* (Paris, 1825), vol. I, pp. 34–5.

16. J. F. Michaud, *Histoire des Croisades*, fourth edition (Paris, 1825–29), vol. I, p. 107, note 1.

17. Thierry, *Histoire de la Conquête*, p. 35.

18. Thierry, *Histoire de la Conquête*, English translation by William Hazlitt (London, 1856), p. xxi.

19. Cf. ten articles of drama criticism, some unsigned and some identified by the initials A.M., which Barante contributed to *Le Publiciste* in the summer of 1806.

20. Feuilleton of *Le Publiciste*, 21 April 1806.

21. *Ibid.*

22. Michaud, *Histoire des Croisades*, vol. I, p. 6.

23. Thierry, *Histoire de la Conquête*, Hazlitt translation, p. xxi.

24. Michaud, *Histoire des Croisades*, vol. I, p. 7.

25. Letter from Barante to Guizot, 28 October 1826, repr. in Barante, *Souvenirs* (Paris, 1890–1901), vol. III, p. 358.

26. Cf. Barthes, *Elements of Semiology*, p. 64.

27. Thierry, *Histoire de la Conquête*, Hazlitt translation, p. xxiii.

28. Cf. Barthes, *Elements of Semiology*, p. 60: Jakobson has extended 'the opposition of the *metaphor* (of the systematic order) and the *metonymy* (of the syntagmatic order) to non-linguistic languages . . .'.

29. Thierry, *Histoire de la Conquête*, fifth edition (Paris, 1838), vol. III, p. 79, plate 22.

30. The edition of the 'Atlas' which has been used here is bound up with the 'Table alphabétique' in the thirteenth volume of the edition held by the British Library (Shelf-mark, 1058.h.18).

31. Lévi-Strauss, *Le cru et le cuit*, *loc. cit.*

32. Michelet, *Histoire de France* (Paris, 1833), vol. I, p. v.

33. *Ibid.*, p. ciii.

34. Rudler, *Michelet*, vol. I, p. 186, note.

35. Cf. Roland Barthes, *Michelet par lui-même* (Paris, 1954), p. 22.

36. Thomas de Quincey, *The English Mail Coach and other essays* (London, 1970), p. 136.

37. Roland Barthes, 'The reality effect', trans. R. Carter, in Tzvetan Todorov (ed.), *French Literary Theory Today* (Cambridge, 1982), p. 11. For the 'five hundred bells of Rouen', see Jules Michelet, *Joan of Arc*, trans. Albert Guérard (Ann Arbor, Michigan, 1974), p. 94.

38. Cf. Allan Nevins, *The Gateway to History* (New York, 1962), p. 63: 'Parkman's work shows how even when sources are meagre, the "vivid authentic detail" . . . may often be supplied; and it shows how literary art, with its triple support of

imagination, vivid language and graceful periods, is not merely a valuable ally of history, but is indispensable to its highest attainments.'

39. Rudler, *Michelet*, vol. I, p. 75.
40. Michelet, *Joan of Arc*, trans. Guérard, *op. cit.*, p. 3: Michelet, *Jeanne d'Arc*, ed. Rudler (Paris, 1925), vol. I, p. 11.
41. I borrow the term from the psychologist Charles Osgood: cf. E. H. Gombrich, *Meditations on a hobby-horse* (London, 1963), p. 140.
42. Michelet, *Jeanne d'Arc*, vol. I, p. 12.
43. Quoted in O. Haac, *Les principes inspirateurs de Michelet* (Paris, 1951), p. 173.
44. *Ibid.*
45. Barthes, *Michelet par lui-même*, pp. 28–9.
46. Michelet, *Jeanne d'Arc*, vol. I, p. 9.
47. Barthes, *Michelet par lui-même*, p. 88.
48. Cf. K. Marx, *The Eighteenth Brumaire of Louis Bonaparte* (Moscow, 1967), p. 9: the quotation is from Engels' Preface to the third edition (Hamburg, 1885).

3.   IMAGE AND LETTER IN THE REDISCOVERY OF THE PAST:
      DAGUERRE, CHARLES ALFRED STOTHARD, LANDSEER,
      DELAROCHE

1. Roy Strong, *And when did you last see your father? The Victorian painter and British History* (London, 1978), p. 66.
2. *Ibid.*, p. 12.
3. *Ibid.*, p. 43.
4. Cf. Arthur Gill, 'The London Diorama', *History of Photography*, art. cit. For a further comparison between Daguerre's paintings and the diorama, see the discussion of 'Personnages visitant une ruine mediévale' (1826) in *De David à Delacroix – La peinture française de 1774 à 1830*, catalogue of exhibition held at the Grand Palais (Paris, 1974), p. 356. While no definite identification can be made because of the lack of records of the diorama, Robert Rosenblum finds that the dramatic light effects and 'plunging perspective' of this picture are strongly reminiscent of the diorama technique.
5. Cf. Roland Barthes, 'The reality effect', in Todorov (ed.), *French Literary Theory Today*, p. 11.
6. Cf. M. F. Collins, *Talma – a biography of an actor* (London, 1964), and John Lough, *Paris theatre audiences* (Oxford, 1957).
7. Strong, *The Victorian painter*, p. 50.
8. Cf. article on Kean in *New Encyclopaedia Britannica* (Macropaedia), vol. 10, p. 411.
9. *De David à Delacroix*, p. 33 (Preface by Frederick Cummings): 'Their subjects, borrowed from medieval France, already announce the themes of the "style troubadour", which will flourish later, but their facture is still that of the first years of Louis XVI's reign. It is only at a later stage that the "troubadour" artists make use not only of the subjects but also of the techniques of medieval miniaturists.'
10. The painting in question is part of the collection of the Musée des Beaux-Arts, Angers (see the exhibition catalogue, *Le Gothique retrouvé*, Caisse nationale des monuments historiques et des sites (Paris, 1979), pp. 121ff and 165).
11. Cf. *ibid.*, pp. 107–9.
12. *Ibid.*

13. Cf. *An Historical and Descriptive Account of the Battle of Poictiers compiled from the best authorities, explanatory of Mr. Charles Bullock's Panstereomachia, or Model of that Memorable Victory, now exhibiting at the Spacious Room, 209 Regent Street*, 1826. A more extensive discussion of this spectacle will follow in the next chapter.

14. Cf. Michel Foucault, *Discipline and Punish* (London, 1977), p. 217 (quoting N. H. Julius); also Eric de Kuyper and Emile Poppe, 'Voir et regarder', in *Communications*, 34 (1981), 85–96.

15. Cf. Hayden White, 'The value of narrativity in the representation of reality', in *Critical Enquiry*, 7, no. 1 (Autumn 1980), 5–27.

16. Strong, *The Victorian painter*, p. 21.

17. *Ibid.*

18. *Ibid.*, illustration no. 11.

19. Charles Alfred Stothard, *Monumental effigies* . . . (London, 1811–33). This passage is quoted in Kempe's 1832 introduction, p. 2.

20. *Ibid.*

21. For a full documentation of all these works, see *Landseer* exhibition catalogue, Tate Gallery, London, 1982.

22. Quoted in Strong, *The Victorian painter*, p. 60.

23. *Ibid.*, pp. 74–5.

24. Lee Johnson, *Delacroix* (London, 1963), p. 19.

25. *De David à Delacroix*, p. 387.

26. *Ibid.*

27. *Ibid.*

28. Strong, *The Victorian painter*, pp. 120–1.

29. Cf. Roland Barthes, *La chambre claire – Note sur la photographie* (Paris, 1980), p. 150; Barthes refers specifically to Alexander Gardner's 'Portrait of Lewis Payne', 1865, which shows a condemned man in his cell, awaiting execution.

30. Henry James, *Autobiography* (New York, 1956), pp. 194–5. It is noteworthy that Henry James insists on his brother William's more mature preference for Delacroix. Indeed he implies that his own youthful fascination with the paintings of Delaroche was to be decisively repudiated: 'the pendulum was at last to be arrested at a very different point'.

4.   POETICS OF THE MUSEUM: LENOIR AND DU SOMMERARD

1. Cf. Roland Barthes, *Elements of Semiology*, p. 21.

2. Cf. p. 4.

3. Cf. Augustin Thierry, *Lettres sur l'histoire de France* (Paris, 1842), p. 81.

4. A. du Sommerard, *Les Arts au moyen âge* . . . (Paris, 1838–46), vol. 1, p. iii.

5. Cf. 'The Author of the Sketch-Book' (i.e. Washington Irving), *Abbotsford and Newstead Abbey* (London, 1835); this will be cited abundantly in the next chapter.

6. *Les Arts au moyen âge*, vol. 1, p. viii. The biographical details which follow are largely taken from the obituary of Du Sommerard which appeared in *Bulletin de la Société de l'Histoire de France* (Année 1841), pp. 294–7.

7. *Catalogue d'une belle collection de tableaux* . . . *provenant du Cabinet de M. Du S.* (March 1826), p. 3.

8. Quoted in *Les Arts au moyen âge*, p. v. Evidently, for Du Sommerard, the attraction of the Hôtel de Cluny lay in its unique condensation of different aspects of French

architectural history. It combined, in his words, 'des parties presque intactes de grands travaux des trois belles époques de l'histoire de l'art en France . . . Edifice à base et étais romains, élevé et décoré en partie par les dernières inspirations de l'architecture gothique . . ., et terminé presque immédiatement sous la gracieuse influence de style dit de la renaissance' (Notice sur l'Hôtel de Cluny et sur le Palais des Thermes avec des notes sur la culture des Arts . . . (Paris, Dec. 1934), p. 6).

9. *Ibid.*, p. 234 (Emile Deschamps, 'Visite à l'hôtel de Cluny', 1834).

10. For early estimates of Lenoir's work, see the biographical article in Michaud, *Biographie universelle* (nouvelle edition), vol. XXIV, p. 133; also the anonymous *Paris à travers les âges* (Paris, 1875–82), vol. II, 53 livre, p. 40. A useful modern summary of his achievement, with many relevant illustrations, is included in the previously cited catalogue, *Le 'Gothique' retrouvé*, Paris, 1979, pp. 75ff (article and notes by Alain Erlande-Brandenburg). This includes a full bibliography. There is a more recent summary of Lenoir's achievement in D. Poulot, 'The birth of the museum of architecture in France during the Revolution', *Lotus International*, 35 (1982/11), 32–5.

11. Journal of Lord John Campbell (Inveraray Castle Archives), p. 12 (entry for 24 Feb. 1803).

12. *Nouvelles archives de l'art français*, Deuxième série, vol. II (Paris, 1880–81), p. 378.

13. *Ibid.*, p. 381.

14. Cf. Hayden White, 'Foucault decoded: notes from underground', *History and Theory*, 12 (1973), 23–54.

15. Cf. Hayden White, *Metahistory* (Baltimore, 1973), p. 35.

16. Prosper de Barante, *Etudes littéraires et historiques* (Paris, 1858), vol. II, p. 421.

17. *Bulletin de la Société de l'Histoire de France*, p. 296.

18. Cf. Michel Foucault, *Les Mots et les Choses*, p. 7.

19. Reproduced in *Les Arts au moyen âge, op. cit.*, Album, plates X (Vue de la Chambre dite de François Ier) and XXXIX (L'Antiquaire, réunion d'objets mobiliers de diverses époques, constituant l'ancien cabinet de Mr. D. S. D. en 1825, époque où fut exécuté sur nature le Tableau de l'Antiquaire par M. Renoux).

20. Cf. Michel Foucault, *L'Archéologie du savoir* (Paris, 1969), *passim*.

21. Cf. further discussion of the fortunes of Barante's text at the beginning of Chapter 6.

22. *Vues de Provins, dessinées et lithographiées, en 1822, par plusieurs artistes* . . . (Paris, 1822), pp. 1–2.

23. E. Du Sommerard, *Musée des Thermes et de l'Hôtel de Cluny: catalogue et description des objets d'art* (Paris, s.d.), p. 681 (Notice on Du Sommerard père by P. Mérimée).

24. *Vues de Provins*, p. 37.

25. *Les Arts au moyen âge*, vol. I, p. i.

26. Cf. *An Historical and Descriptive account of the Battle of Poictiers compiled from the best authorities, explanatory of Mr. Charles Bullock's Panstereomachia, or Model of that Memorable Victory* . . . (London, 1826), p. 6.

27. Cf. *ibid.*, pp. 42ff.

28. Cf. Alfreda Murck and Wen Fong, *A Chinese Garden Court – The Astor Court at the Metropolitan Museum of Art*, reprinted from *The Metropolitan Museum of Art Bulletin* (Winter 1980/81). A special expedition was mounted in the Chinese province of Sichuan to secure supplies of the traditional *nan* wood for the project, and an old imperial kiln in the village of Lumu, outside Suzhou, was reopened in order to obtain the distinctive tiles of local clay, 'fired by burning rice-husks' (*ibid.*, pp. 60–1).

5.   THE HISTORICAL COMPOSITION OF PLACE: BYRON AND SCOTT

1. *Abbotsford and Newstead Abbey*, by the Author of 'The Sketch-Book' (London, John Murray, 1835). A further edition of the work was published in London in 1850, 'with an Appendix peculiar to the present edition' (which is however not by Washington Irving).
2. Cf. entry on Irving in *Dictionary of American Biography* (1932 edition): the failure of his family firm and the death of his mother in the same year had together brought about a crisis in his life, which the visit to Scott appears to have helped to resolve; in the same entry it is suggested that 'save the meeting of Emerson and Carlyle at Craigenputtock, no literary encounter between an American writer and an English writer has been more seminal'.
3. *Abbotsford and Newstead Abbey*, p. 5.
4. Quoted *ibid.*, p. 141.
5. Maynard Mack, *The Garden and the City – Retirement and Politics in the Later Poetry of Pope 1731–1743* (London and Toronto, 1969), p. 9.
6. Cf. pp. 79–88.
7. Byron, *Poetical Works* (Oxford, 1970), p. 815.
8. *Abbotsford and Newstead Abbey*, p. 141.
9. Byron, *Poetical Works*, p. 816.
10. *Ibid.*, p. 181.
11. Byron, *Childe Harold's Pilgrimage and other Romantic poems*, ed. Samuel C. Chew (New York, 1936), p. 5.
12. Byron, *Poetical Works*, p. 224.
13. Edward Gibbon, *Autobiography* (Oxford, 1962), p. 160.
14. *Abbotsford and Newstead Abbey*, p. 144.
15. Cf. p. 81.
16. *Abbotsford and Newstead Abbey*, p. 202.
17. *Ibid.*, p. 207.
18. *Ibid.*, p. 53.
19. *Ibid.*
20. Cf. p. 16.
21. *Abbotsford and Newstead Abbey*, pp. 53–4.
22. *Ibid.* Although Irving notes that this possible germ of a story was not developed by Scott, it is worth pointing out that his novel *The Talisman* (1825) makes use of a very similar device. The 'talisman' in question, which reveals its magical powers in the course of the novel, is also identified as an authentic relic in the possession of a historic Scottish family.
23. Letter of 1852 to his father, quoted in John Unrau, *Looking at architecture with Ruskin* (London, 1978), p. 20.
24. See in particular *Smooth and Rough* (first published 1951), in Adrian Stokes, *Critical Writings*, vol. II (London, 1978).
25. Melanie Klein, *Contributions to Psycho-analysis* (New York, 1964), p. 283.
26. *Ibid.*, p. 284.
27. *Ibid.*, pp. 289–90.
28. Byron, *Poetical Works*, p. 248.
29. Cf. Byron, *Childe Harold's Pilgrimage and other Romantic poems*, p. 191.
30. *Abbotsford and Newstead Abbey*, p. 90.
31. J. G. Lockhart, *The Life of Sir Walter Scott Bart.* (London, 1912), p. 441.
32. It is a carved memorial pillar, purporting to represent 'James Ye First' of Scotland,

among other things, and stands in the grounds to the south of the Abbey Gatehouse. Buchan was probably also responsible for a spurious inscription, reading 'Hic jacet Archibaldus' beside the entrance to the chapter-house. (See the official guide-book to Dryburgh Abbey, Stationery Office, Edinburgh, 1948, p. 8.)

33. *Abbotsford and Newstead Abbey*, p. 94.
34. Cf. p. 40.
35. Walter Scott, *Quentin Durward*, Signet Classics (New York, 1963), p. 30.
36. Cf. Roland Barthes, 'The reality effect', in Todorov (ed.), *French Literary Theory Today*, p. 11.
37. Walter Scott, *The Antiquary*, Everyman Edition (London and New York, undated), p. 142.
38. *Ibid.*, p. 102.
39. Cf. p. 89.
40. *Ibid.*, my translation.
41. Scott, *The Antiquary*, pp. 31–2. It is worth mentioning that Washington Irving specifically suggests that 'many of the antiquarian humours of Monkbarns were taken from his [Scott's] own richly compounded character' (*Abbotsford and Newstead Abbey*, p. 72). However the occasion which Irving takes for making this point, which is his visit with Scott to 'the remains of a Roman camp', reminds us of the necessary deviousness of the identification. After all, the Antiquary also has a theory about the siting of a Roman camp. But he is confuted in his hypotheses by the more pragmatic knowledge of the countryside displayed by Edie Ochiltree (*The Antiquary*, pp. 40ff).
42. *Ibid.*, p. 45.
43. *Ibid.*, p. 38.
44. Michel Foucault, *L'Archéologie du savoir* (Paris, 1969), pp. 21–2.
45. Lionel Gossman, *Augustin Thierry and Liberal Historiography*, History and Theory, Beiheft 15 (1976), p. 2.
46. *Ibid.*, p. 74.
47. *Abbotsford and Newstead Abbey*, p. 135.
48. Quoted in Lockhart, *The Life of Sir Walter Scott Bart.*, pp. 6–7.
49. *Abbotsford and Newstead Abbey*, pp. 80–1. The phrase 'a grandame's child', quoted here, is from Scott's 'Marmion'.
50. Lockhart, *The Life of Sir Walter Scott Bart.*, p. 6. 'Robert Scott of Sandy-Knowe, married, in 1728, Barbara Haliburton, daughter of Thomas Haliburton of Newmains . . .'.

6.   DEFENCES AGAINST IRONY: BARHAM, RUSKIN, FOX TALBOT

1. Extract from *Journal de Bruxelles* (undated), preserved in black box labelled 'Brochures diverses de Prosper de Barante', No. 1516, Archives of the Château de Barante, near Thiers, Puy-de-Dôme, France.
2. Anatole France, 'La jeunesse de M. de Barante', in *La vie littéraire*, vol. IV (Paris, 1897), p. 28.
3. Barry St Leger, *Stories from Froissart* (London, 1834), vol. I, p. viii.
4. *Ibid.*, p. 84.
5. *Ibid.*, pp. xxi–xxii.
6. Thomas de Quincey, *The English Mail Coach and other essays*, p. 143.
7. Lionel Gossman, *The Empire Unpossess'd* (Cambridge, 1981), p. 74.

8. (Richard Barham), *The Ingoldsby Legends or Mirth and Marvels by Thomas Ingoldsby Esquire* (Third Series, second edition, London, 1847), p. 40.

9. *Ibid.*, p. 73.

10. *Ibid.*, pp. 3–4. A notable point in common between the real and the fantastic Tappington is the 'blood-stained stair, the scene of the remarkable fratricide, which is a genuine tradition, and the sanguinary evidence of which is pointed out with enviable faith by the present tenants' (*ibid.*). Tappington Farm can still be seen to the right of the Canterbury–Folkestone road, a little to the south of the village of Denton.

11. J. G. Lockhart, *The Life of Sir Walter Scott*, abridged version (London, 1912), p. 767.

12. Victor Hugo, *Oeuvres complètes* (Paris, 1967), vol. IV, p. 135: quoted in Jeffrey Mehlman's highly stimulating study, *Revolution and Repetition – Marx, Hugo, Balzac* (Berkeley and London, 1977), pp. 72–3.

13. *The Ingoldsby Legends* (Second Series, second edition, 1842). p. 110; cf. also *The Ingoldsby Legends* (First Series, second edition, 1843), p. 334.

14. *Ibid.*, p. 167; young Lochinvar also comes in useful later in the same collection, in the 'Lay of St. Odile' (p. 252).

15. *Ibid.*, p. 178.

16. *Ibid.*, p. 224.

17. *The Ingoldsby Legends*, Third Series, p. 71.

18. *The Ingoldsby Legends*, First Series, p. 229.

19. Cf. 'Some French Caricaturists', translated in Charles Baudelaire, *The Painter of Modern Life and other essays* (London, 1964), pp. 166–86.

20. *The Ingoldsby Legends*, Third Series, p. 139.

21. *The Ingoldsby Legends*, First Series, p. 242.

22. *Ibid.*, p. 248.

23. Baudelaire, *The Painter of Modern Life*, p. 178; Baudelaire is quoting from the first line of a satire by Joseph Berchoux.

24. Thierry, *Histoire de la Conquête* (fifth edition, Paris, 1838), vol. III, p. 79 (plate 22). Cf. p. 43.

25. *Ruskin in Italy – Letters to his parents 1845*, ed. Harold I. Shapiro (Oxford, 1972), p. 52 (letter dated Lucca, 6 May).

26. Gibbon, *Autobiography* (Oxford, 1962), p. 160.

27. *Ruskin in Italy*, p. 136 (letter dated Florence, 2 July).

28. *Ibid.*, p. 54 (letter dated Lucca, 6 May).

29. *Ibid.*

30. *Ibid.*

31. *Ibid.*, pp. 57–8 (letter dated Lucca, 10 May).

32. Cf. Harold Bloom, 'Introduction', in *The Literary Criticism of John Ruskin* (New York, 1965), p. xii.

33. *Ruskin in Italy*, p. 58 (letter dated Lucca, 10 May).

34. *Ibid.*, p. 149.

35. Adrian Stokes, *Critical Writings*, ed. Lawrence Gowing (London, 1978), vol. III, p. 173.

36. Proust, *Pastiches et Mélanges* (Paris, 1947), p. 176. The succeeding quotation is taken from the same page.

37. For a succinct statement of Proust's relationship to Ruskin's writing, see Richard A. Macksey, 'Proust on the margins of Ruskin', in J. D. Hunt (ed.), *The Ruskin Polygon* (Manchester, 1982), pp. 172–97.

38. Ruskin, *Modern Painters* (London, 1897), vol. IV, p. 3.
39. Cf. Washington Irving, *The Sketch-Book of Geoffrey Crayon, Gent.* (New York, 1961) (first published 1819–20), for innumerable illustrations of the historical flavour of English buildings and the English landscape; the description of Annesley Hall already cited (p. 100) is a further example (*Abbotsford and Newstead Abbey*, p. 207).
40. Stokes, *Critical Writings*, vol. II, p. 153.
41. W. Pater, *The Renaissance* (London, 1906), p. 148.
42. Ruskin, *Praeterita* (London, 1978), p. 341.
43. *Ruskin in Italy*, p. 220 (letter dated Venice, 7 Oct.).
44. *Praeterita, loc. cit.*
45. Ann Wilsher, 'Horace Walpole, William Storer and the Accurate Delineator', in *History of Photography*, vol. IV, no. 3 (July 1980), p. 249.
46. *Ibid.*
47. Cf. Larry Schaaf, 'Herschel, Talbot and Photography', in *History of Photography*, vol. IV, no. 3 (July 1980), p. 181.
48. *Ibid.*, p. 192 (letter dated 11 Feb. 1839).
49. Cf. John Berger, *Selected Essays and Articles* (Harmondsworth, 1972). In his valuable article, 'Photography and aesthetics' (*Screen*, 19, no. 4, Winter 1978/79, 9–28), Peter Wollen reviews the general positions of Barthes, Berger, Sontag and Benjamin. However he gives surprisingly scanty consideration to the aspects of their work which are being considered here.
50. Roland Barthes, *Image, Music, Text*, trans. Stephen Heath (London, 1977), p. 44.
51. Roland Barthes, 'The reality effect', in Todorov (ed.), *French Literary Theory Today*, p. 11.
52. Walter Benjamin, 'A short history of photography', in *Screen*, 13, no. 1 (Spring 1972), p. 7. The reference is to David Octavius Hill's photograph, 'Elizabeth Johnstone, the beautiful fishwife'.
53. Cf. Susan Sontag, *On Photography* (London, 1977).
54. Roland Barthes, *La chambre claire – Note sur la photographie* (Paris, 1980), pp. 146–7.
55. Cf. Pierre de Lagarde, *La memoire des pierres* (Paris, 1979). Although written on a popular level, this study is extremely suggestive in the connections which it draws between nineteenth-century pioneers and the contemporary institutions which embody their ideals.

7.   ANTI-HISTORY AND THE ANTE-HERO: THACKERAY, READE,
      BROWNING, JAMES

1. Thomas Gray, *Poems and Letters*, Chiswick Press (London, 1874): the edition seems to have been commissioned by Eton College, for prize awards.
2. Cf. Izaak Walton, *The Compleat Angler or The Contemplative Man's Recreation*, being a Fac-simile reprint of the first edition, published in 1653 (London, s.d.), pp. ix–x; George Herbert, *The Temple* . . . being a Facsimile Reprint of the First Edition (London, 1885), p. xv.
3. Cf. p. 70.
4. William Thackeray, *Barry Lyndon* (London, 1967), p. 181.
5. *Ibid.*, p. 248.
6. The edition referred to, which is in the Pierpont Morgan Library, New York, is presumably a second impression; another edition in the same collection, which is

cloth-bound, bears the date 1852. The printer who was persuaded to use eighteenth-century type for the manuscript was Bradbury & Evans, 'In the precinct of Whitefriars'.

7. *The Letters and Private Papers of William Makepeace Thackeray*, ed. Gordon N. Ray (Oxford, 1945–46), vol. III, p. 27.

8. Quoted in G. Tillotson and D. Hawes (eds.), *Thackeray – The Critical Heritage* (London, 1968), p. 156.

9. Roland Barthes, *S/Z* (Paris, 1970), p. 206.

10. Cf. Georg Lukàcs, *Der historische Roman* (Berlin, 1965), pp. 244ff.

11. Walter Scott, *Quentin Durward*, Signet Classics (New York, 1963), p. xl.

12. *Ibid.*, p. 30. Like the Marquis, Scott also has fun in 'showing the code' during this Preface; the Marquis is made to refer to 'one of your *gens de lettres, qu'on appelle, je crois, le Chevalier Scott'* (p. xxvii). *Quentin Durward* was, of course, first published when the author of Waverley remained incognito. Scott's own introduction to the novel, dated 1 December 1831, clearly renders the framing 'Preface' somewhat problematic. Yet it seems odd that he should have chosen to undercut its effect with the note, attached to the first page: 'It is scarcely necessary to say that all that follows is imaginary' (p. xvii).

13. *Ibid.*, pp. 48–9.

14. *Ibid.*

15. *Ibid.*, p. 126.

16. *Ibid.*, p. 501.

17. *Thackeray – The Critical Heritage*, p. 139.

18. For a more extensive discussion of this aspect of the novel, see my article 'L'anti-histoire de Henri Esmond', in *Poétique*, 9 (1972).

19. William Thackeray, *The History of Henry Esmond* (Harmondsworth, 1970), p. 109.

20. *Ibid.*, p. 135.

21. *Ibid.*, p. 253.

22. *Ibid.*, p. 259.

23. *Ibid.*, p. 262.

24. *Ibid.*, pp. 460–1.

25. *Ibid.*, p. 347.

26. *Ibid.*, p. 307.

27. *Ibid.*, p. 513.

28. *Ibid.*, p. 221.

29. Barthes, *S/Z*, pp. 108–9.

30. Thackeray, *The History of Henry Esmond*, p. 185.

31. *Ibid.*

32. *Ibid.*, p. 203.

33. *Ibid.*, p. 205.

34. *Ibid.*, p. 206.

35. *Ibid.*, p. 463.

36. Cf. Thackeray, *Letters*, vol. III, p. 69 (letter to his family, 16 August 1852); also vol. III, p. 15 for comments by Charlotte Brontë (letter to Mrs Carmichael-Smyth, 26 Feb. 1852).

37. Algernon Swinburne, 'Appreciation', reprinted from *Miscellanies* (1886): in Charles Reade, *The Cloister and the Hearth* (London, 1938), p. 10.

38. *Ibid.*, p. 9.

39. *Ibid.*, p. 10.

40. *Ibid.*, p. 7.

41. Cf. letter dated 21 July ?1859 in Pierpont Morgan Library, New York; Reade writes to Millais: 'Either I am an idiot or it is an immortal work.'
42. Hayden White, *Metahistory*, p. 233.
43. Reade, *The Cloister and the Hearth*, p. 182.
44. *Ibid.*, p. 15.
45. *Ibid.*
46. *Ibid.*, p. 105.
47. *Ibid.*, p. 317.
48. *Ibid.*, p. 702.
49. Cf. his introduction to the 1894 edition of *The Cloister and the Hearth*.
50. Walter Pater, *Imaginary Portraits* (London, 1903), p. 153; Pater's narrator writes of the young Goethe: 'In that amiable figure I seem to see the fulfilment of the *Resurgam* on Carl's empty coffin – the aspiring soul of Carl himself, in freedom and effective, at last.'
51. Cf. in particular the closing pages of the chapter: Walter Pater, *Gaston de Latour* (London, 1928), pp. 70–2: for Pater's concern to 'father the future', see Harold Bloom, 'Walter Pater: The Intoxication of Belatedness', *Yale French Studies*, no. 50 (1974).
52. Robert Browning, *The Ring and the Book* (London, 1927), p. 2.
53. Cf. introduction by Charles W. Hodell, *ibid.*, p. vii.
54. *Ibid.*, p. 513, note 1.
55. *Ibid.*, p. 17.
56. *Ibid.*, p. 509.
57. Cf. Henry James, *The Sense of the Past*, Collins edition: Prefatory Note by J. C. Squire (p. v).
58. Henry James, *The Sense of the Past* (London, 1917), p. 101.
59. *Ibid.*
60. *Ibid.*, pp. 112–13.

POSTSCRIPT

1. Cf. p. 123.
2. Uderzo and Goscinny, *Astérix chez les Bretons* (Paris, 1966), p. 5.
3. Cf. Roland Barthes, *Mythologies*, trans. Annette Lavers (London, 1973), p. 78.
4. Alan Colquhoun, 'Classicismo e ideologia', in *Casabella*, 489 (March 1983), p. 37: Colquhoun in effect uses a terminology which is close to our own when he defines 'certain columns and pediments' in Aldo Rossi's work as remaining 'detached and enigmatic, bursts of memory that refuse to be integrated as a synecdoche'.
5. Burrow, *A Liberal Descent*, p. 299: the particular novel quoted in this connection is John Fowles's *The French Lieutenant's Woman*.
6. Cf. Mary Stewart, *The Hollow Hills* (London, 1973) and Peter Vansittart, *Three Six Seven* (London, 1983): I choose to compare these two historical novels because both are concerned with the period at the end of 'Roman Britain'. Mary Stewart follows the boyhood of Arthur, with Merlin as first person narrator. Peter Vansittart makes his fiction much more credible by creating a 'very important man' who perceives the making of history from a distance, and whose narration is permeated with a 'Tacitean' irony.
7. I am indebted for many of the ideas in this section to my colleagues Ben Brewster and John Ellis, whose choice of films for their course on 'Realism in the cinema' has also enabled me to see the range of works by Rossellini mentioned below.

8. Cf. interviews with Roberto Rossellini by Mario Verdone (translated by Judith White), republished in *Screen*, 14, no. 4 (Winter 1973/74), 69–111; also Pascal Kané's useful article on 'Cinema and history' (with particular reference to Renoir and Rossellini) in *Cahiers du cinéma*, no. 254/55 (Dec. 1974/Jan. 1975).

9. Cf. p. 70.

10. The scenario of the film, and Natalie Zemon Davis's version of the story, are published together in Daniel Vigne, Natalie Zemon Davis and Jean-Claude Carrière, *Le Retour de Martin Guerre* (Paris, 1982).

11. Cf. Frederick A. Olafson, *The Dialectic of Action – A philosophical interpretation of History and the Humanities* (Chicago, 1979): esp. Chapter 2 on 'Literature and intentional process'.

12. *Le Retour de Martin Guerre*, p. 106.

13. *Ibid.*, p. 125.

14. Cf. Louis Mink, 'Narrative form as a cognitive instrument', in Robert H. Canary and Henry Kozicki (eds.), *The Writing of History – Literary Form and Historical Understanding* (Madison, Wisconsin, 1978), pp. 148–9.

15. Hans Kellner, 'Disorderly conduct: Braudel's Mediterranean satire', in *History and Theory*, 19 (1980), p. 222.

16. Adrian Wilson, 'The infancy of the history of childhood: an appraisal of Philippe Ariès', in *History and Theory*, 18, no. 2 (1979), pp. 136, 148.

17. Cf. p. 4.

18. Cf. p. 28.

19. Wilson, 'The infancy of the history of childhood', p. 139.

20. Philippe Ariès, *L'Homme devant la mort* (Paris, 1977), p. 36.

21. Wilson, 'The infancy of the history of childhood', p. 139.

22. Roland Barthes, 'The discourse of history', trans. Stephen Bann, in E. S. Shaffer (ed.), *Comparative Criticism Yearbook* no. 3 (Cambridge, 1981), p. 18.

23. E. Le Roy Ladurie, *Carnival – A People's Uprising at Romans*, trans. Mary Feeney (London, 1979), p. 370.

24. Jean-Baptiste Castor Fabre, *Jean-l'ont-pris*, trans. Alan Sheridan: extract from E. Le Roy Ladurie, *Love, Death and Money in the Pays d'Oc* (London, 1982), issued separately by the publisher, Scolar Press: this quotation comes from the brief publisher's preface (unpaged).

25. Cf. Le Roy Ladurie, *Carnival*, advertisement for *Montaillou* on the rear cover of the dust jacket (the phrases are quoted from Michael Ratcliffe, Hugh Trevor-Roper and Geoffrey Grigson, respectively).

26. *Ibid.*, pp. 41, 42, 80.

Index

CPSIA information can be obtained at www.ICGtesting.com
Printed in the USA
BVOW071908030412

286781BV00002B/15/P